Legacies of Great Men in World Soccer

Soccer, the world's most popular mass spectator sport, gives birth to great achievers on the field of play all the time. While some of them become heroes and stars during their playing career, transforming themselves into national as well as global icons, very few come to be remembered as all-time greats. They leave an enduring legacy and thereby claim to be legends by their own rights. While the rise and achievements of these soccer greats have drawn considerable attention from scholars across the world, their legacies across time and space have mostly been overlooked. This volume intends to reconstruct the significance of the legacies of such great men of world soccer particularly in a globalized world. It will attempt to show that these luminous personalities not only represent their national identity at the global stage, but also highlight the proven role of the players or coaches in projecting a global image, cutting across affiliations of nation, region, class, community, religion, gender and so on. In other words, the true heroes, icons and legends of the world's most popular sport have always floated at a transnational global space, transcending the limits of space, identity or culture of a nation.

This book was originally published as a special issue of *Soccer & Society*.

Kausik Bandyopadhyay, an editor of *Soccer & Society*, teaches History at West Bengal State University, India. He was a Fellow of the International Olympic Museum, Lausanne, Switzerland. His recent works include *Bangladesh Playing: Sport, Culture, Nation* (2012) and *Scoring Off the Field: Football Culture in Bengal, 1911–80* (2011).

Sport in the Global Society – Contemporary Perspectives

Series Editor: Boria Majumdar

The social, cultural (including media) and political study of sport is an expanding area of scholarship and related research. While this area has been well served by the *Sport in the Global Society* series, the surge in quality scholarship over the last few years has necessitated the creation of *Sport in the Global Society: Contemporary Perspectives*. The series will publish the work of leading scholars in fields as diverse as sociology, cultural studies, media studies, gender studies, cultural geography and history, political science and political economy. If the social and cultural study of sport is to receive the scholarly attention and readership it warrants, a cross-disciplinary series dedicated to taking sport beyond the narrow confines of physical education and sport science academic domains is necessary. *Sport in the Global Society: Contemporary Perspectives* will answer this need.

Titles in the Series

Legacies of Great Men in World Soccer

Heroes, icons, legends

Edited by
Kausik Bandyopadhyay

Routledge
Taylor & Francis Group

LONDON AND NEW YORK

First published 2016
by Routledge

2 Park Square, Milton Park, Abingdon, Oxon OX14 4RN
711 Third Avenue, New York, NY 10017, USA

Routledge is an imprint of the Taylor & Francis Group, an informa business

First issued in paperback 2017

British Library Cataloguing in Publication Data
A catalogue record for this book is available from the British Library

ISBN 13: 978-1-138-92921-0 (hbk)
ISBN 13: 978-1-138-09501-4 (pbk)

Typeset in Times New Roman
by RefineCatch Limited, Bungay, Suffolk

Publisher's Note
The publisher accepts responsibility for any inconsistencies that may have
arisen during the conversion of this book from journal articles to book chapters,
namely the possible inclusion of journal terminology.

Disclaimer
Every effort has been made to contact copyright holders for their permission to
reprint material in this book. The publishers would be grateful to hear from any
copyright holder who is not here acknowledged and will undertake to rectify
any errors or omissions in future editions of this book.

Contents

CONTENTS

Citation Information

The chapters in this book were originally published in *Soccer & Society*, volume 15, issue 5 (September 2014). When citing this material, please use the original page numbering for each article, as follows:

Chapter 1
Prologue
Kausik Bandyopadhyay
Soccer & Society, volume 15, issue 5 (September 2014) pp. 629–634

Chapter 2
Playing for freedom: Sócrates, futebol-arte *and democratic struggle in Brazil*
Jorge Knijnik
Soccer & Society, volume 15, issue 5 (September 2014) pp. 635–654

Chapter 3
Pibes, Cracks *and* Caudillos: *Argentina, the World Cup and identity politics*
Rwany Sibaja and Charles Parrish
Soccer & Society, volume 15, issue 5 (September 2014) pp. 655–670

Chapter 4
The Hand of God, the Hand of the Devil: a sociological interpretation of Maradona's hand goal
Simone Magalhães Britto, Jorge Ventura de Morais and Túlio Velho Barreto
Soccer & Society, volume 15, issue 5 (September 2014) pp. 671–684

Chapter 5
Zinedine Zidane's return to the land of his ancestors: politics, diplomacy or something else?
Yvan Gastaut and Steven Apostolov
Soccer & Society, volume 15, issue 5 (September 2014) pp. 685–695

Chapter 6
A tale of two Kaisers: Ballack and Beckenbauer, and the battle for legacy
Rebecca Chabot
Soccer & Society, volume 15, issue 5 (September 2014) pp. 696–708

Chapter 7

Spanish football: from underachievers to world beaters
Shakya Mitra
Soccer & Society, volume 15, issue 5 (September 2014) pp. 709–719

Chapter 8

Looking at the extraordinary success of the 'Clockwork Orange': examining the brilliance of total football played by the Netherlands
Ric Jensen
Soccer & Society, volume 15, issue 5 (September 2014) pp. 720–731

Chapter 9

Hristo the 'Terrible', Stoitchkov the misunderstood: a biographical sketch of Bulgaria's most famous athlete
Steven Apostolov
Soccer & Society, volume 15, issue 5 (September 2014) pp. 732–741

Chapter 10

David Beckham's re-invention of the winger
Søren Frank
Soccer & Society, volume 15, issue 5 (September 2014) pp. 742–750

Chapter 11

From local heroism to global celebrity stardom: a critical reflection of the social, cultural and political changes in British football culture from the 1950s to the formation of the premier league
Mark Turner
Soccer & Society, volume 15, issue 5 (September 2014) pp. 751–760

Chapter 12

Iconic figures in African football: from Roger Milla to Didier Drogba
Wycliffe W. Simiyu Njororai
Soccer & Society, volume 15, issue 5 (September 2014) pp. 761–779

Chapter 13

Flawed heroes and great talents: the challenges associated with framing soccer legends in the NASL
Fernando Delgado
Soccer & Society, volume 15, issue 5 (September 2014) pp. 780–793

Chapter 14

Why Zico is called the 'God of Soccer' in Japan: the legacy of Zico to Japanese soccer
Yoshio Takahashi
Soccer & Society, volume 15, issue 5 (September 2014) pp. 794–803

Chapter 15
Of magic and mania: reflections on the fan following of Brazilian football and Pelé in Calcutta
Souvik Naha
Soccer & Society, volume 15, issue 5 (September 2014) pp. 804–821

For any permission-related enquiries please visit:
http://www.tandfonline.com/page/help/permissions

Prologue

Kausik Bandyopadhyay

Department of History, West Bengal State University, Kolkata, India

Soccer, world's most popular mass spectator sport, gives birth to great achievers on the field of play all the time. While some of them become stars and heroes during their playing career, transforming themselves into national as well as global icons, very few come to be remembered as all-time greats, leaving an enduring legacy and thereby claiming to be legends by their own rights. While the rise and achievements of these soccer greats have drawn considerable attention from journalists and scholars across the world,[1] their legacies across time and space have mostly been overlooked.[2] While you have hundreds and thousands of popular biographies of footballers across the world,[3] there is almost a vacuum in terms of academic studies on their legacies.[4] This volume, on the eve of the 2014 World Cup to be played in Brazil, intends to reconstruct the significance of the legacies of such great men of world soccer particularly in a globalized world. It will attempt to show that these luminous personalities not only represent their national identity at the global stage, but also highlight the proven role of players or coaches in projecting a global image, cutting across affiliations of nation, region, class, community, religion, gender and so on. In other words, the true heroes, icons and legends of the world's most popular sport have always floated at a transnational global space, transcending the limits of space, identity or culture of a nation. The iconic figures, who will play in the volume by dint of their legacies from a variety of perspectives, include Pele, Socrates and Zico (Brazil); Rattin, Menotti, De Stefano, Bilardo, Maradona and Messi (Argentina); Beckenbauer and Ballack (Germany); Zidane (France); Michels, Cryuff, Neeskens, Gullit-Basten-Rijkaard and Bergkamp (Holland); Best-Charlton to Best and Beckham (England); Stoitchkov (Bulgaria); Drogba (Ivory Coast); and Milla (Cameroon).

The volume unfolds with Jorge Knijnik's study of the life of one of the most skilled, intelligent and respected Brazilian footballers of the late 1970s and 1980s – Socrates. The author intends to make clear how the manner of Socrates' play and his political ideology had a strong impact not only in the football world but also on the social order. Through a historical analysis of newspapers and Socrates' writings from that period, and using journalistic interviews and personal memories, the essay demonstrates the unique contribution made by Socrates to Brazilian society and politics. It makes evident that apart from his technical and tactical football skills and sportsmanship, he has left a legacy of political awareness.

Following up Brazil, the other Latin American giant in world football Argentina with its unique style of play in the vortex of national identity comes under scrutiny of Rwany Sibaja and Charles Parrish. Their essay focuses on the performance of key Argentine personalities including Rattin, Menotti, Bilardo, Maradona and Messi at the FIFA World Cup from 1958 to 2010 to understand how *fútbol* represented a contested vision of the nation across seven decades. It addresses the long-standing debate around the team's style of play and the question of national identity as evident in popular discourses. The manner in which the national team, players and coaches continue to be the subject of intense debate reveals how the discourse over Argentine identity in terms of its contested styles of play – *criollo* and European – remains unsettled. In this context, a momentous legacy of Argentine triumph at the World Cup 1986 came from Diego Maradona's (in)famous hand goal, which is the theme of sociological analysis by Simone Magalhães Britto, Jorge Ventura de Morais and Túlio Velho Barreto. Using the perspective of figurational sociology, their essay addresses the moral problem of Maradona's goal, known as the 'Hand of God'. Taking the event as paradigmatic event for sociological reasoning, it tries to eke out its long-term significance focusing on notions of civilizing process, morality, fair play and gentleman's game in the broader perspective of Argentina–England soccer relations. The legacy of Maradona's hand goal still remains one of the most celebrated debates in football history.

Yvan Gastaut and Steven Apostolov look at the legacy of another greatest footballing personality of the late 1990s and early 2000s – Zinedine Zidane. One of the outstanding players of the French national side that won the 1998 World Cup, Zidane's achievements on the field of play have been well documented. The authors therefore explore and assess his contributions in the arena of charity, humanity and diplomacy. Analysing Zidane's historic visit to Algeria in 2006, using media discourses, it throws light on its diplomatic and political significance.

Rebecca Chabot makes a comparative assessment of the two Kaisers of German football – Franz Beckenbauer and Michael Ballack – in terms of their legacies. She raises a pertinent point in examining the legacy of such icon footballers – what weighs more in remembering a soccer celebrity after retirement – success or failure on the pitch or scandals off the pitch? While Beckenbauer's legacy, despite being repeatedly touched by scandals, remains largely positive because of his tremendous success on the pitch, Ballack's legacy, disturbed by similar scandals, remains somewhat vulnerable to date due to his unfortunate failures or absences on the pitch.

It is said that Spain has been going through the greatest period of success in its football history in the last five years or so. The present Spanish national team invites comparison with the greatest in global football history while its two premier clubs – Real Madrid and FC Barcelona – dominate international club football. Shakya Mitra traces the evolution of Spain from underachievers to world beaters in the context of long-standing tension between Spain and Catalonia, represented by Real Madrid and FC Barcelona. However, as Mitra's essay suggests, Spain's stunning success has been due to a great extent to players from Catalonia. To illustrate his point, he focuses on the impact of Xavi Hernandez, a Catalan, who has played a key role on Spain's rejuvenation as an international football power house.

Ric Jensen takes up the case of one of the most transformative football teams in the history of world football – the Netherlands led by Johan Cruyff – to illustrate the legacy of 'total football' across the globe. The author's analysis of 'the clockwork orange' as perfected by Dutch legends like Cruyff, Neeskens and Rensenbrink under the able guidance of Rinus Michels shows how a fundamental change ushered in the style of play in the football world. He also contrasts the Dutch performances in post-Cruyff age with that of the earlier, focusing on key players such as Ruud Gullit, van Basten, Frank Rijkaard, Dennis Bergkamp, Ruud van Nistelrooy, Wesley Sneijder and Arjen Robben, relating simultaneously with issues of fandom, hooliganism, racism and anti-semitism.

Steven Apostolov, in his essay on the legendary Bulgarian footballer Hristo Stoitchkov, challenges the conventional image of an obnoxious and racist football star as built up in media discourses, and offers a corrective to these received notions about Stoitchkov. Apostolov's reconstruction of Hristo is interesting because he does this not by discussing Hristo's achievements as a star player of Bulgarian national team or the FC Barcelona, but by looking at some lesser known yet important aspects of his life. It assesses his contributions in grooming young talents in the US and his coaching career in Spain and South Africa.

When one talks about celebrity culture around modern-day footballers in the age of globalization, probably the best possible example of a football icon who is known more for his celebrity status than for his football talent is David Beckham. Søren Frank challenges this construction of Bekham as an iconic celebrity overshadowing his footballing talent and qualities. For Frank, despite unhealthy comparisons Beckham has always been pitted against as a winger with the likes of George Best, Raymond Kopa, Cristiano Ronaldo, Ryan Giggs or Luis Figo, he represented a unique combination of central midfielder and winger, thereby inventing a completely new type of winger. Frank churns out in Beckham's unique style of play a legacy of soccer art that offers a fusion of Bergson and Nietzche on the one hand and Euclid and Einstein on the other.

Celebrity culture around soccer stardom increasingly became one of the core issues of international football in the second half of the twentieth century. The passage from local heroism to global celebrity status has often been a critical process. Mark Turner looks into this process in the context of evolution of British football culture from the 1950s to the 1990s when the formation of the English Premier League transformed the British soccer space. Tuner's essay attempts to identify the key factors in society, culture, politics and economy in late twentieth-century Britain, which facilitated the transformation of local football heroes into global stars or icons. These relate to the paradox of Keynesianism, growth of consumer culture, the rise of television and sponsorship, and last but not the least the development of 'new' football and modern 24 h news culture. The birth of the English Premier League Turner places in the twin contexts of the politics of post-Fordist Britain and Thatcherism and the rise of global consumerism around the game. The legacy of modern day football superstar may be addressed to this changing paradigm of British popular culture where football came to play a central role.

In the last three decades, Africa has come a long way to captivate the football world with their dazzling playing techniques and soccer heroes. African football stars who made headlines at the World Cups since the 1980s showed the way forward for burgeoning footballers to play for European club teams for fuller fruition of their talent. The chief legacy of these soccer icons was to instil immense confidence in African youngsters to chart out a professional career in the global game. At the same time, football provided a space to assert national identity in global eyes. Njororai Wycliffe W. Simiyu focuses on two of the most iconic football heroes of Africa – Roger Milla of Cameroon and Didier Drogba of Ivory Coast, to analyse the essence of celebrity status in relation to debates surrounding African soccer. He situates their contributions and legacies in the context of sports labour migration, the state of the domestic game and the success of national teams. The transition of African soccer from Milla to Drogba also encapsulates the increasing legendary status these iconic figures have come to enjoy as a result of transnational fandom. Post-retirement humanitarian concerns often redefine their legacies as more than footballing personalities as Simiyu shows in the case of Milla.

The last there essays of the volume deal with the legacy of football legends from Europe and Latin America in developing or underdeveloped countries of the football world – the USA and Asia. The first of these, authored by Fernando Delgado, tries to explore how the media attempted to educate its American readers and popularize and legitimize soccer to US sports fans, and framed the import, quality and characteristics of legendary players who used to play in the North American Soccer Leagues (NASL) between 1968 and 1984. Emphasizing the role of various stake holders in the process – investors, marketers and journalists – the essay discusses the Pelé model that characterized framing of icon footballers in the NASL and examines how far the model was applicable to understand the legacies of soccer icons such as Franz Beckenbauer, George Best and Johann Cruyff.

Takahashi Yoshio, in his attempt to highlight Zico's lasting contributions to Japanese football, addresses the question of unique deification of the Brazilian soccer legend in Japanese society. Yoshio attributes Zico's image as the 'God of Soccer' in Japan to his character, actions and the social condition surrounding him. Using mainly Zico's own writings along with those of his trainer, coach and a Japanese Brazilian journalist, he reconstructs Zico's enduring legacies in Japan in terms of his style of play, his image of a father figure and his emphasis on the importance of family – virtues that concurred with values embedded in Japanese society and culture.

The last essay of the volume offers a nuanced understanding of legacies of Brazilian soccer in India. Souvik Naha tries to explore the roots of the celebration of Brazilian soccer and its greatest legend Pelé in Indian football capital Calcutta. His essay analyses transnational football fandom from perspectives of cultural diffusion and image-making. Discussing what Brazilian football and Pelé meant to a generation of Bengalis through the lens of Bengali sports writings and media responses to Pelé's actual visit of Calcutta in 1977, it examines the nature of transnational fan culture and hero worship in Calcutta as evident in the impact of Brazilian football on Bengali fandom. It also shows how soccer legends float at a transnational space through moral/cultural networks.

As understandable, this volume is an attempt to scratch the surface of burgeoning legacy studies on soccer greats. It draws on eclectic scholarship as available to the editor, and does not claim to offer any holistic appraisal of legacies of footballing achievements on and off the field. Naturally, there are many worthy names which escape attention: the likes of Romario and Ronaldo (Brazil); Rossi, Baggio and Lippi (Italy); Matthaus (Germany); Francescoli and Forlan (Uruguay); Platini (France); Suarez, Butragueno, Raul and Hierro (Spain); Eusebio, Fig. and Ronaldo (Portugal); Puskus and Hidegcuti (Hungary); Charlton, Lineker and Rooney (England); Lev Yashin (Soviet Russia); Scifo (Belgium); Hagi (Rumania); Ibrahimović (Sweden); Guus Hiddink (Netherlands); Shevchenko (Ukraine); George Weah (Liberia); Abedi Pele (Ghana); Kanu (Nigeria); Park Ji-Sung (South Korea); Nakata (Japan); and so on.

More importantly, I believe, reminiscences and autobiographies of footballers, coaches, managers and administrators can augment new ways of looking at their legacies both during and after the end of their professional career. Although memoirs of footballing personalities, in many cases, are either ghost-written or written with the acknowledgement of a co-author, these bring to us a personalized view of their perception of their own legacies, or rather how they would like to be remembered. Think of world's two greatest footballers – Pele and Maradona. An insightful journey into their autobiographies reveals two most enigmatic yet opposedly contradictory characters of soccer history.[5] Similarly, as we come close to more contemporary times, and particularly the age of information technology, we are able to use the wherewithal of the Internet and social media in reconstructing the legacies of soccer personalities from a more popular perspective.

Notes

1. An example of general works in this regard is: Bingham, *Sports Heroes*. Besides this, thousands of biographical works deal with the career and achievements of footballers across the world in various languages, too numerous too mention here.
2. Even when legacies of soccer have drawn attention, in most cases they concentrate on a country's glory and tradition focusing on a few legendary players rather than the legacies and future contributions of such legends. For example, see Levine, *Brazilian Legacies*; Dubois, *Soccer Empire: The World Cup and the Future of France*. However, renowned clubs of world's top leagues such as Manchester United, FC Barcelona or FC Bayern Munich also have their official and scholastic histories.
3. Understandably, as I have already mentioned, since such biographies abound in number, it is needless to mention such works here. One can access the same through the internet, browsing various book sites like the google books. However, there are a few works which try to look at soccer stars/icons/legends from a popular perspective: Trusdell, *Pele*; Morgan, *In Search of Alan Gilzean*.
4. In fact, in sports, the tradition of legacy studies is stronger in case of events such as the Olympics, or sports writings and journalism. A few examples are illustrative: Kassens-Noor, *Planning Olympic Legacies*; Rogan and Rogan, *Britain and Olympic Games*; Caffrey, *The Beijing Olympics*; Qing and Richeri, *Encoding the Olympics*; Mangan and Dyreson, *Olympic Legacies*; Bloom, *There You Have It*.
5. Pele with Duarte and Bellos, *Pele*; Maradona, *El Diego*.

References

Bingham, Jane. *Sports Heroes*. New York: Rosen Publishing Group, 2011.

Bloom, John. *There You Have It: The Life, Legacy, and Legend of Howard Cosell*. Amherst, MA: University of Massachusetts Press, 2010.

Caffrey, Kevin, ed. *The Beijing Olympics: Promoting China – Soft and Hard Power in Global Politics*. London: Routledge, 2011.

Dubois, Laurent. *Soccer Empire: The World Cup and the Future of France*. Berkeley, CA: University of California Press, 2010.

Kassens-Noor, Eva. *Planning Olympic Legacies: Transport and Urban Realities*. London: Routledge, 2012.

Levine, Robert M. *Brazilian Legacies*. New York: M.E. Sharpe Inc, 1997.

Mangan, J.A., and Mark Dyreson, eds., *Olympic Legacies: Intended and Unintended – Political, Cultural, Economic and Educational*. London: Routledge, 2010.

Maradona, Diego. *El Diego: The Autobiography of the World's Greatest Footballer*. London: Yellow Jersey Press, 2004.

Morgan, James. *In Search of Alan Gilzean: The Lost Legacy of a Dundee and Spurs Legend*. Glasgow: BackPage Press, 2011.

Pele, Orlando Duarte, and Alex Bellos. *Pele: The Autobiography*. London: Simon & Schuster, 2006.

Qing, Luo, and Giuseppe Richeri, eds., *Encoding the Olympics: The Beijing Olympic Games and the Communication Impact Worldwide*. London: Routledge, 2010.

Rogan, Matt, and Martin Rogan. *Britain and Olympic Games: Past Present Legacy*. Leicester: Matador, 2011.

Trusdell, Brian. *Pele: Soccer Star and Ambassador*. Minneapolis, MN: ABDO Publishing Company, 2014.

Playing for freedom: Sócrates, *futebol-arte* and democratic struggle in Brazil

Jorge Knijnik

School of Education and Institute for Culture and Society, University of Western Sydney, Penrith, Australia

Brazilian *futebol* has provided the world with several first-class players who have left their footprint on football history. However, no player can be compared to Sócrates; Sócrates was not only an icon of *futebol-arte* who mastered the 'back heel' and played for the Brazilian team in two FIFA World Cups (1982 and 1986), he was also a political activist who fought for democracy from inside the football world and who joined the Brazilian struggle for civil liberties during the 1980s. Interviews with sport journalists, an exploration of my personal memories of Brazilian *futebol* and the political scene, and a revisiting of Sócrates' chronicles and testimonies together demonstrate Sócrates' belief that the *futebol* arena was a privileged place to fight for social change. Sócrates passed away in 2011, leaving an inspiring heritage of joy, *futebol-arte* and freedom struggle. His libertarian legacy must be acknowledged in a country where, despite being acclaimed as one of the most authentic cultural expressions of the people, *futebol* is controlled by a corrupted and authoritarian elite.

Introduction

Gorgeous! What a marvellous dance, this game of futebol![1]

I clearly remember that day in April, 1984. It was a warm autumn evening in São Paulo. I was amongst nearly two million people who paraded in a huge park known as *Vale do Anhagabau*, located in the heart of the Brazil's most populous city. It was the largest demonstration of a social movement which had begun a year earlier and which had, after a few months, taken over the streets of all moderate-sized and main Brazilian cities. In every gathering across the country, peaceful demonstrators wore white head bands and carried placards and banners demanding *Free elections now!*[2] We wanted to elect our president, a civil right that had been taken from us 20 years earlier by the 1964 military *coup d'état*.[3]

This April rally in São Paulo was a crucial one, as it was taking place only one week before the National Parliament would assemble to vote for a bill that could allow free elections again in the country. On the edge of the *Vale do Anhagabau* one could see a huge stage packed with musicians, intellectuals, artists and politicians waiting for their time to sing or talk. The official spokespersons of the day were left-wing traditional leaders who had been in political exile overseas during the military dictatorship, and who had returned to the country after the 1979 Amnesty Law.[4] Emerging political leaders such as Lula,[5] the unionist who led the first enormous workers' strikes during the military government, were also scheduled to talk.

Sócrates, the famous football player and leader of the revolutionary democratic movement in his club, was also one of the featured speakers.[6] There was a mix of happiness, freedom, fear and anxiety in the park atmosphere. Speakers from diverse political views were cheered by their supporters. When Sócrates' turn to speak arrived, the crowd became silent. As he was a very tall man, it was possible to see him, wearing his familiar white head band, amongst the artists, journalists and politicians on the stage. He did not take too much time as he announced his profound personal decision: if the bill passed, he would reject any millionaire proposal from European teams and be more than happy to stay playing in what he thought would be a 'new Brazil'; however, if the bill did not pass, he would leave the country to play in Italy. He would no longer tolerate living in a non-democratic society.[7]

Sócrates was not only one of the 'greatest Brazilian footballers',[8] but he was also a distinctive democratic leader.[9] Yet, in spite of the abundance of material (books, documentaries and articles) about Sócrates that exists in Portuguese, there is no significant academic material about him available for an international audience.[10] In this essay, I discuss the unique life of *Dr Sócrates*, the master of the 'back heel' who played for the Brazilian team in two FIFA World Cups (1982, when he was also the team's captain, and 1986, both teams coached by Telê Santana, the legendary guru of *futebol arte*[11]). I intend to make clear how Sócrates' playing style, his political ideology and his actions had a strong impact, not only on the football world but also on Brazilian social order. Through a historical analysis of Sócrates' testimonies[12] and written chronicles,[13] interviews with Brazilian sports journalists and an exploration of my personal memories of these effervescent historical times, I demonstrate the unique contribution made by Sócrates to Brazilian football and to political life.

Kaufman and Wolff argue that the use of the voices of athletes who have a direct connection to the people who support them is a powerful vehicle for social change.[14] The authors give empirical evidence of the ways athletes can use their sport experiences to engage with social change. Following their theoretical insights, I intend to demonstrate that Sócrates was a pioneer not only as a player and an 'athlete-activist'; he was an innovator who made an inspiring and unique impact both on the *futebol* world and on Brazilian society. I ask: will Sócrates' legacy be seen in the 2014 World Cup?

I start by describing the several sets of data that comprise my research, explaining how these data assist the reader to understand Sócrates' multifaceted life. The subsequent section focuses on Sócrates' sports life: I look at his career and football style through the lens of several South American researchers and writers who found in *futebol* their inspiration to reflect on Brazilian history, culture and society.[15] Next, I explore Sócrates' political and social engagement, both in his time as a player and also after his retirement from the football field. In this section I discuss his activism in the light of recent theoretical understandings that consider the possible avenues for political renovation through sport.[16] Finally, I approach the issue of Sócrates' legacy for twenty-first century football.

The research (mid) field

> *But what good are roots if you can't take them with you?*[17]

One set of my data comes from Sócrates' own words. During his life, he gave countless interviews and testimonies; some have been filmed and can be found on the internet, and many have been published, in magazines, newspapers and books. My focus here is on three documents in particular, as they provide a full range of Sócrates' ideas across different times of his life:

(1) A book edited by the journalist Jorge Vasconcellos[18] in which he interviewed 12 retired 'masters of Brazilian *futebol*', Socrates among them; in the book the 'masters' reflect on their careers, tell football anecdotes and talk about episodes of the football world. However, as Vasconcellos affirms, political engagement and leadership makes Sócrates' testimony unique; he is a 'rare character in the football realm'.[19]

(2) A book written by Sócrates and the journalist Ricardo Gozzi about the Corinthians Democracy.[20] This book is a valuable resource because its chapters contain, firstly, Gozzi's extensive historical research (including testimonies by other actors in the political movement, such as players, football managers, directors and coaches): secondly, details about games, scores and championships; and thirdly, after each passage in which Gozzi discloses and analyses historical facts in chronological order, Sócrates' reflections on the episodes reported by Gozzi;

(3) Sócrates' chronicles: From 2001 to 2011, Sócrates wrote articles for *Carta Capital*, a left-oriented Brazilian weekly magazine. In each of his approximately 1000-word articles, he reflects on football, reports anecdotic football histories and talks about Brazilian politics and culture. The articles offer genuine insight into Sócrates' ideology.[21]

As a second set of data, I also interviewed two Brazilian sports journalists who not only followed Sócrates' career, but also had close relationships with him; the first is Juca Kfouri, the most widely read Brazilian sports journalist and Sócrates' closest friend; and the second is Victor Birner, who continues to have a daily presence on several Brazilian sport press channels (internet, TV and newspapers).

Finally, I was witness – and a few times a participant – to many of the historical passages I refer to in this essay. As a Brazilian teenager living in São Paulo in that period, I saw Sócrates playing against my team and I also cheered him when he played for Brazil. As a high school student, I was involved in the country's political life. I went to every student union gathering or parade, where we demanded freedom of speech and better schooling conditions. As a consequence of being witness to and participant in Brazil's social life and of employing my personal memories[22] as a background to many of the histories I report and analyse, I 'move in and out'[23] of the paper, since I cannot remove myself from certain images, such as the demonstration I described at the beginning of this paper.

Sócrates is a central character in Brazilian history. The wide spread of my data shows the ways that he transcended the football field to become more than a sports legend, a libertarian icon who inspires every freedom fighter around the world.

Sócrates, the footballer

Football without art is not futebol.[24]

Freeing the body ... and the spirit

Following a tradition originated by Brazilian sociologist Gilberto Freyre,[25] several authors[26] emphasize a particular feature in Brazilian *futebol* that makes it so worthwhile to watch as well as distinctive compared to other play styles: its *poetry*. Transforming the mechanical way that Europeans played the game of football into *futebol-arte* is what made Brazilian *futebol* so extraordinary. In opposition to the Apollonian European play style, the so-called 'prose',[27] Brazilians have a Dionysian play style, which is closer to pleasure, to improvisation and to the aesthetics of dance steps.[28] The real *futebol-arte* is 'artful dribbling and sending the ball around opponents in sweeping arcs, spontaneous and efficient, capable of creating unexpected spaces'[29]; it 'is based on short rather than long passes: players are more likely to dribble and pass the ball (...) than to send a long kick into their half of the field'.[30]

Sócrates once declared that football appeared to be a 'route accident'[31] in his life. He thought that, given his personal circumstances, he was not meant to be a good player.[32] However, external events allied with his particular skills transformed him into a unique example of poetry on the football fields. A closer look at Sócrates' life assists in a better understanding of the ways his football style developed. Sócrates never played 'football'; he played *futebol-arte* which is more than just a game style, it is inextricably linked to autonomy. *Futebol-arte* is poetry and freedom.[33]

Sócrates Brasileiro Sampaio de Souza Vieira de Oliveira[34] was born in 1954 in *Belém do Pará*, the capital city of *Pará*, a state located in Brazilian North, close to the Amazon forest. He was six when his family moved to Ribeirão Preto, a medium-sized city in the state of São Paulo. As with many Brazilian players, he started playing futsal at school, and at the age of 14, he and other school colleagues were called by Haroldo Soares, their school coach, to play in Botafogo de Ribeirão Preto, one of the two major teams in the city.[35] It was in this team that Sócrates built his fame as a talented player. Yet, reconciling training, weekend games and studies at the university was hard[36]; Botafogo coaches and directors supported him in an 'exclusive exemption regime; as I could not miss classes, I could not practice, my workload was extremely hard, and many times I only showed up for the Sunday matches after 24 h without sleeping working in the hospital'.[37]

These particular situations may have influenced Sócrates' football style. As he could not practice, when he became a professional, he had no physical strength to resist his opponents. He considered himself to be an 'anti-athlete: no muscles, very tall and thin, with zero conditions to cope with opponents' tackling'.[38] In a very short period of time, he fostered an alternate technique, totally different from what had been seen on the field so far; he started to pass the ball very quickly, using no more than one touch on the ball: 'I did everything to avoid physical contact and tackling from the opponents; it was only one touch: my bottom, my knee, elbow, whatever I could use to pass the ball; and of course, my heels, what later became my trademark'.[39]

Another way to explain Sócrates' playing style – a version heard my whole life from journalists and football commentators on TV shows and in every gathering in which I have discussed football – referred to the disproportion between his height and the size of his feet. As he was tall and his feet were small, if he turned too fast, he lost his balance; therefore, he mastered the back heel kick to overcome this obstacle. Lirio disagrees with this version.[40] He believes that Sócrates used the back heel to celebrate *futebol-arte*. In his chronicles, Sócrates supports this version; he tells a history about a festive game to celebrate a Brazilian singer, in front of 30,000 supporters,

> I played the whole game using back heel kicks; the crowd went crazy at each touch; it was a collective catharsis, it was so good to look towards the stands and see that happiness (...). At the end of the game, I kicked a penalty with my heel. The ball touched the bar. Never was a missed penalty so cheered![41]

It is clear that Sócrates' play style made him an artist on the fields. Just like one of the best examples of Brazilian *futebol-arte,* Garrincha – with his 'famous crooked legs' that made it impossible for his opponents to foresee his movements[42] – Sócrates used his intelligence to transform physical disadvantages into technical resources.[43] His talent gave him freedom to develop a new style and to overcome brutal untalented opponents.[44]

In a 2010 chronicle entitled 'The Brazilian way of playing', Sócrates adopted Freyre's *futebol-arte* concepts. He explains the idea of combat by opposing the Brazilian Dionysian and the European Apollonian football styles:

> our *futebol,* with its creativity and joy, is the expression of our social formation, our nonconformity to an excess of order and standardization (...) whilst European football is an expression of scientific method, we enjoy the surprises and the flexibility that remind us of dance steps and individual spontaneity.[45]

Juca Kfouri stated that Sócrates had 'magical heels and a privileged mind'. According to Victor Birner, besides his amazing skills that gave him his exclusive and elegant style, Sócrates had an 'enviable capacity for reading the game'. By the end of the 1970s, Botafogo was gaining good results against the major state teams.[46] It did not take too long for Sócrates to receive the attention of major club coaches and managers.

In the beginning, he rejected proposals from bigger clubs, deciding to finish his medical degree. However, as soon as he finished his university studies, Sócrates put aside his medical career and focused his energies on football. He was aiming to play in a bigger team which could lead him to the Brazilian team.[47] São Paulo FC and Sport Club Corinthians entered into a bid to hire him. Following a few negotiation rounds, he accepted the offer from Vicente Matheus, the legendary Corinthians' president. It was 1978. Sócrates was moving from the modest Botafogo to the powerful Corinthians, one of the most popular football clubs in Brazil, a move that would change not only his and the Corinthians' life, but also make a resounding difference to Brazilian's football and social history.

Next, I examine the relationship between Sócrates, his new club and its enormous cohort of fans. I explain the ways which, in a dialectical process, they changed each other – for the better.

Sócrates and S.C. Corinthians: A synergistic dance

Poetry is to prose as dancing is to walking.[48]

Founded in 1910 by lower-class workers, S.C. Corinthians was the second Brazilian club to accept black players into its team. Over the decades, the club became a symbol of social cohesion and 'class and race integration'.[49] On the other hand, it was also the club which best represented the poor migrants from Brazil's north and north-east, a good number of whom were socially marginalized black or *mulatos* inhabitants of the *favelas*.

The club increased its supporter base during a long period of losses. From 1954 to 1977, Corinthians did not win a single title. During this 23 years of 'desert crossing',[50] instead of losing fans, Corinthians' aura of suffering and penitence attracted hundreds of thousands of people. Winning any title became an obsession for the team and its supporters. The crowd developed a fanatic and rather religious sense, naming itself 'The Faithful'. The expectations on the players' shoulders were massive: they should adore the team as fans did; players were expected to show *raça*,[51] meaning that they were involved in a war and must give everything – their flesh and their blood – to win it. A mainstream Corinthians player was not an artist who displayed *futebol-arte*, but one who, even if not particularly skilled, would sacrifice himself for the club's sake.

Therefore, it was no surprise that Sócrates and 'The Faithful' had difficulties in accepting and understanding each other. As Florenzano remembers, Sócrates, on his very first day wearing a Corinthians jersey, in August 1978, in front of the TV cameras, said 'I have been a fan of Pelé and Santos F.C. since I was a child, but now as a Corinthians player, I will be a professional'.[52] This statement was heresy for 'The Faithful'. They were hoping for a *raçudo* warrior, not for a cold-blooded professional.

Sócrates' play style was a problem too. Fans did not initially enjoy his slower rhythm or his *futebol-arte*. Even with the 1979 state title win, 'the Faithful' still had trouble accepting his style. In May 1980, after being beaten in the semi-finals of an important national championship, fans followed Sócrates to the club's parking area and tried to lynch him. They were familiar with players who displayed virility, heart and *raça,* and did not accept Sócrates' refinement, art and intelligence. They strongly resented his lack of passion. Sócrates blamed the media for these misunderstandings: 'Journalists have created a myth that a Corinthians' player must be ignorant and vibrant; as I am not that, they think I don't fit in the club'.[53]

Sócrates also had conflicts with the president of the club, the legendary Vicente Matheus. Over the previous 10 years, Matheus had been at the top of the club, managing everything with his iron hand; he was the self-proclaimed 'fighter for Corinthians' rights'.[54] However, all the players suffered when attempting to renew their contracts with him.[55] At the beginning of 1980, Sócrates wanted a raise in his wages. He both deserved and needed it:

> After one year in Corinthians, I was called to the National Team – however, I was struggling with my bills – I signed with the club for the same wages I had in Botafogo, but life in São Paulo was far more expensive. So, I came up with a proposal to Matheus: he would give me a salary raise and I would sign up a year extension in my contract. But he refused my request, and I entered into a fight with the club to preserve my rights.[56]

As Sócrates had not signed a new contract, and as the old one had ended by the first semester of 1980, he stopped playing for two months. He was angry with both Matheus and the supporters. He thought he would not return to Corinthians. 'It is not only about money, but also about my principles'.[57]

After a hard negotiation, Matheus, who was being pushed by club members and supporters, gave in and signed a better contract with Sócrates. But Sócrates was still in doubt about returning, as he wanted to be himself as a player, not the passionate idol 'the Faithful' were looking for. Additionally, he intended to be listened to about the ways Corinthians would play. His friend Juca Kfouri, editor at that time of *Placar* magazine, persuaded him to change his mind and to come back to the team.[58]

After two months, Sócrates reappeared on the team, marking his 'conversion' with a beard and long hair – to illustrate that he was no longer that icy player. Little by little, he was adopting a new style, mixing his intellectualism and *futebol-arte* with the *raça* required by his fans. He started to create a new way to communicate with his public:

> A few times I did not celebrate a goal, as a reaction against aggressive behaviour of 'the Faithful' I did not approve of. I was creating a new dialogue with the fans so I could use that immense communal energy working for the team. I was using psychology and being honest with them by saying "look, I am like this; when I don't like something I tell you, let's be fair to each other". In fact, I was creating an emotional bond.[59]

The fans supported his new attitude from his first game back. They cheered him on, showing him they were on his side in his work rights struggle. At the beginning of 1981, they paraded in the city making a symbolic funeral of president Matheus, calling him an 'incompetent dictator'.[60] By displaying *raça* allied with his natural talent, Sócrates demonstrated to the fans he was another 'Faithful'. In this sense, 'The Faithful' changed Sócrates as a player and as a man.

The bond worked very well for all sides. Sócrates played nearly five years for Corinthians, appearing in 297 games where he scored 172 goals. He won three state championships[61] and is ranked as one of the top ten players in the club's history.[62]

After leaving the club in 1984, Sócrates played with Fiorentina (Italy), and with two other great Brazilian teams, Flamengo and Santos, before retiring. Nonetheless, for him nothing was the same as playing in Corinthians. In a 2011 chronicle entitled 'The weight of a Corinthians jersey' he expressed his feelings for the team:

> Playing in Corinthians is different. It is an uncontested love. It is your soul mate. It is respecting a culture, a people, a nation. It is like being called up to an irrational war and never questioning that it is the most important war that ever existed. It is being requested to think as Marx, fight as Napoleon, pray as Dalai-Lama and donate your life just like Mandela.[63]

The important role that Corinthians played in Sócrates' life is well established. Their mutual love and admiration is recognised by all. However, it was due to his participation in the Brazilian national team, *the* Seleção, that Sócrates became acknowledged as one of the 100 top players of the twentieth century.[64]

Wearing the 'mythical' yellow jersey: Sócrates in the Seleção

Magic and dreams are finished in football. We have to combine technique and efficiency.[65]

During the twentieth century, *futebol* played a central role in the construction of Brazilian national identity. After winning its first World Cup in Sweden (1958), the Brazilian national football team, the *Seleção*, became the biggest source of national pride in the country. Following each international win, the prowess of the players in the yellow jerseys was incessantly retold, increasing the 'myths and magic' of the team in Brazilian hearts. *Futebol* is so central to Brazilian identity that the 'nationwide identification with the Brazilian National Team paralyses the country and makes its players national heroes'.[66] Wearing a yellow jersey makes a player an ambassador of Brazilianness to the world. The *Seleção* has become the 'motherland in booths'.[67] The so-called 'inferiority complex' that Brazilians feel when comparing any aspect of their society to Europe or North America is only overcome on the football field. The futebol played by the *Seleção* in the 1970s has been admired and feared by teams around the world.[68]

After becoming a professional, Sócrates thought he could make it into the *Seleção*. He was short-listed for the *Seleção* for the first time just before the 1978 Argentine World Cup. He was chosen as one of 40 players who would make up the team, but was not called to the competition. He believed that he would have made it if at that time he had been playing for a bigger team; this had also accelerated his decision to go and play for Corinthians.[69] After that World Cup, he was a frequent name on the team, and was the captain of the *Seleção* when it was defeated by Italy in the 1982 Spain World Cup. He considers that one of the best teams he has played on in his life. Being its captain was 'the major honour I had in my life'.[70] His trauma of being defeated was proportional to the happiness of being there.

Sócrates loved the 1982 team. He was thrilled about playing that World Cup. The 1982 *Seleção* had a play style that he thought represented the players' feelings, their beliefs, the way they lived and cried. He described his goal in his World Cup debut against USSR as an 'endless orgasm'.[71] At the same time though, Sócrates considered the 'tragedy of *Sarria*', as Brazilians call the defeat against Italy in the 1982 World Cup, his life's most important lesson. After the tragic defeat, as he had no other objectives in his life than the World Cup, he had to 'start again from zero'.[72] He had to rethink his professional objectives and found strength deep inside to continue his life as a player.

However, and agreeing with Victor Birner and other sports commentators, he recognized the paradox that will surround that team forever. Although the team lost, the 1982 *Seleção* continues to be recognized as one of the best teams in football history; Sócrates thought this was evidence that Brazilians should recognize not only the winners, but also the 'aesthetic outcome'.[73] Within Brazilian society there continues to be an endless debate about the 1982 *Seleção*; many commentators show an enormous reverence for this team. They constantly affirm they would rather have seen the 1982 team displaying their art, even if defeated, than the bureaucratic football displayed by the 1994 *Seleção*.[74] The argument becomes more interesting as the 1994 national team won the world championship, but it is still not considered by the critics to be as remarkable as the 1982 *Seleção*

Victor Birner, when answering my questions about Sócrates and the *Seleção*, confirmed this paradox, but also reaffirms the place that Sócrates had in that team:

How many times have you seen a defeated team receiving countless compliments? Sócrates was so special that even with the *Seleção* he was able to contradict a historical sporting rule that establishes that the winners become beloved heroes and the losers hated villains. He was the *Seleção's* face, they matched each other. The unmatched side was the results of that 1982 magic team.

Sócrates acknowledges that the members of the 1982 team were a very special group of people; according to him, the dialogue and the relationship among them were fantastic. This was in part due to the team's coach, Telê Santana, who Sócrates nominates as 'the most democratic coach I have ever worked with'.[75] The close relationship with Telê Santana, master of *futebol-arte*, was crucial to understand Sócrates' passage in the *Seleção*. Sócrates felt at home in the team and he and Telê Santana talked about everything. Sócrates enjoyed being part of and discussing game plans with coaches and other players. Juca Kfouri stated that 'Sócrates admired Telê as much as he admired his idol, his father Raimundo'. Victor Birner adds that 'Sócrates and Telê not only shared an ideological view about *futebol-arte*, they had it embedded in their souls'.

It was this spirit that accompanied Telê and Sócrates to the 1986 México World Cup. Unlike 1982 though, Sócrates' memories of this team are solely of 'hard pain'.[76] He declared that the heart of the 1982 *Seleção* was there, but sick. He and team-mates such as Zico were recovering from injuries, and struggling with pain. The intimacy they had had in 1982 was lost. It was in México where he made what Juca Kfouri considers his major mistake on a football field: the missed penalty against France that cost Brazil's qualification for the semi-finals of the tournament. Sócrates did not sleep after that defeat in the World Cup. He complains that the media promotes the idea that Brazil must win, and if the team loses, whoever is culpable must be found. He defends himself, saying that in that period he was developing his penalty shots techniques. Hence, mistakes were part of the drill.[77]

Sócrates made 60 appearances in a yellow jersey, scoring 22 goals. Even if he did not win a title with the *Seleção*, he contributed to one of the most beautiful chapters in the *Seleção*'s history. Sócrates' international football achievements were accepted by Pelé, who listed him on his 2004 FIFA 100 list.

Sócrates used his position as a football idol in a different way from other players – he transformed the football stage into a place where he could make a social difference. He wanted to make a contribution to his community. He refused to comply with undemocratic relationships, whether in his team or in the broader society; he did not accept social injustice. The following section will reveal other facets of Sócrates' life – his political and social activism.

Sócrates, the social activist

Sport as a vehicle for social change

We need an educational revolution – and sport is the cheapest tool for this aim.[78] Scholars in the field of sociology of sport agree that sport has been long regarded as a conservative institution.[79] They maintain that athletes have been called to play rather than think, and there is no stimulus for them to engage in critical thinking or social/political causes – and if they do engage in such activities, they are more likely to be scorned than movie or music stars who do the same. A Marxist perspective on the sociology of sport criticizes the sports world for 'fostering alienation'[80]; as the pursuit of excellence in sport is so focused on individual performance, the assumption is that sport is not the right place for social concerns.

However, many researchers and social organizations have begun to develop a different agenda for sport, conceiving it as a tool for social change. The United Nations state that 'organized and competitive sport is a powerful and cost-effective way to support development and peace objectives'.[81] They see sport as a tool to promote world peace, gender equity, better communication between communities, anti-racism campaigns, as well as health and educational values.

Several scholars believe that sport, through its inherent qualities, 'can and indeed should, be a vehicle for progressive change'.[82] Kaufman and Wolf maintain that sport experience provides athletes with many opportunities to develop social consciousness, through a familiarity with feelings of power and powerlessness and through experiences of working towards mutual goals in a team. Jarvie provides a range of practical examples in which sport has aided social change, in either an actual or a symbolic manner.[83] Other authors call for human rights in sport itself, stating that 'human rights cannot be achieved without all sports participants fully enjoying those rights'.[84] They point to a range of human rights concerns – such as women's rights, good sports facilities and quality sport programmes for all – that must be part of the progressive social agenda of the sporting world.

Kaufman and Wolf make use of activist athletes' voices to outline the ways that sport might be a tool for advancing social and political causes. The authors have identified four dimensions of sport – 'social consciousness, meritocracy, responsible citizenship and interdependency'[85] – which have important connections to social activism. If they had known Sócrates and his teammates, these scholars would certainly have agreed that the social and historical conditions of their struggle, the content of their demands and their methods made them pioneers among athletes who 'play and protest'.[86] Sócrates shared the UN sport taskforce's understandings about sport being a powerful and inexpensive tool to promote education and development; he promoted this idea continually and was a strong advocate of human rights within sports.

In 1981, Sócrates started putting his political activism into practice within the sports milieu. He and his Corinthians team-mates wanted to have voice in their own team. Fortunate political circumstances allowed them to begin a self-government experience in the club, which later became known as Corinthians Democracy. Next, I explain the development and importance of this movement to Brazil's struggle for democracy.

The Corinthians Democracy: Roots

Athletes have the power in a football team, but they do not know it yet [87]
As previously mentioned, in the 1980 quarrel Sócrates had with Corinthians – which caused him to stop playing for two months – wages were one among several issues in dispute. Another was that Sócrates wanted to have a say in the way the team played, but his coach, Oswaldo Brandão, backed by president Matheus, did not want players to have tactical opinions – they were there to play not to think.

Sócrates' demands found echoes in Brazil's football history. Before and even after the 1964 military coup, there was much more autonomy within the *futebol* context. Players made decisions together with coaches. Florenzano argues that this autonomy of opinion had parallels with the *futebol-arte* displayed by Brazilian players[88]; they nourished each other, as both were 'freedom practices' – autonomy for the soul, *futebol-arte* for the body. The author claims that this practice was evident in the magic 1970 *Seleção*; Pelé, Gerson, Tostão and others, although under the military's close surveillance, had their say in the way the team played; they convened meetings to modify tactics and they even pushed the coach to put on the field those team-mates they thought were better for the team.

This democratic tradition suffered during the 1970s – a period known as the *years of lead* – in which the country's 'modernization project' undertaken by the military imposed its ideology on the football world: intensive fitness training and body control; rigid discipline and centralized command; and the presence of the military and their allies as coaches and on club boards, as directors and presidents – people like *capo* Vicente Matheus in Corinthians. One of the arguments that Matheus used to convince Sócrates to come back to Corinthians after the 1980 contract dispute was that he would be given greater voice in the team's tactics. But this turned out to be untrue. Matheus had employed every sort of political and juridical trick to remain club president during the previous 10 years. His methods of running the club were aligned with the years of lead that were taking place in Brazil; he declared that Corinthians was a 'soft dictatorship'.[89]

However, in the 1981 club election, Matheus, unable to find a legal way to continue as club president, proposed his old friend and political ally, Waldemar Pires, for president with himself as vice-president, expecting Pires to be his figurehead, while he – Matheus – would remain in charge. The Pires/Matheus ticket won the election, and in the first month, things went as planned. Matheus still sat, literally, in the president's chair and controlled all decisions. Nevertheless, after a few months, tired of and humiliated by being 'Matheus' puppet', Pires turned things around, moved away from Matheus and nominated a new person to be in charge of the professional football department, the 33-year-old sociologist, Adilson Monteiro Alves, son of one of the club deputy-presidents. This was the beginning of the revolution.[90]

The year 1981 had been awful for Corinthians: the athletes were unmotivated, brought down by the lack of dialogue in the team; in the national championship the team had been relegated to the second division; the team did not play well in the state tournament. On the other hand, civil society in Brazil – after several years of tough oppression, censorship, torture and killings – was coming alive again. The 1979 Amnesty Law had brought back to the country many of the political, cultural and intellectual leaders who had been in exile abroad. All sectors of the population – students, workers, and women – were demonstrating their desire to change the country.[91] The desires of Corinthians players to share in this movement point to the 'potential intersectionality between sport, reflexivity and activism'.[92]

The new football director, Adilson Alves, had his first talk with the players at the beginning of November during the 'confinement' before a match. He started by breaking down the traditional hierarchy. Aligning with the changes occurring in Brazil, he wanted free expression of ideas in the team. He told the players that he did not know too much about football, hence he needed their ideas; coincidently, Mario Travaglini, a new coach known as a man of dialogue, arrived in the club in the same period. Sócrates and the other team leaders (Wladimir and Casagrande) did not waste a minute. They wanted to have a voice in their own work as athletes; they knew they could make a difference in the club's life; they had strong social consciousness and aspired to exercise it. In short, they aspired to be not only athletes, but 'activist-athletes'.[93] The Corinthians Democracy was born.

The Corinthians Democracy – implementation

It was a revolutionary movement, isolated, in a very reactionary milieu called
football[94]

'One person, one vote'. The universal suffrage slogan could be used to define the
Corinthians Democracy. The team members employed polls to decide everything
concerning the group. As voting was central in their relationship and it was embedded in their professional lives, democracy was the name given to the movement by
Juca Kfouri at a round table at the Catholic University at the beginning of 1982.[95]
They voted for everything, from the practice timetable to the days or times they
would travel to a match in another city, and even the hotel they would stay in.
Before hiring or firing a player, Adilson Monteiro Alves would present the
candidate's name to the group, and after a discussion, the issue would be decided by
vote. It is important to highlight that every professional in the team had the right
to vote: players voted, but also medical doctors, coaches, directors (Alves had just
one vote too – he represented the club executive) and even the most humble
employees – cleaners, bus drivers, cooks – were entitled to vote.

Enemies of the Corinthians Democracy – and according to Sócrates there were
plenty of them, both inside and outside the club – claimed that it was a 'democracy
of four people'. These enemies stated (and many currently claim this) that Sócrates'
group prevailed in all polls. However, this is easily denied by the facts: Sócrates lost
many of the polls. For example, Alves wanted to bring in a talented goalkeeper also
known to be an authoritarian person. Sócrates thought he would not fit the democratic atmosphere, but the group believed they needed a good goalkeeper, and he
was hired. Sócrates also narrates with pleasure a few humorous stories, such as,
once, after a fiery debate about which day the team should travel to Rio de Janeiro
to a match, they started the poll, which was even until the end; the last man was to
uneven it. He was a shy goalkeeper who rarely expressed his opinion – and he voted
against Sócrates' point of view![96]

Most significant, though, in Sócrates' view, was that all involved were growing
as professionals as well as human beings. This democratic process demanded education, political formation and information, as many players and employees had no
idea how to manifest their opinions. A few also feared what would happen to them
if they disagreed with the directors or with the most influential players. Sócrates had
the consciousness that he, with a few other players, had more information and education, so the members of this group were more prepared to make decisions, and
were more skilled to stand up and speak for the movement when called. As
described many years later by Kaufman and Wolf, the activism of the Corinthians
Democracy raised everyone's political and social consciousness.

These freedom practices of autonomy in voting and decision-making also
increased the responsibility and interdependence of all players.[97] They knew that if
they did not play well, the conservative sectors of the club, the media and the society more generally would blame the democracy. The major newspapers were already
writing against the club's self-governance, stating that this would not work in a football team. So, the fight to rebuild the 1981 defeated team was directly linked to the
struggle to implement the democratic project. Many Corinthians 'war horse' players,
motivated by the project, renewed their strength to practice and play better.[98] The
1982/1983 team, playing high level *futebol-arte*, won two state championships and

performed well in the national championships. Democracy and success walked side by side.

At the beginning, the need to be part of the decisions that affected their daily work lives was a key goal of the players. However, although self-government praxis in a popular football club was per se a revolutionary idea, the players soon wanted more. Being an athlete-activist, as Kaufman and Wolf maintain, requires social consciousness and involvement in the broader social issues of the society. Therefore, Corinthians players began to engage themselves in political causes: a few subscribed to new political parties that were forming at that period; others became members of the players' union. However, the main element of their political engagement was their contribution, both as individuals and also as a team, to the *Free Elections Now* movement.

Sócrates had a clear vision that everything that happened in Corinthians had a huge repercussion within the society: whether losing or winning, the Corinthians made Brazilian newspaper covers every day. Hence, they soon constituted a focal point of the civil rights movement, contributing to the delivery of its messages to bigger audiences.

The Corinthians Democracy and the society

We employed the word democracy in the best way, both socially as within the football world.[99]

In December of 1983, 115,000 fans went to the Morumbi stadium to watch the state championship grand final. Corinthians was playing my beloved São Paulo FC. I was there in the middle of the São Paulo crowd, singing and supporting my team. However, it was impossible not to feel empathy for the Corinthians players as well.

Just before the start of the game, when both sides made their appearance on the field, the whole Corinthians team paraded around the pitch, with an enormous banner reading: *Winning or losing, but always with democracy.* In the centre of their formation, holding the banner was a tall, bearded man – Sócrates – with his white head band, looking like the natural leader of that parade.

The *Free elections now* movement and the Corinthians Democracy were closely connected. As Juca Kfouri stated in his interview, the best things Sócrates did outside the field were his leadership of the club's revolutionary movement and his active involvement with the democratization process. A few historical events demonstrate this link.

By participating in the *Free elections now* movement, Sócrates and his teammates were not only surfing the wave of a successful and popular movement. A few years earlier, Sócrates had participated in fundraising matches for civil rights causes. He used his popular profile to support democratic causes, such as the Worker's Party Foundation. He was also very happy as on these occasions he could meet democratic leaders, famous actors and singers. He describes these events as 'orgasmic moments of Brazilianness'.[100]

The members of the country's progressive political scene also backed the club's utopic movement. In 1982, at the end of Corinthians Democracy's first year, Vicente Matheus' political group tried to stage a 'coup d'état' to recover power in the club. However, the Brazilian progressive intelligentsia leadership promptly protested and made enough noise in the press to abort the reactionary try. Democracy prevailed.

The revolutionary players left their mark additionally on other important areas within Brazilian society. Sócrates sang in rock and roll shows, alongside eminent singers like Rita Lee. Wladimir and Casagrande took roles as actors in movies that contested the hegemonic gender and sexual order.[101] They wanted to show that footballers should be regarded as integral participants of Brazilian culture, on and off the field.

At the beginning of 1984 Corinthians Democracy and the *Free elections now* were at their climax. The following events would once again demonstrate the deep connections between both. Regrettably, to all democrats, that was a sad link. Despite the vast democratic and civil euphoria that was going on across the country, the federal parliament – intimidated by the military – did not approve the *Free elections now* bill. A huge wave of frustration invaded the country's heart. Brazilians would have to wait five more years until they could elect their president ourselves. Sócrates' memories of that day are sorrowful: 'as soon as I heard the bad news, I started to cry. I never cried like I did on that day. I told the Corinthians' directors that I would leave'.[102]

Carrying out his promise, Sócrates left Corinthians in the middle of the year to play in Italy. Following him, other key players such as Casagrande and Juninho left the club to play elsewhere. In 1985, Adilson Monteiro Alves bid to be Corinthians' president, but lost the club's elections to the conservative forces. It was the end of the dream.

Sócrates' legacy and the future of football

If I can't dance to it, it's not my revolution.[103]

After his retirement, Sócrates continued to be politically active. In 2002, he participated in Lula's campaign to become president. As with most people, Sócrates had big expectations of Lula's government, as Lula was the first left-oriented worker to be elected as the country's president. However, over time, Sócrates became frustrated with the ways things went, and he kept a critical eye on the government.

During the first four years of Lula's government, the president and his ministers were constantly asking Sócrates for his opinions on key sports issues. Sócrates participated fully in the application of Lula's political proposals to the sports arena. Despite Lula's frequent requests to Sócrates to take a place in the government, Sócrates did not accept. In his interview, Victor Birner conveyed to me that, unlike Sócrates' *Free elections now* colleagues, 'Sócrates never accepted any public employment, which would be easy for him as he had good connections and popularity. But he opted to stay out of the system and to keep his critical point of view'.

Sócrates passed away in December 2011. He was only 56 years old. His death was caused by diseases related to alcohol-consumption. He had never denied that he enjoyed a 'few beers'. He once declared 'Let's put away the hypocrisy. Everybody drinks in this country. Every player drinks. Don't they want me to smoke, drink and think? But I smoke, I drink and I think'.[104]

Far from being perfect, Sócrates was a human being. As Juca Kfouri told me, he was a 'passionate human being, who needed to be constantly in love – which made him, his women and his children suffer a lot; but as a Brazilian Che Guevara, he also taught us that a footballer must go far beyond the field'.

Unlike many players who made a fortune as players and who, after their retirement, became entrepreneurs or TV commentators, Sócrates remained a fighter for better life conditions for the Brazilian people throughout his life. He maintained his political position that futebol should be used to advance the social changes that are urgent in the country. He had a perfect understanding of the power emanating from the football field. He knew that there was nothing more popular or more political than football in the country. So, if conservative forces use football to promote their beliefs, progressive sides should use it as well. He was also keen on a project to make high school studies compulsory for every professional footballer; in his opinion, when footballers became more educated, they would be better role models for the countless children who dream of being a professional footballer. Furthermore, education would provide these kids with other prospects for their future if they could not achieve a good position in the football world.

Sócrates' legacy is also part of Brazilian history. From a historical perspective, it can be seen that, after two decades, the country has a consolidated democracy, and Sócrates was an integral part of the realization of this. The journalists who supported the Corinthians Democracy are currently putting all their strength into denouncing the web of corruption involved in the 2014 Brazil World Cup.[105] This denouncement is only possible as there is now a free press in the country, which was not the reality 30 years ago. Sócrates' struggles were essential for this achievement.

Sócrates' legacy, however, is broader than role modelling athlete-activism and citizenship and the poetry of *futebol-arte* discussed earlier. Above all, Sócrates left a legacy of happiness and freedom to the football world. After scoring a goal, he celebrated with his right fist raised, mimicking the Black Panthers gesture at the Mexico Olympics. However, this was not merely an attitude of defiance against anything non-democratic. His celebration was accompanied by an immense smile, showing the world that one must struggle with joy. His major legacy, then, is that he was able to combine the aesthetics of *futebol-arte* with the ethics of a freedom fighter, without missing the joyfulness of play and life. Although Sócrates was unique, *futebol* needs many more players like him.

Acknowledgements

I would like to acknowledge: the kindness of Juca Kfouri and Victor Birner in responding to my questions so quickly; the consideration I received from Ademir Takara, librarian of the São Paulo Football Museum, who sent precious research material to Australia; the patience of Dr Kausik Bandyopadhyay with my delay in finishing this paper. Last but not least, I would like to express my profound gratitude to Dr Constance Ellwood for her more than careful English editing of this paper.

Notes

1. Andrade, *Os filhos da Candinha*.
2. *'Diretas-já' Campaign*.
3. Bertoncelo, *I Want to Vote for President*.
4. Reis, 'Ditadura, anistia e reconciliação'.
5. Lula, 18 years later, was twice elected Brazilian president. He governed the country from 2002 to 2010. His friendship with Sócrates has been reaffirmed in the many episodes when they were together, such as at the 1984 Sócrates' farewell dinner – he was leaving to play in Italy – and Lula made a speech at the party, calling on Sócrates to remain connected to the Brazilian political scene (Florenzano, *A democracia corintiana*).
6. Shirts, 'Playing Soccer in Brazil'.
7. Sócrates and Gozzi, *Democracia Corintiana*.

8. Toledo, *Logicas no Futebol*.
9. Sócrates and Gozzi, *Democracia Corintiana*.
10. The two papers by M. Shirts ('Sócrates, Corinthians' and 'Playing Soccer in Brazil') are the only exemptions I have found so far; however, and despite their good analytical content, Shirts' papers lack historical accuracy. Later in this essay, I clarify the history of the beginning of the Corinthians Democracy; on Sócrates see also Eric Cantona's documentary 'Football Rebels'.
11. Camargo, ed., *Tecnicos: deuses e diabos na terra do Futebol*.
12. Vasconcellos, ed., *Recados da Bola*; Sócrates and Gozzi, *Democracia Corintiana*.
13. Lirio, ed., *Sócrates, Brasileiro*.
14. Kaufman and Wolff, 'Playing and Protesting'.
15. Wisnik, *Veneno remedio*; Florenzano, *A democracia corintiana*; Toledo, *Logicas no Futebol*; Bellos, *Futebol*; Natali, 'The Realm of the Possible'; Alvito, 'Our Piece of the Pie'; Knijnik, 'Visions of Gender Justice'; Pardue, 'Jogada Linguistica'. I apply here a broader definition of 'South American', not only those born there, but also researchers who wrote on the theme.
16. Kaufman and Wolff, 'Playing and Protesting'; Harvey, Horne, and Safai, 'Alterglobal-ization, Gobal Social Movements'; Jarvie, 'Sport, Social Change'.
17. Stein, *Three Lives*.
18. Vasconcellos, ed., *Recados da Bola*.
19. Ibid., 32.
20. Sócrates and Gozzi, *Democracia Corintiana*.
21. After his death, 87 of these articles were put together in a book edited by Lirio op cit., my source here.
22. Evelyn, 'Telling Stories of Research'.
23. Humberstone, 'Sport Management, Gender', 255.
24. Sócrates, in Lirio, *Sócrates, Brasileiro*, 60.
25. Freyre, *New World in the Tropics*; de Hollanda, 'In Praise of Improvisation', Toledo, *No pais do futebol*; Wisnik, 'The Riddle of Brazilian Soccer'.
26. Wisnik, 'The Riddle of Brazilian Soccer'; Campos, 'On the Value and Meaning of Football'; Gordon and Helal, 'The Crisis of Brazilian Football'; Natali, 'The Realm of the Possible'.
27. Freyre, *New World in the Tropics*; Buarque de Hollanda, 'In Praise of Improvisation in Brazilian Soccer'.
28. Maranhao, 'Apollonians and Dionysians'; Maranhao and Knijnik, 'Futebol Mulato'; Natali, 'The Realm of the Possible'.
29. Wisnik, *Veneno remédio*, 207.
30. Natali, 'The Realm of the Possible', 273.
31. Sócrates in Vasconcellos, *Recados da bola*, 208.
32. Sócrates, *Placar Magazine*, (score magazine, Brazilian weekly sports) special edition on Sócrates, December 2011.
33. Florenzano, *A democracia corinthiana*, 33.
34. Sócrates was also known as *Doctor*, Dr Sócrates or *Magrão* (tall thin buddy). He was the oldest of a six-brother family and his youngest brother is Rai, also a footballer who played in the 1990s for São Paulo F.C., Paris Saint-Germain and won the 1994 FIFA World Cup with the Brazilian Team.
35. Unzelte, *Os dez mais do Corinthians*.
36. In 1972 Sócrates entered the Faculty of Medicine at University of São Paulo, one of the largest and best South American universities. He graduated as a medical doctor there.
37. Sócrates, in Vasconcellos, *Recados da bola*, 209.
38. Ibid., 210.
39. Ibid.
40. Lirio, ed., *Sócrates Brasileiro*, dusk jacket.
41. Sócrates, ibid., 50.
42. Wisnik, 'The Riddle of Brazilian Soccer', 205.
43. 'A writer, or any man, must believe that whatever happens to him is an instrument; everything has been given for an end. This is even stronger in the case of the artist

(…) all has been given like clay, like material for one's art. One must accept it.' (Jorge Luis Borges, 'Blindness', in *Seven Nights*, 385)

44. Florenzano, *A democracia corinthiana*.
45. Sócrates, in Lirio, *Sócrates Brasileiro*, 102.
46. São Paulo, Corinthians, Palmeiras and Santos.
47. Unzelte, *Os dez mais do Corinthians*.
48. John B. Wain, *Wildtrack*.
49. Florenzano, *A democracia corinthiana*, 149.
50. Ibid., 145.
51. Bellos, *Futebol*.
52. Florenzano, *A democracia corinthiana*, 161.
53. *Placar Magazine*, August 1980, 535.
54. Sócrates and Gozzi, *Democracia Corintiana*, 29.
55. On that time, Brazilians footballers were under the '*Lei do Passe*' ('Bond Law' – cf. Toledo, *No país do futebol*). They 'belonged' to their club even when their contracts had expired, so they could not move to another club unless their club agreed. This Law was even harder than the equivalent European rules which were changed after 'The Bosman ruling' (cf. Frick, 'Globalization and Factor Mobility').
56. Sócrates and Gozzi, *Democracia Corintiana*, 26.
57. *Placar Magazine*, August 1980, 538.
58. Ibid., 539. 'The Doctor is Back'.
59. Vasconcellos, ed., *Recados da bola*, 211.
60. Florenzano, *A democracia corinthiana*, 176.
61. Vasconcellos, ed., *Recados da bola*, 206.
62. Unzelte, *Os dez mais do Corinthians*.
63. Lirio, ed., *Sócrates Brasileiro*, 27.
64. According to the *World Soccer* magazine list, published in 1999, Sócrates was ranked as the 61st Greatest Player of the twentieth century, drawing with Frenchman David Ginola and Englishman Glenn Hoddle.
65. Carlos Alberto Parreira, 1994 and 2006 Brazilian Team Coach, quoted in *New Straits Times*, July 2, 1994.
66. Maranhao and Knijnik, 'Futebol Mulato', 62.
67. Rodrigues, *A Patria de Chuteiras*.
68. Wisnik, *Veneno remédio*.
69. Unzelte, *Os dez mais do Corinthians*.
70. Vasconcellos, ed., *Recados da bola*, 280.
71. Sócrates, in Lirio, *Sócrates Brasileiro*, 74.
72. Vasconcellos, ed., *Recados da bola*, 221.
73. Ibid., 220.
74. Natali, 'The Realm of the Possible'.
75. Vasconcellos, ed., *Recados da bola*, 220.
76. Ibid., 222.
77. Ibid.
78. Sócrates, in Lirio, *Sócrates Brasileiro*, 188.
79. Kaufman and Wolf, op cit.; Davis-Delano and Crosset, 'Using Social Movement Theory'; Jarvie, 'Sport, Social Change'.
80. Kaufman and Wolf, 'Playing and Protesting', 155.
81. United Nations, 'Sport for Development', 24.
82. Kaufman and Wolf, 'Playing and Protesting', 156.
83. Jarvie, 'Sport, Social Change', 415 – one of his examples is Cathy Freeman, the Olympic medallist who became a powerful symbol of the Aboriginal Australians' fight for civil and political rights.
84. Kidd and Donnelly, 'Human Rights in Sports', 131.
85. Kaufman and Wolf, 'Playing and Protesting', 158.
86. Ibid.
87. Sócrates, in Sócrates and Gozzi, *Democracia Corintiana*, 57.
88. Florenzano, *A democracia corinthiana*.
89. Sócrates and Gozzi, *Democracia Corintiana*, 29.

90. I have added these historical passages here in order to bring more accuracy to the events related by Shirts in his two papers, where he affirms that the Corinthians Democracy began with the 1982 elections in the club; however, there were no elections in the club that year, and Adilson Monteiro Alves never ran for director of football; in 1981 he was invited to the position, and only in 1985 did he try to become the club's president but was defeated by the conservatives. Sócrates and Gozzi, *Democracia Corintiana*; Florenzano, *A democracia corinthiana*.
91. Reis, 'anistia e reconciliação'.
92. Kaufman and Wolf, 'Playing and Protesting', 159.
93. Ibid., 158.
94. Sócrates, in Sócrates and Gozzi, *Democracia Corintiana*, 100.
95. Kfouri, 'Preface', in Sócrates and Gozzi, *Democracia Corintiana*, 12.
96. Sócrates, 'My Corinthians', 2010, in Lirio, *Sócrates Brasileiro*, 25–6.
97. As was the case with the players interviewed by Kaufman and Wolf, 'Playing and Protesting'.
98. Florenzano, *A democracia corinthiana*.
99. Solito, Corinthians' goalkeeper, in Sócrates and Gozzi, *Democracia Corintiana*, 121.
100. Sócrates, 2002, in Lirio, *Sócrates Brasileiro*, 168.
101. Knijnik and Melo, 'Football, Cinema and New Sensibilities in the Masculine Territory'.
102. Sócrates, in Vasconcellos, *Recados da bola*, 223.
103. Emma Goldman.
104. Vasconcellos, ed., *Recados da bola*, 205.
105. Schausteck et al., 'Rationales, Rhetoric and Realities'.

References

Alvito, M. 'Our Piece of the Pie: Brazilian Football and Globalization'. *Soccer & Society* 8, no. 4 (2007): 524–44.
Andrade, M. *"Brasil-Argentina" in Os filhos da Candinha* [Candinha's Sons]. São Paulo: Martins Fontes, 1963.
Bellos, A. *Futebol: The Brazilian Way of Life*. London: Bloomsbury, 2002.
Bertoncelo, E. *"Eu quero votar para presidente": uma análise sobre a Campanha das Diretas* ["I Want to Vote for President": An Analysis of the 'diretas-já' Campaign], 169–96. Lua Nova: Revista de Cultura e Política, 2009.
Borges, J.L. 'Blindness'. *Seven Nights*. New York: New Directions Book, 1984.
Camargo, L.O.C., ed. *Técnicos: deuses e diabos da terra do futebol* [Coaches: Gods and Devils from the Football Land]. 1st ed. SESC-Ipiranga: São Paulo, 2002.
Campos, D. 'On the Value and Meaning of Football: Recent Philosophical Perspectives in Latin America'. *Journal of the Philosophy of Sport* 37, no. 1 (2010): 69–87.
Davis-Delano, L.R., and T. Crosset. 'Using Social Movement Theory to Study Outcomes in Sport-related Social Movements'. *International Review for the Sociology of Sport* 43, no. 2 (2008): 115–34.
Evelyn, D. 'Telling Stories of Research'. *Qualitative Research Journal* 5, no. 2 (2005): 125–50.
Florenzano, J.P. *A democracia corinthiana: práticas de liberdade no futebol brasileiro* [Corinthians Democracy: Freedom Practices in Brazilian football]. São Paulo: Educ/ Fapesp, 2010.
Freyre, G. *New World in the Tropics: The Culture of Modern Brazil*. New York: Knopf, 1959.
Frick, B. 'Globalization and Factor Mobility: The Impact of the "Bosman-ruling" on Player Migration in Professional Soccer'. *Journal of Sports Economics* 10, no. 1 (2009): 88–106.
Gordon, C., and R. Helal. 'The Crisis of Brazilian Football: Perspectives for the Twenty-first Century'. *The International Journal of the History of Sport* 18, no. 3 (2001): 139–58.
Harvey, J., J. Horne, and P. Safai. 'Alterglobalization, Global Social Movements and the Possibility of Political Transformation through Sport'. *Sociology of Sport Journal* 26 (2009): 383–403.

de Hollanda, B.B.B. 'In Praise of Improvisation in Brazilian Soccer: Modernism, Popular Music and a Brasilidade of Sports'. *Critical Studies in Improvisation/Études critiques en improvisation* 7, no. 1 (2011). http://www.criticalimprov.com/article/viewArticle/1229/2051.

Humberstone, B. 'Sport Management, Gender and the "bigger picture" Challenging Changes in Higher Education—A Partial Auto/ethnographical Account'. *Sport Management Review* 12, no. 4 (2009): 255–62.

Jarvie, G. 'Sport, Social Change and the Public Intellectual'. *International Review for the Sociology of Sport* 42 (2007): 411–24.

Kaufman, P., and E. Wolff. 'Playing and Protesting: Sport as a Vehicle for Social Change'. *Journal of Sport & Social Issues* 34, no. 2 (2010): 154–75.

Kidd, B., and P. Donnelly. 'Human Rights in Sports'. *International Review for the Sociology of Sport* 35, no. 2 (2000): 131–48.

Knijnik, J. 'Visions of Gender Justice Untested Feasibility on the Football Fields of Brazil'. *Journal of Sport & Social Issues* 37, no. 1 (2013): 8–30.

Knijnik, J., and V.A. Melo. 'Football, Cinema and New Sensibilities in the Masculine Territory: An Analysis of *Asa Branca, a Brazilian dream* (1981) and *New Wave* (1983)'. In *Embodied Masculinities in Global Sports*, ed. J. Knijnik and Daryl Adair. WV: FIT, 2014.

Lirio, S., ed., *Sócrates Brasileiro: as crônicas do Doutor em Carta Capital* [Sócrates Brasileiro: Doctor's Chronicles in Carta Capital]. Editora Confiança: São Paulo, 2012.

Maranhão, T. 'Apollonians and Dionysians: The Role of Football in Gilberto Freyre's Vision of Brazilian People'. *Soccer & Society* 8, no. 4 (2007): 510–23.

Maranhão, T., and J. Knijnik. 'Futebol Mulato: Racial Constructs in Brazilian Football'. *Cosmopolitan Civil Societies: An Interdisciplinary Journal* 3, no. 2 (2011): 18–34.

Natali, M. 'The Realm of the Possible: Remembering Brazilian Futebol'. *Soccer & Society* 8, no. 2–3 (2007): 267–82.

Pardue, D. 'Jogada Linguistica: Discursive Play and the Hegemonic Force of Soccer in Brazil'. *Journal of Sport & Social Issues* 26, no. 4 (2002): 360–80.

Reis, D.A. 'Ditadura, anistia e reconciliação [Dictatorship, Amnesty and Reconciliation]'. *Estudos Históricos (Rio de Janeiro)* 23 (2010): 171–86.

Rodrigues, N., and R. Castro. *A pátria em chuteiras: novas crônicas de futebol* [Homeland in Football Boots: New Chronicles of Football]. Sao Paulo: Companhia das Letras, 1994.

Schausteck de Almeida B., C. Bolsmann, W. Marchi Jr., and J. de Souza. 'Rationales, Rhetoric and Realities: FIFA's World Cup in South Africa 2010 and Brazil 2014'. *International Review for the Sociology of Sport* (2013), doi: 10.1177/1012690213481970

Shirts, M. 'Playing Soccer in Brazil: Sócrates, Corinthians, and Democracy'. *The Wilson Quarterly (1976–)* 13, no. 2 (1989): 119–23.

Shirts, M. 'Sócrates, Corinthians, and Questions of Democracy and Citizenship'. In *Sport and Society in Latin America: Diffusion, Dependency, and the Rise of Mass Culture*, ed. J.L. Arena, 97–112. New York: Greenwood Press, 1988.

Sócrates, and R. Gozzi. *Democracia Corintiana: a utopia em jogo* [Corinthians Democracy: The Utopy in Question]. São Paulo: Boitempo, 2002.

Stein, G. *Three Lives: Stories of the Good Anna, Melanctha and the Gentle Lena*. New York: Grafton Press, 1909.

Toledo LHd. *No país do futebol* [In the Football Country]. Rio de Janeiro: Jorge Zahar Editor Ltda, 2000.

Toledo LHd. *Lógicas do futebol* [Football Logics]. São Paulo: Hucitec, 2002.

United Nations. *Sport for Development and Peace: Towards Achieving the Millennium Development Goals. Report from the United Nations Inter-Agency Task Force on Sport for Development and Peace*. New York: United Nations Publications, 2003. Available at http://www.un.org/wcm/webdav/site/sport/shared/sport/pdfs/Reports/2003_interagency_report_ENGLISH.pdf.

Unzelte, C. *Os dez mais do Corinthians* [The Top 10 of Corinthians]. Rio de Janeiro: Maquinária, 2008.

Vasconcellos, J., ed. *Recados da bola: depoimentos de doze mestres do futebol brasileiro* [Messages from the Ball: Testimonials of Twelve Brazilian Football Masters], São Paulo: Cosac Naify, 2010.

Wain, J. *Wildtrack*. New York: Penguim Group, 1966.
Wisnik, J.M. 'The Riddle of Brazilian Soccer: Reflections on the Emancipatory Dimensions of Culture'. *Review: Literature and Arts of the Americas* 39, no. 2 (2006): 198–209.
Wisnik, J.M. *Veneno remédio: o futebol e o Brasil* [Poison Remedy: Football and Brazil]. São Paulo: Companhia das Letras, 2008.

Pibes, Cracks and *Caudillos*: Argentina, the World Cup and identity politics

Rwany Sibaja and Charles Parrish

School of Recreation, Health, and Tourism, George Mason University, Fairfax, VA, USA

Scholars of Argentine *fútbol* have explored the construction of *fútbol criollo* and how this style of play has factored into the broader debate over national identity in Argentina. Focusing on the performance of the key Argentine personalities at the FIFA World Cup from 1958 to 1990, this essay explores how *fútbol* represented a contested vision of the nation across five decades. After a 24-year absence at the FIFA World Cup, and in the wake of the overthrow of President Juan Perón, Argentina underachieved at the 1958 tournament. The country would later experience a number of disappointments en route to eventually winning the 1978 and 1986 World Cups. However, across this time span (and beyond) the team's style of play and identity became the subject of intense debate. Popular discourse revealed a preference between two approaches seemingly in juxtaposition to each other. On the one hand, traditionalists favoured the *criollo* style, which celebrated the *pibe* (the young kid from the streets) and the *potrero* (the dusty fields where *fútbol* is practised) as emblematic of the nation. These symbols represented the working class and elevated the life of the barrio as an anchor to the nation's humble beginnings. On the other hand, reformers preferred approaches that proved successful in Europe. Sometimes described by critics as *anti-fútbol*, the emphasis was on physicality, strict adherence to tactics and data-driven training. Proponents in Argentina equated this European approach to progress and modernity. Between 1958 and 1990, notable Argentine personalities at the FIFA World Cup embodied both of these philosophies.

Introduction

For many, sports can serve as a lens with which to gain useful insight into issues related to identity.[1] From an analytical and practical standpoint, they 'provide people with a sense of difference and a way of classifying themselves and others, whether latitudinally or hierarchically.'[2] This is particularly true with respect to Argentina as soccer, or *fútbol*, has consistently been a focus of popular public discourse with respect to national identity since the first quarter of the twentieth century.[3] Perhaps the prevailing dominant work on *fútbol* and identity politics in Argentina is the scholarship of the late anthropologist Eduardo Archetti, which emphasizes how the sport emerged as a cultural representation and an embodied expression of a hybrid national identity.[4] His work, along with that of historian Julio Frydenberg, emphasizes football's role in the construction of national and local identities during the first three decades of the twentieth century.[5] Others have noted the emergence of competing

---

Rwany Sibaja is currently at University of Maryland, Baltimore County, Baltimore, MD, USA

philosophies of the creative and spontaneous *fútbol criollo* and the physical, methodical and defensive-minded *anti-fútbol* during the 1960s and into the 1980s.[6] The former embodied a traditional and authentic version of national identity while the latter represented a more liberal and progressive notion of nationalism modelled after European styles associated with modernity.[7] The manner in which the national team, players and coaches have been the focus of intense politicized debates reveals how the discourse over Argentine identity remains unsettled in the twenty-first century.

Similar in approach to Andrews and Jackson's edited collection *Sport Stars*, this essay will diverge from the works previously mentioned by making the individual, rather than football in the abstract, the unit of analysis.[8] Specifically, legendary personalities such as Antonio Ubaldo Rattín, César Luis Menotti, Carlos Bilardo and Diego Maradona will be analysed and placed into context to emphasize their cultural and historical relevance within the larger debate over national identity in Argentina. These individuals represent one of two culturally relevant figures in Argentine society, the *pibe* and *caudillo*. They also embody the two competing philosophies that lie in juxtaposition to each other, fútbol criollo and anti-fútbol. At the conclusion of the article, a third category, the *crack* forward, will be introduced to suggest that not all Argentine soccer icons fit neatly into this binary taxonomy. In fact, one could argue that two of Argentina's greatest players of all time, Alfredo Di Stéfano and Lionel Messi, are examples of this conundrum. While both are celebrated as football legends and icons, they exist in the margins in terms of relevance with respect to national identity politics. However, before attempting such an analysis, it is necessary to provide some context with respect to Argentina's national identity debate.

National identity in Argentina

The construction of modern Argentina began in earnest during the last half of the nineteenth century after the defeat of caudillo Juan Manuel de Rosas.[9] During this period, the country's liberal-minded leaders and intellectuals aggressively sought to 'civilize' the nation by facilitating massive European immigration. Theoretically, this strategy would efficiently transform society from cultural and political 'barbarism' into a modern nation governed by a strong central government and informed by rationalized and objective scientific thinking. Intellectuals such as Domingo Sarmiento and Juan Bautista Alberdi espoused Europe as a model of civility in opposition to the 'barbarie' typified by strongmen such as Rosas. The opposition to this Unitarian agenda was the prevailing Federalist post-colonial system of rule in which caudillos, or authoritarian rural strong men in Argentina's interior, and their gaucho militias sought to conserve and maintain regional control.[10]

By the turn of the century, the civilizing efforts of the 'Generation of 1880' had successfully supplanted the 'backwards' indigenous ways of the past. Even more, by the First World War locals and foreign observers identified Argentina among the most developed and prosperous countries in the world. This process was, however, not a seamless and uncontested transition. Social 'maladies' and political unrest, among other challenges, worked to undermine the utopian and overtly racist vision of the late nineteenth-century reformers.[11] Further, the massive influx of Italian, Spanish, Jewish and eastern European migrants yielded a national identity crisis.[12] The 1910s and 1920s were decades in which intense public debate ensued over what and who was considered to be Argentine.[13]

The nation's fledging love affair with British football was not immune from this political debate. However, as historian Matthew Karush points out, the sport became a particular target of public debate during this period.[14] Journalists and literary critics from traditional publications in Buenos Aires, as well as popular print sources, sought to construct and define a distinguishable style of play. Their writings portrayed a particular emerging national identity embedded within the increasingly popular practice of fútbol. In the end, the ethnically based *criollo* (creole) style championed by the popular press outlets *El Gráfico* and *Crítica* emerged as the dominant discourse that defined and represented a national style of play symbolic of a distinctive Argentine race. As Archetti outlines, fútbol criollo emerged as a product of both cultural hybridity and environmental factors.[15] Sports writers associated a national style of play with the imagery of the pibe (young kid) who developed a knack for *viveza* (trickery or cunning) on the *potreros* (abandoned dusty fields and vacant urban lots) in and around the city of Buenos Aires. This undisciplined and playful approach to the game stands in contrast to the methodical British style taught in private schools and athletic clubs. Therefore, the pibe and the newly defined fútbol criollo constituted a distinct cultural product that helped construct an emerging *Argentinidad* (Argentineaness) in the 1920s and 1930s – a process that also occurred in Argentine art and cinema.[16] The popular press, for example, lauded the success of Racing Club's seven consecutive league titles as evidence of the positive virtues associated with fútbol criollo alongside an emerging national race responsible for its production.[17] Likewise, Argentines could point to the championship matches of the 1928 Olympics and the inaugural World Cup in 1930 – both played by Argentina and Uruguay – as evidence of the superiority of fútbol played in the Rio de La Plata region. Even when Argentina underperformed at the 1934 World Cup, when it sent an improvised squad, the popular press focused on the presence of three Argentines on the Italian national team as the reason for why Italy won the tournament.

In the midst of a national identity crisis brought on by massive immigration and migration, Archetti shows how football provided a context in which the creativity of immigrants and their children 'allowed a national style to appear, strengthen and reproduce over time. National identity in football … is a cultural form created on the margins of the nationalist's *criollismo*.'[18] This national identity was not immune from challenges and threats over time. In the aftermath of the first Perón era (1946–1955), Argentine society entered into a turbulent period characterized by social and political unrest. Fútbol, like other forms of mass culture, such as art and cinema, became sites where national identity could be contested along class lines. Much like the debates over national identity at the turn of the century, fútbol and identity politics once again became the focus of heated public discourse over the nation's past and future.

1958 and the turn to the caudillo

The national team's arrival in Sweden in 1958 generated excitement and optimism for a whole generation of fans. After hearing legendary stories about the 1928 Olympics and 1930 World Cup, and recently witnessing an impressive performance at the 1957 South American Championship, this was Argentina's chance to finally breakthrough and win at a global tournament. But the young 'cracks' of 1957 who mesmerized observers – Enrique Omar Sívori, Humberto Maschio, and Antonio Angelillo – all left to play in Italy. The Argentine Football Association (AFA), unwilling to select players from overseas leagues, turned to veteran players such as

Ángel Labruna, who were well past their prime. But after losing 3–1 to West Germany in the opening match of the World Cup, sports magazines such as *Mundo Deportivo* drew on stereotypes to question the efficacy of the supposedly beautiful *rioplatense* game against the methodical, and efficient, German approach.[19] Veteran journalist Borocotó even argued that Argentine players possessed too much 'potrero' in their style of play, although he cautioned that it would also be unwise for Argentine players to try to match their European rivals' physicality.[20]

An unconvincing victory over Northern Ireland meant that Argentina needed to defeat Czechoslovakia in order to advance to the second round of the tournament. Instead, few people expected the final score line: Czechoslovakia 6, Argentina 1. Sports writers grasped for ways to explain this lopsided result to readers back home. Some attributed this 'disaster' to the decaying morals of Argentine players who lived off fútbol, but did not live *for* fútbol. Unlike the Germans, who trained incessantly, one journalist argued that the Argentine player was lazy.[21] Fans in Buenos Aires waited many hours for the arrival of the national team at Ezeiza airport. As players descended from the aircraft, fans threw coins and called them 'drunkards', among other names.[22]

Two of the players who received abuse from fans at Ezeiza airport were Pedro Dellacha and Néstor Rossi. Both men were unquestioned leaders on the national team and earned a reputation as 'caudillos' on their club teams (Racing and River Plate, respectively). These were tough players, who like the caudillo leaders of nineteenth-century Argentina, controlled their teams in the middle of the field by the sheer force of their personality and their toughness. However, it was not their toughness that was under question; rather, critics of the national team questioned the commitment of Argentine players. Were they willing to change? Was fútbol criollo out of date? This debate over whether to import European approaches and modernize, or remain firm to the artistry of the 'crack' player, consumed fútbol discourse in Argentina in the wake of the 'disaster' in Sweden.[23] More problematically for Argentine fans, one of their fiercest rivals in South America, Brazil, won the World Cup in 1958 and joined Uruguay as the only American nations to lift the trophy. *El Gráfico* noted with admiration how the Brazilians moulded the latest training methods and tactical approaches from Europe with their own fluid style of play, whereas AFA seemed clueless on how to improve the national team.[24]

In search for new types of players who could embody the discipline and toughness needed to match European teams, various coaches of the national team of the 1960s appropriated modern tactics and training. They also leaned on a 'number 5' midfield player from Boca Juniors: Antonio Ubaldo Rattín.[25] Already tabbed by Rossi as the next leader of the national team, Rattín stood at an imposing 6 feet 5 inches and earned a reputation as a hard-nosed 'caudillo' leader – a true *guapo*.[26] More importantly, he was a disciplined athlete unconcerned with Argentina maintaining a certain style of play. Like many of the players who came of age in the 1960s, Rattín sensed the impatience of fans who wanted to win at all costs. He was the type of player head coach Juan Carlos Lorenzo – hired by AFA for his coaching experience in Europe – counted on as Argentina prepared for the 1962 World Cup in neighbouring Chile.

Critics of *lo moderno* warned that this trend towards modern tactics was a displaced sense of 'patriotic *garra* (or grit)', and the wrong course for Argentine fútbol. AFA, they argued, was favouring a culture where the ultra-defensive *cerrojo* tactical approach (also dubbed as the 'Swiss bolt', or *catenaccio* in Italy) was the only way to win.[27] When Argentina, once again, exited after the first round of the 1962 World Cup, and Brazil won its second consecutive title, the reaction was less severe.[28] Argentines recognized that any claim to superiority was nonsense. Despite the historic rivalry with their South American neighbours, many Argentines acknowledged that best practitioners of the sport were the Brazilians.[29] Yet, Lorenzo, Rattín and the rest of the national team did not come under fire for the new European-like and disciplined approach to the game. If anything, coaches and players argued that Argentina needed more time to adapt to new tactical systems and training habits.

A string of positive results in 1964 justified Argentina's shift to a more pragmatic and physical approach to the game. In a small four-nation tournament hosted by Brazil – dubbed the 'Cup of Nations' – Argentina defeated Portugal, Brazil and England. Rattín, in particular, earned respect for his ability to nullify the potent Brazilian attack. Boca Juniors fans showered him with praise upon his return by chanting 'Rattín … Rattín … Rattín el capo de Brasil'.[30] The term *capo* originated in Italy and stood for a boss (usually the head of a Mafia group). In Argentine fútbol, a 'capo' dominated rivals; he was the best at his profession and a true leader. In this case, Rattín was the caudillo who dominated the Brazilians to the delight of Argentine fans. Not only was he more 'macho' than the Brazilians, he also instilled fear in them like a true Mafioso.[31]

Rattín embodied the new type of caudillo player. This version of the midfield general made sure that teammates stuck to the tactics designed for a particular game. For Rattín, discipline and adherence to the game plan were the keys to success; playing as if one was still on the potrero was a recipe for failure. From a tactical standpoint, however, new caudillos like Rattín were less of a pure 'number 5'. Instead of dictating the tempo of the game, his job was to compliment the defence by double-teaming the player with the ball, or by marking the best player on the opposing team (like he did to Brazil's Pelé). On offence, his job was to try to score with his head when outside midfielders or forwards crossed the ball into the penalty area, or to take shots from long distance.[32]

Rattín's ultimate legacy as a caudillo would come two years later at the 1966 World Cup in England. In the run-up to the tournament, the AFA struggled to find a permanent coach to prepare the national team. When Estudiantes' coach, Osvaldo Zubeldía, resigned in April, the AFA turned to Lorenzo once again. The outspoken coach returned from a second stint in Europe even more convinced about the superiority of European training methods and tactics, which annoyed those who felt that he denigrated Argentine fútbol.[33] He also angered players by keeping them confused about their status on the team, refusing to look them in the eye, and his overall detachment. Reports soon surfaced of a player mutiny led by Rattín.[34] The rift inside the national team caused a sensation back home in Argentina, precisely at the same time that the military overthrew the elected government of President Arturo Illia and assumed power for itself.[35] It is hard to ignore the parallels between the two caudillo figures, Rattín and General Juan Carlos Onganía, and the two leaders portrayed in the press as inept and losing control (Lorenzo and Illia). Desperate to save face, the new military government intervened and sent an assessor to mediate the situation.[36]

Eventually, victories over Spain and Switzerland and a tie against tournament-favourite West Germany soothed tensions in the national team. For the first time since 1930, Argentina advanced to the second round of a World Cup.[37] Next for Argentina was a quarterfinal match against the host nation, England, at the historic Wembley Stadium. Because of the historic relationship between both countries, the

Argentine press suddenly raised expectations that Argentina would finally fulfil its destiny and win a World Cup. Some journalists, however, hedged their bets and warned of a plot to prevent Argentina's victory and ensure the host nation's success.[38] Sure enough, when German referee Rudolf Kreitlein expelled Rattín after thirty minutes of play for 'violence of the tongue' – despite not understanding Spanish – his teammates stormed off the field sensing that an act of injustice had taken place. As captain, Rattín was entitled to ask for a translator per FIFA rules. Afterwards, he claimed that the diminutive referee mistook his request as an insult. For his part, Kreitlein claimed that the towering midfielder stared him down and confronted him with a threatening pose.[39] All the same, Rattín refused to leave the field and eventually walked off, but not before squatting for a few minutes in the Queen's box in an ultimate act of defiance.

Upon their return to Buenos Aires, journalists, fans and government officials hailed the national team as the nation's 'moral champions' (See Figure 1). As captain, Rattín was one of the first to shake hands with Onganía at the presidential house. Images of this exchange appeared across news outlets in Argentina (See Figure 2). It was a moment of patriotic fervour that the government was sure to capitalize on for good publicity. For Argentines already possessed of anti-imperialist sentiment, Rattín represented the defiant figure that stood up to yet another injustice perpetrated by the English.[40]

Figure 1. '¡Bravo Argentinos!' Front cover to *El Gráfico*, July 26, 1966.

Figure 2. 'El saludo de 22 millones' (The Salute of 22 Million), *El Gráfico*, August 16, 1966. Rattín (left) shakes hands with General Juan Carlos Onganía, leader of the ruling military junta.
*Images courtesy of the Biblioteca del Círculo de Periodistas Deportivos in Buenos Aires, Argentina.

Menotti and *Menottismo* in the 1970s

Not every player in Argentina adhered to the new approaches from Europe that valued physicality and adherence to tactics above all else. More than any other player from the 1960s, César Luis Menotti professed a particular philosophy about fútbol in line with older journalists such as Borocotó, or the outspoken Dante Panzeri (who also wrote at *El Gráfico* until 1962). These writers at *El Gráfico* maintained an affinity for skilful players who still relied on trickery and artistry in the fútbol criollo style. Rosario Central's Menotti reminded the veteran writers at *El Gráfico* of the 'cracks' of the past.[41] For his part, Menotti believed that players were more critical than coaches to the outcome of a match. He argued that players should 'feel' fútbol; true players learned the game by playing, not by adhering to structured tactical systems. In short, he did not believe in 'modern fútbol'.[42] As a result, Menotti became the subject of numerous positive articles in *El Gráfico*. His lucrative transfer from Rosario Central to Racing, for example, garnered headlines in the magazine, which labelled his signing as a shift back towards the age of 'crack' players.[43]

With goal averages at an all-time low, Menotti's ascendancy raised hopes for a revival of high-scoring fútbol.[44] Menotti, however, would not enjoy the same level of success in Buenos Aires, either at Racing or later at Boca Juniors. Some observers wondered whether it was difficult for him to adapt to Buenos Aires, due to the size of the city and the scrutiny of the national press. Menotti argued that his approach to the game did not fit with the physicality that dominated the league. *El Gráfico* avoided articles that discussed his decline. But rival publications such as *Campeón*, which targeted a less middle-class audience, published pieces that either described his decline or ridiculed Menotti's self-assuredness about his knowledge of the game.[45] Tired of the criticism, as well as the state of professional fútbol in Argentina, Menotti eventually left Argentina for a brief spell with the New York Generals of the rogue National Professional Soccer League in the United States before finding a kindred spirit in Pelé. He joined Pelé's successful Santos team before retiring and pursuing a career as a head coach. Despite his up-and-down career as a player, Menotti remained convinced in his philosophy about fútbol. He continued to see the game as a paradox, which required professional players to study each aspect of the game, but then to depend on their natural instincts and skill on the field.[46]

Menotti was not alone in seeing the value of returning to a free-flowing attack by 1969. Teams such as San Lorenzo and Boca Juniors won national championships with potent offences. Boca Juniors' coach that year, Alfredo Di Stéfano, was widely regarded as one of the greatest players of his time when he retired at Real Madrid in 1966.[47] Argentines followed his exploits in Europe and his return to Argentina in 1969 was akin to a prodigal son returning home, perhaps even to save fútbol in Argentina. According to Di Stéfano, playing cautiously had become the trademark of Argentine teams fearful of losing. For Pelé, Di Stéfano's approach to coaching was the welcome return of Argentine fútbol.[48] San Lorenzo and Boca Juniors brought renewed attention to playing styles. After a decade of 'cerrojo', or *catenaccio,* approaches, Argentine fútbol seemed to be in no better position than after the 'disaster in Sweden' of 1958. Many fans saw hope in a return to a more visually aesthetic style of play.

The shift back towards fútbol criollo occurred in 1973, when Menotti, now a coach at Huracán, led his to team to great success with a visually attractive style of play. Huracán won the national title that year, a rare feat for a team not considered as a major club association in Argentina. Because Argentina failed to even make the 1970 World Cup, and then underperformed at the 1974 tournament, the AFA offered Menotti the reigns to the national team. Fútbol officials agreed to his demands, including a request that he remains in charge for the duration of the four years leading to the 1978 World Cup, which Argentina would host for the first time. Menotti also demanded complete control over tactics, training and player selection. His mission was to show the world that fútbol criollo could succeed at the highest level.[49] With Menotti firmly in control of the national team, Argentina went on to win the 1978 FIFA World Cup. Argentina also displayed the fútbol criollo mentality that Menotti preferred behind the exploits of goal scorer Mario Kempes, and talented players such as Osvlado Ardiles and Daniel Pasarella.[50]

Bilardo, *Bilardismo* and competing identities at the 1986 and 1990 World Cups

Although Menotti enjoyed success with Huracán and the Argentine national team, the 'modern' approach of the 1960s did not completely disappear. Perhaps the greatest legacy of the tough and hard-nosed Estudiantes team of the late 1960s, which won consecutive world club championships, was its caudillo midfielder Carlos

Bilardo. A disciple of head coach Osvaldo Zubeldía's obsession with strict adherence to strategy, relentless training and winning at any cost, Bilardo moved into coaching and adopted what many dubbed as *anti-fútbol*.[51] Thus, *Bilardismo* stood in direct contrast to *Menottismo*; or, in terms of identity politics, Bilardismo represented a quest for modernity based on European tactics while Menottismo resonated more with traditional notions of potrero life. When Menotti eventually stepped down in 1982 after an unsuccessful World Cup, Bilardo took over and changed the complexion of the team. He supported the genius talent of his star player, Diego Maradona, with a team of players in the Estudiantes mould. In the end, Bilardo's 'modern' approach worked and Argentina won its second World Cup in 1986 at the Azteca Stadium in Mexico.

However, whether the team as a collective unit performed a style that successfully achieved an embodiment of a consensus modern style of play is less clear. On the one hand, the enduring images of Argentina at the 1986 FIFA World Cup are not representative of physicality and toughness. Instead, Maradona's two goals against England in the quarterfinals summarized the 1986 team: talented, but prone to trickery and deceit when needed. If any team embodied the 'win at all costs' and anti-fútbol mentality of Bilardismo, it was the 1990 World Cup squad. In Italy, Bilardo's Argentina applied an ultra-defensive approach predicated on quick counter-attacks led by Maradona and striker Claudio Caniggia.[52] Although Argentina lost the final against West Germany, the most notable episode was the allegation that someone on the national team drugged Brazilian player Branco by offering him tainted water during their Round of 16 encounter. This issue resurfaced in 2005 when Maradona himself admitted that Branco received water laced with sedatives.[53]

Embodying the pibe: Maradona and working class identity

In 2000, Rodrigo (Bueno), the late popular musician from Córdoba, cast the regional and niche *cuerteto* musical style into the national spotlight with his song *La Mano de Dios* (Hand of God). Written in honour of soccer legend and national hero Diego Maradona, the title is an obvious reference to the infamous goal he scored against England during the 1986 FIFA World Cup quarterfinals. However, the song's lyrics reveal much more about Maradona's place with respect to playing styles and identity politics.

> He was born in a villa (slum), it was God's desire
> to grow and survive the humble expression, to face adversity
> with the desire to earn a living, with every step.
> On the potrero he forged an immortal lefty with experience and a thirsty ambition to make it.
> As a little onion[54] he dreamed of playing in the World Cup,
> and to be glorified in the First Division.
> Maybe playing, he could help his family ...
> Marado, Marado
> His dream had a star, full of goals and gambetas ... The hand of God was born

Rodrigo's song is less about Maradona's actual 'Hand of God' goal and more about his humble upbringing in one of the many Buenos Aires *villas* (slums). It is also a celebration of the style of play embodied by Maradona given the singer's reference to the aforementioned *gambeta* and potrero. It may be useful here to draw parallels between the modern day villas and the emerging barrios and *conventillos* of *fin de siècle* Buenos Aires, which journalist in the past attributed to potreros. Today's urban villas and their potreros (which are often littered with trash and debris) resonate with Argentina's popular sectors, which are familiar with economic hardships and often eager to celebrate the positive elements of working class Argentine culture and identity. In this case, the object of affection is the triumph of 'their' distinct fútbol criollo style of play as performed by Maradona.

Following the failure of the national team at the 1982 FIFA World Cup in Spain and on the heels of a disappointing and narrow qualifying effort, Argentina entered the 1986 World Cup under the guidance of Bilardo and his preference for anti-fútbol and winning at all costs. However, the head coach was astute enough to grant Maradona and his partner in attack, Valdano, enough freedom to use their creativity and spontaneity in space. Ironically, the lasting impressions on popular consciousness from the 1986 World Cup are anything but anti-fútbol. Fulfilling popular expectations of a traditional mythical national identity through playing styles, Maradona's two goals against England in the quarterfinal can be read as an embodiment of fútbol criollo.

The first goal was allowed to stand even though Diego employed the 'Hand of God' to poke the ball into the net as he and English goalkeeper Peter Shilton were in midair. Despite the infraction, which went unnoticed by the referee, working class Argentines see this as a necessary form of a *viveza* (trickery), or *picardía criolla* (conniving), which is an acceptable and celebrated characteristic of the romanticized gaucho (cowboy) of Argentina's interior. Where the gaucho's use of trickery for survival serves as a source of pride for criollo nationalism, likewise, football on the potrero is consistent with winning at all costs even if it requires gaining a clever, or 'unfair', advantage over the opponent.

For the second goal, which many consider one of the greatest ever scored at the World Cup, Maradona received the ball near midfield with his back to the goal, made a turn and performed the gambeta through the English midfield and defensive back line en route to scoring what turned out to be the game winning goal. While he later indicated the victory over England contained emotional elements of retribution for the Malvinas conflict,[55] this particular goal was symbolically a triumph of the pibe of the potrero. Though the stakes were much higher and opponents more skilled, Maradona's run resembled that of the typical young Argentinean kid who creatively uses his dribbling skills to manoeuvre towards the goal during pick-up games in the streets or on one of the rudimentary empty lots of the modern day villa.

Maradona's playing career, at both the club and national team level, contains a number of moments that embody the essence of the pibe of the potrero (both on and off the field) yet recollections of the 1986 moments are crystallized in popular memory. For the working class of Argentine society, Maradona's individual success as a player is complimentary to his representation of the traditional Argentine identity constructed in the sports pages in the 1920s. His humble beginnings in the *Villa Fiorito* slum resonates with the Argentine popular sectors and his youthful mastery of the creative, undisciplined and celebrated fútbol criollo afford him the ability embody the mythical pibe of the potrero. For many, this imagery represents the traditional version of fútbol that forms a part of Argentine national identity. Alabarces and Rodríguez argue that the story of Maradona and the villas 'is the continuity of the myth of the Argentinian style embodied by Maradona that allows this identity to survive.' With Maradona's exit as a playing icon in world football, 'the local-global mediation of the national hero is put in crisis' until another Maradona-like figure emerges to ensure its place in future identity debates.[56]

Discussion

In his analysis of the role of football and Argentine identity, Alabarces has argued that football lacks the capacity to impart any real lasting effects on the political structure. On the occasion where these two spheres of public life collide, he sees the effect as temporary. Analysing people's behaviour, television, radio, and print media discourse, and Argentina's disastrous performance at the 2002 FIFA World Cup in the context of the 2001–2002 economic crises, Alabarces reaffirms his earlier hypothesis that 'Football was again only football, and politics only politics.'[57] Of course, here he is speaking to what Tobin discusses as big 'P' politics, or macro-political institutions.[58] With respect to little 'p' politics, which includes identity politics, we have outlined that football, and more specifically football icons, provides a lens with which to discuss the negotiated and dynamic politics of national identity. In agreement with Marshall's description of celebrities, the notable iconic Argentine personalities of the FIFA World Cup from 1958–1986 and the popular discourse that translate and define their actions help to structure meaning, crystallize constructed ideologies and help embody 'collective configurations' of the social world.[59] They provide conceptual maps or points of reference for working class perceptions of national identity in Argentine society.

The negotiation of identity as it relates to fútbol in Argentina emerged in the first quarter of the twentieth century. As this article has pointed out, fútbol and identity politics in Argentina is a contested and ongoing process that has fluctuated along a spectrum. On one end of the spectrum lies a hybridized traditional identity embodied by the imagery of the pibe, potrero and fútbol criollo. At the other end rests the quest for modernity through the emulation of European tastes and is embodied by the caudillo and anti-fútbol.

So where does Argentina's most famous contemporary soccer star, Lionel Messi, fit within the framework of fútbol and national identity? A celebrated and depoliticized component of fútbol criollo during the middle of the twentieth century was the role of the 'crack' forward. A term typically reserved for the player in the 'number 9' position, this player was often a 'crack', or the best player. Fans and journalists alike admired the prolific goal-scorer. This seems to be the most appropriate descriptive category to place Messi as he, like Alfredo Di Stéfano before him, is a relatively marginal personality in the national identity debate.[60] First, Messi hails from a family that, if not necessarily of middle-class origin, is not from the villas. Second, he never made an impact in Argentina's domestic league. When Argentine club teams refused to pay for medical treatment for his stunted growth, Spanish club FC Barcelona stepped in and paid for the teenage Messi's treatment as part of his contract to play in Europe. Third, aside from a gold medal at the 2008 Olympics, Messi has yet to deliver for the full national team in international tournaments such as the World Cup or Copa América. A last consideration is that for professional reasons, Messi pursued dual Spanish citizenship and spends the majority of the year in Spain.[61]

Perhaps the most important distinction to make as part of this argument is that Messi does not represent the dramatic 'rags to riches' story that resonates with the popular sectors. Unlike contemporaries such as Carlos Tévez, an argument can be made that he lacks the embodied imagery of the poor pibe honing his skills in the streets and potreros of impoverished neighbourhoods. Simply stated, Messi is a player whose career has been defined within the context of European football, not the Argentine league. Although he is clearly Argentina's crack player and has, in recent years, dispelled the notion that he is a 'pecho frio' (a term to denote that he lacks passion for the colours of the national team jersey), Messi lacks a connection to the nation's working class. Barring the emergence of a new hero who fully embodies the hybridized Argentine national style at the 2014 FIFA World Cup in Brazil, the continuation of the mythical poor pibe of the potrero will remain in nostalgic recollections of the past.

Notes

1. See Harris and Parker, *Sport and Social Identities*; Maguire, *Global Sport*, 176–206; Smith and Porter, *Sport and National Identity*.
2. MacClancy, *Sport, Identity, and Ethnicity*, 2.
3. Karush, 'National Identity in the Sports Pages'.
4. Archetti's *Masculinities* and 'Playing Football and Dancing Tango' draw on a theory of hybridization by Néstor García Canclini, which explains processes of identity formation in Latin America, such as *mestizaje* or *criollismo*. See Canclini, *Hybrid Cultures*.
5. Frydenberg, *Historia social del fútbol*.
6. Alabarces et al., 'Treacheries and Traditions in Argentinian Football Styles'; Goldblatt, *The Ball is Round*, 384–9 and 612–9; Kuper, *Football Against the* Enemy, 181–3; Mason, *Passion of the People?*, 127–9. For an account of discourse in the sports pages see Downing, *England v Argentina*, 94–143.
7. Alabarces, *Fútbol y patria*; Alabarces et al., 'Treacheries and Traditions in Argentinian Football Styles'; Goldblatt, *The Ball is Round*.
8. Andrews and Jackson's edited collection entitled *Sports Stars* profiles the effects sixteen celebrity athletes from around the world have on the manner in which individuals negotiate their everyday lives.
9. Though Argentina began its struggle and won independence from Spain in 1810 and 1816, respectively, the first constitution was written in 1853 and fully ratified in 1860 once Buenos Aires province rejoined the newly constructed Argentine Republic.
10. de la Fuente, *Children of Facundo*; Hedges, *Argentina: A Modern History*; Scobie, *Argentina: A City and a Nation*.
11. Ablard, *Madness in Buenos Aires*; Rodríguez, *Civilizing Argentina*.
12. Baily, *Immigrants in the Lands of Promise*; Deutsch, *Crossing Borders, Claiming a Nation*; Moya, *Cousins and Strangers*.
13. For examples of how the Argentine elite used science, notions of proper hygiene, penal codes and measures against youth delinquency to 'civilize' the masses, *see*: Armus, *The Ailing City*; Caimari, ed. *La ley de los prófanos;* Guy, *Sex and Danger in Buenos Aires*; Rodríguez, *Civilizing Argentina*; Ruggiero, *Modernity in the Flesh*.
14. Karush, 'National Identity in the Sports Pages', 14–8.
15. Archetti, *Masculinities*, 70–2.
16. Karush, *Culture of Class*; Giunta, *Avant-Garde, Internationalism, and Politics*.
17. Racing Club, which is based in the southern Avelleneda barrio, was considered a team comprised of *criollo* players rather than British or Anglo-Argentines.
18. Archetti, Masculinities, 71.
19. *Mundo Deportivo*, June 16, 1958, 4–7.
20. *El Gráfico*, June 13, 1958, 10–2.
21. *El Gráfico*, June 20, 1958, 4–8. Among the problems listed by journalists as examples of a lack of discipline among players were their tendency to stay out late on the streets, their preoccupation with meeting Swedish women, their insistence on having Argentine beef and chicken sent to Sweden, ignoring the instructions of the physical trainers, and the coaching staff allowing players to take days off from training (unlike the Germans).

22. *Campeón*, June 25, 1958, 3; *Mundo Deportivo*, June 23, 1958, 7; *El Gráfico*, June 27, 1958, 62–5.

23. A few examples can be found in *El Gráfico*, June 27, 1958, 21 and *Mundo Deportivo*, June 23, 1958, 4–9 and 28–32.

24. *El Gráfico*, June 27, 1958, 10–2. Among the complaints listed here was that Brazilian coaches wisely imported balls made in Sweden – lighter than those used in South America – in the event that they were used for the tournament. The Argentine player, on the other hand, feigned injury, refused to play differently and publicly complained whenever physical training proved to be too excessive for their tastes.

25. Traditionally, players wore jersey numbers that corresponded to their position on the field. This practice lost its universal application by the 1960s, but the 'number 5' player was typically a defensive midfielder or a defender that played either in front, or behind, the line of three defenders. The number 5 player was usually tasked with breaking up the opposing team's offence in the middle of the field.

26. *Campeón*, September 23, 1964, 4.

27. *El Gráfico*, April 4, 1962, 10–8; *El Gráfico*, April 25, 1962, 10–4.

28. *El Gráfico*, June 6, 1962, 20–9; *Campeón*, June 6, 1962, 3–5; *El Gráfico*, June 7, 1962, 3–8.

29. For Juan Carlos Lorenzo's thoughts on the importance of the Brazilian model, *see*: *El Gráfico*, July 11, 1962, 52–4. *Also see*: *Gráfico*, August 16, 1966, 96.

30. *Campeón*, June 17, 1964, 3.

31. Today, 'capo' is a term reserved for the head of Argentina's violent fan groups known as *barras bravas*.

32. *Campeón*, December 22, 1965, 3. Other 'caudillos' of the 1960s that played in a similar manner to Rattín were Racing's Alfio Basile and Estudiantes' Carlos Bilardo, *see*: *Campeón*, October 27, 1965, 2; *Clarín*, January 1, 1966; *El Gráfico*, July 19, 1966, 8–9.

33. *El Gráfico*, April 5, 1966, 42–4; *El Gráfico*, April 26, 1966, 3; *El Gráfico*, May 3, 1966, 14–5.

34. *Clarín*, July 5, 1966, 33; *Clarín,* July 6, 1966, 28; *Clarín*, July 9, 1966, 4–5.

35. César Tcach and Celso Rodríguez, *Arturo Illia: Un sueño breve-El rol del peronismo y de los Estados Unidos en el golpe militar de 1966* (Buenos Aires: Edhasa, 2006), 154–5.

36. *Campeón*, June 29, 1966, 2; *Gente y la actualidad*, July 14, 1966, 42–5; *Primera Plana*, July 12, 1966, 54.

37. *Clarín*, July 14, 1966, 3; *El Gráfico*, July 19, 1966, 4–9 and 21–4; *Clarín*, July 20, 1966, 3; *Clarín*, July 21, 1966, 7.

38. *Clarín,* July 2, 1966; *Clarín,* July 11, 1966, 3; *Primera Plana*, July 24, 1966, 66; *Clarín*, July 23, 1966, 1–8.

39. *La Prensa*, July 24, 1966, 12. Match footage shows Rattín confronting the referee, but Kreitlein's description is accurate only after he expels Rattín, leaving the situation unclear to this day.

40. Among the explanations for Argentina's loss to England was that the English head of FIFA, Sir Stanley Rous, used his powers to ensure that no South American team would win the World Cup in England. Many Argentines (and South Americans) were suspicious that a German referee officiated England's match against Argentina, and that an Englishman refereed the West Germany–Uruguay match. Brazil also endured a tough tournament as teams targeted Pelé, who wound up injured from excessive tackles. The proof for conspiracy theorists was that the semi-finalists were all European and the final pitted England against West Germany, with the host nation lifting its first World Cup.

41. *El Gráfico*, August 22, 1962, 4–9.

42. *El Gráfico*, September 12, 1962, 20–3; *El Gráfico*, April 10, 1963, 51.

43. *El Gráfico*, March 25, 1964, 54–7. Menotti's signing for 16 million pesos was evidence for *El Gráfico*'s writers that fútbol criollo could still succeed in an age of *catenaccio* and overly defensive tactics.

44. Juvenal, 'La inyección rosarina que necesita nuestro fútbol', *El Gráfico*, January 2, 1963, 14–7.

45. *Campeón*, June 17, 1964, 6–7. After missing a penalty shot in a meaningless exhibition match against Real Madrid in Morocco, popular magazine *Gente y la actualidad* wondered why Menotti failed to score when he possessed so much knowledge of the game.

It felt that maybe Menotti could learn a lesson of humility, *see: Gente y la actualidad*, September 1, 1966, 47.

46. *Así*, July 12, 1974, 20–1. After brief co-coaching spells at Central Córdoba (Rosario) and Newell's Old Boys (Rosario), he became head coach at Huracán in 1972 and led the team to the national team a year later. Menotti's team earned admiration from fans for its return to 'la vieja', or traditional style.

47. A youth prospect at River Plate during the late 1940s, Di Stéfano left amid the 1948 players' strike. He signed with Millionarios of Colombia before ultimately heading to Spain to play for Real Madrid. Di Stéfano's signing with Real Madrid remains a controversial topic in Spain. The rivalry between Real Madrid and FC Barcelona – one of the most heated in all of sports – is rooted in Spanish history, between Catalans and Castilians, and even linked to the Spanish Civil War. Much has been written about Di Stéfano's initial signing with Barcelona, only to have Real Madrid swoop in and take the Argentine star in a dubious manner that still rankles Barcelona fans to this day. For a current, Catalan, view of the coup, *see:* Xavier G. Luque, 'El golpe del siglo', *La Vanguardia* (Barcelona, September 27, 2012), Online edition, sec. Deportes, 49. http://t.co/CXgyPOgr.

48. *El Gráfico*, December 16, 1969, 46–7.

49. Menotti, *Como ganamos la Copa del Mundo*.

50. It should be noted that the 1978 squad did not display the same attacking prowess of Menotti's 1973 Huracán team. Argentina struggled in the early stages of the tournament. It needed a four-goal margin victory over Peru to advance to the final – a match still marred by controversy and accusations of threats and bribery by the military regime ruling Argentina at the time (Argentina defeated Peru 6–0). However, Argentina's best performance came precisely in the championship match against the Netherlands, with Kempes scoring twice in a 3–1 victory. Although critics associate Menotti with the military regime, he believed that his duty was to his nation first and that his team's free-flowing approach was actually a contrast to the rigidity imposed by the military junta.

51. Alabarces et al., 'Treacheries and Traditions'.

52. Argentina's five goals in the entire tournament was the lowest total for a World Cup finalist. The entire 1990 tournament was among the lowest scoring editions.

53. *La Nación*, March 1, 2005, Online edition, sec. Deportes, http://www.lanacion.com.ar/683820-maradona-ratifico-la-historia-del-bidon-y-avivo-la-polemica; *La Nación*, March 1, 2005, Online edition, sec. Deportes, http://www.lanacion.com.ar/683847-branco-podrian-haber-terminado-con-mi-carrera; *El País*, January 24, 2005, Online edition, sec. Archivo, http://elpais.com/diario/2005/01/24/deportes/1106521223_850215.html; *The Guardian*, January 20, 2005, sec. Football, http://www.guardian.co.uk/football/2005/jan/21/newsstory.sport5.

54. In his youth, Maradona developed as a player through the youth team of Argentinos Juniors, which is known as the Little Onions (Cebollitas).

55. 'In our skin was the pain of all those kids who had died there … Emotionally, I blame every one of the English players-our rivals-for what happened.' Maradona quoted in *El Gráfico's* (no. 4003, 25 June 1996, 78) ten year World Cup anniversary feature article 'Por Siempre Heroes: Suplemento Extraordinario de Argentina Campeón Mundial en Mexico'.

56. Alabarces and Rodríguez, 'Football and Fatherland', 128.

57. Alabarces, 'Football Fans and the Argentine Crisis of 2001–2002', 67.

58. Tobin, 'Soccer Conspiracies', 55–7.

59. Marshall, *Celebrity and Power*, IX–XI.

60. A similar argument can be made for Enrique Omar Sívori, who after a few years at River Plate, spent the rest of his career in Italy to great success.

61. One should also consider in any discussion of identity politics that Messi is not from Buenos Aires and openly professes his longing for his hometown of Rosario. Because the national media is heavily, if not exclusively, from Buenos Aires, Messi's identity is more *rosarino* than it is *argentino*. His recent appointment as captain of the national team may change that perception, especially if he guides Argentina to a World Cup title.

References

Ablard, Jonathan. *Madness in Buenos Aires: Patients, Psychiatrists and the Argentine State, 1880–1983*. Athens: Ohio University Press, 2008.

Alabarces, Pablo. *Fútbol y patria: El fútbol y las narrativas de la nación en la Argentina* [Football and the Homeland: Football and Narratives of the Nation in Argentina]. Buenos Aires: Prometeo, Libros de Cnfrontación, 2002.

Alabarces, Pablo. 'Football Fans and the Argentine Crisis of 2001–2002: The Crisis, the World Cup, and the Destiny of the Patria'. In *Fútbol*, ed. Ilan Stavans, 57–70. Santa Barbara, CA: Greenwood, 2011.

Alabarces, Pablo, and María Rodríguez. 'Football and Fatherland: The Crisis of National Representation in Argentinian Soccer'. In *Football Culture: Local Contests, Global Visions*, ed. G.P.T. Finn and R. Guilianotti, 118–33. London: Frank Cass, 2000.

Alabarces, Pablo, Ramiro Coehlo, and Juan Sanguinetti. 'Treacheries and Traditions in Argentinian Football Styles: The Story of Estudiantes de La Plata'. In *Fear and Loathing in World Football*, ed. G. Armstrong and R. Guilianotti, 237–49. Oxford: Berg, 2001.

Andrews, David L., and Steven J. Jackson, eds. *Sports Stars: The Cultural Politics of Sporting Celebrity*. London: Routledge, 2001.

Archetti, Eduardo P. *Masculinities: Football, Polo, and the Tango in Argentina*. New York: Berg, 1999.

Archetti, Eduardo P. 'Playing Football and Dancing Tango: Embodying Argentina in Movement, Style, and Identity'. In *Sport, Dance, and Embodied Identities*, ed. N. Dyke and E.P. Archetti, 217–30. Oxford: Berg, 2003.

Armus, Diego. *The Ailing City: Health, Tuberculosis, and Culture in Buenos Aires, 1870–1950*. Durham, NC: Duke University Press, 2011.

Baily, Samuel. *Immigrants in the Lands of Promise: Italians in Buenos Aires and New York City, 1870–1914*. Ithaca, NY: Cornell University Press, 1999.

Caimari, Lila, ed. *La ley de los prófanos: Delito, justicia y cultura en Buenos Aires (1870–1940)* [The Law of the Profane: Crime, Justice and Culture in Buenos Aires (1870–1940)]. Buenos Aires: Fondo de Cultura Económica, 2007.

Canclini, Néstor García. *Hybrid Cultures. Strategies for Entering and Leaving Modernity*. Minneapolis: University of Minnesota Press, 1989.

Deutsch, Sandra McGee. *Crossing Borders, Claiming a Nation: A History of Argentine Jewish Women, 1880–1955*. Durham, NC: Duke University Press, 2010.

Downing, David. *England v Argentina: World Cups and Other Small Wars*. London: Portrait, 2003.

Frydenberg, Julio. *Historia social del fútbol: Del amateurismo a la profesionalización* [Social History of Football: From Amateurism to Professionalization]. Buenos Aires: Siglo XXI, 2011.

de la Fuente, Ariel. *Children of Facundo: Caudillo and Gaucho Insurgency during the Argentine State-formation Process, La Rioja, 1853–1870*. Durham, NC: Duke University Press, 2000.

Giunta, Andrea. *Avant-garde, Internationalism, and Politics: Argentine Art in the Sixties*. Durham: Duke University Press, 2007.

Goldblatt, David. *The Ball is Round: A Global History of Soccer*. New York: Riverhead Books, 2006.

Guy, Donna. *Sex and Danger in Buenos Aires: Prostitution, Family, and Nation in Argentina*. Lincoln, NE: University of Nebraska Press, 1991.

Harris, John, and Andrew Parker, eds. *Sport and Social Identities*. New York: Palgrave Macmillan, 2009.

Hedges, Jill. *Argentina: A Modern History*. New York: I.B. Taurus, 2011.

Karush, Matthew B. 'National Identity in the Sports Pages: Football and the Mass Media in 1920s Buenos Aires'. *The Americas* 60, no. 1 (2003): 11–32.

Karush, Matthew B. *Culture of Class: Radio and Cinema in the Making of a Divided Argentina*. Durham, NC: Duke University Press, 2012.

Kuper, Simon. *Football Against the Enemy*. London: Orion, 1994.

MacClancy, Jeremy, ed. *Sport, Identity, and Ethnicity*. Oxford: Berg, 1996.

Maguire, Joseph. *Global Sport: Identities, Societies, Civilizations*. Malden, MA: Polity Press, 1999.

Marshall, P. David. *Celebrity and Power: Fame in Contemporary Culture*. Minneapolis: University of Minnesota Press, 1997.

Mason, Tony. *Passion of the People? Football in South America*. London: Verso, 1995.

Menotti, César Luis. *Como ganamos la Copa del Mundo* [How We Won the World Cup]. Buenos Aires: El Gráfico-Editorial Atlántida, 1978.

Moya, José. *Cousins and Strangers: Spanish Immigrants in Buenos Aires, 1850–1930*. Berkley: University of California Press, 1998.

Rodríguez, Julia. *Civilizing Argentina: Science, Medicine, and the Modern State*. Chapel Hill, NC: University of North Carolina Press, 2006.

Ruggiero, Kristin. *Modernity in the Flesh: Medicine, Law, and Society in Turn-of-the-century Argentina*. Stanford: Stanford University Press, 2004.

Scobie, James R. *Argentina: A City and a Nation*. New York: Oxford University Press, 1964.

Smith, Adrian, and Dilwyn Porter, eds. *Sport and National Identity in the Post-War World*. London: Routledge, 2004.

Tobin, Jeffery. 'Soccer Conspiracies: Maradona, the CIA, and Popular Critique'. In *Sport in Latin America and the Caribbean*, ed. Joseph L. Arbena and David G. LaFrance, 51–73. Wilmington, DE: Scholarly Resource, 2002.

The Hand of God, the Hand of the Devil: a sociological interpretation of Maradona's hand goal

Simone Magalhães Britto[a], Jorge Ventura de Morais[b] and Túlio Velho Barreto[c]

[a]Universidade Federal da Paraíba, Ciências Sociais, João Pessoa, Brazil; [b]Universidade Federal de Pernambuco, Ciências Sociais, Av. Acadêmico Hélio Ramos, s/n, Cidade Universitária, Recife, Brazil; [c]Joaquim Nabuco Foundation, Recife, Brazil

Based on the moral problem of Maradona's goal, known as the 'Hand of God', this essay presents a theoretical discussion using the perspective of figurational sociology of how game rules and moral rules are related. It does not aim to solve the moral dispute occasioned by actions like the 'Hand of God', but concentrates on a much more limited discussion (appealing to far fewer people) in which we strive to reach a proper sociological understanding. Indeed, we believe that the 'Hand of God' is a paradigmatic event for sociological reasoning. This is not to claim that sociology can give any final answers, but to suggest the opposite, namely that an understanding of the value of 'hand goals' can be very important for understanding the limits of sociological reason.

After many years in which the world has afforded me many experiences, what I know most surely in the long run about morality and obligations, I owe to football.[1]

Pelé had nearly everything. Maradona has everything. He works harder, does more and is more skilful. Trouble is that he will be remembered for another reason. He bends the rules to suit himself.[2]

Introduction

What could one say about a goal in association football scored with the hands? Since the Laws of the Game were first codified, it is very clear that 'to deliberately touch the ball with one's hands', with the exception of the goalkeeper in the penalty area, is illegal. From a purely formal point of view, there is no doubt about 'hand goals': they do not (and must not) have a place in the practice of association football. Even more, considering that the prohibition on the use of the hands by all field players and also by goalkeepers outside their penalty areas is fundamental to association football's identity, scoring a hand goal is, according to this sport's economy of values, not only a deviation, but a sort of threat or pathology.

However, such goals do happen. Thierry Henry scored one recently.[3] Its most famous version, which could be regarded as a kind of 'cultural trauma' – in Alexander's sense[4] – happened in 1986, in a match between England and Argentina, when Diego Maradona qualified Argentina for the semi-finals of the

Word Cup in Mexico. This goal's moral dimension became much more controversial when Maradona justified it under the label of the 'Hand of God'. The tragic Argentine hero explained how he scored the first goal of the match: 'a bit with the head and a bit with the hand of God'. The discussion about this goal leads to so many passionate debates because it brings in itself the main contradictions of moral life. Would the 'Hand of God' be a result of good luck and, therefore, something we must accept as part of the game and, consequently, of life? Or, would it be only the result of deliberate bad faith? In that case, it needs to be punished and condemned if we wish for justice in games as we do in life. Especially, regarding Maradona's attitude, should we consider it as a lack of fair play, an example of an immoral attitude or as a rational action justified by the necessity of winning? Would it be an example of lack of virtue or that the end justifies the means? Would the English team's supporters feel the same kind of anger if the 'Hand of God' had played in their favour?[5] What should the English team (and its supporters) do in the face of that 'Hand of the Devil'[6]: to claim justice or to accept their fate? Should the development of football be based on an effort to avoid winning by hand goals, or are they inevitable just like misfortune in life?

Despite the fact that hand goals clearly involve a breaking of the rule, attempts at justifying them contain clear moral arguments and ethically defensible positions that become more problematic once we consider their use in everyday social life.

This paper does not aim to solve the moral dispute occasioned by actions like the 'hand of god', but concentrates on a much more limited discussion (appealing to far fewer people) in which we strive to reach a proper sociological understanding.[7] Indeed, we believe that the 'Hand of God' is a paradigmatic event for sociological reasoning. This is not to claim that sociology can give any final answers, but to suggest the opposite, namely that an understanding of the value of 'hand goals' can be very important for understanding the limits of sociological reason.

In this way, this paper attempts to reveal the sociological theory of morality which is arguably implicit in Norbert Elias's figurational or process sociology. It is fundamental to the argument presented here to point out how the civilizing processes also involve changes in moral experience. This argument could be developed by reference to any specific area of figurational sociology, but the effort seems to be easier when we turn to sports figurations because of the possibility of comparing game rules and moral rules. Nevertheless, there is an argument that will be much more difficult to prove, namely that the boundaries of the figurational sociology of morality are the limits of sociology itself. However, once again, we believe that football dilemmas can help our argumentation.

Civilizing process and morality

The comparison between game rules and moral rules seems simple. However, what it is at stake is actually the characterization of moral experience itself and an elaboration of the nature and origin of 'normativity'. In this way, when dealing with the social development of sports, figurational sociology also elaborates a theory of morality: it indirectly constructs a model of a moral subject. One has to ask: what particular kind of morality is this? Who is this moral subject?

One of the key aspects of the characterization of the developing civilizing process is a change in individuals' 'sensibility'. According to Elias:

(…) In the course of centuries the standard of human behaviour on the same occasion very gradually shifts in a specific direction. We see people at table, we see them going to bed or in hostile clashes. In these and other elementary activities the manner in which individuals behave and feel slowly changes.[8]

This change in feelings and behaviour is 'a very specific change in the feelings of shame and delicacy'.[9] People's relations with others, the social expression of their feelings, became a fundamental object for social control, not in a diffuse or dubious way, but as a very strict set of rules:

> [...] The social standard of conduct and sentiment, particularly in some upper-class circles, began to change fairly drastically from the sixteenth century onwards in a particular direction. The ruling of conduct and sentiment became stricter, more differentiated and all embracing, but also more even, more temperate, banishing excesses of self-castigation as well as of self-indulgence.[10]

The rules of etiquette are an important dimension of social life which allows us to understand the course of this historical transformation. However, its sociological scope is broader: it involves a general transformation in our relationships with bodies, the bodies of others as well as our own and with the specific 'aspects' that are allowed to take part in differing ways in social life. Rules for controlling body sounds and fluids, together with rules of overt behaviour and communication, not only came to provide a set of mundane and superficial rules, but are also internalized in a manner in which sensitivity about 'the other' (and 'its' proximity – the very issue of morality) is radically changed. Some behaviours that in past times were not objects of interest started to be considered disgusting. This process led into the establishment of new social prohibitions and the institutionalization of new taboos, setting a new threshold for the feelings of fear, disgust and shame.

The set of activities – that we now call 'sports' – can reveal more directly the nature of these new moral taboos. As an example, we can think of boxing's history where an increasing sensitivity and control of violence manifested itself in a succession of rule changes: prohibition of using the legs and feet; wearing gloves, eventually padding; the division of fighters by weight categories and the delimitation of size and shape of the battle field. Even if an ethos of the imitation of battle remains in sports,[11] the main feature of these 'mock battles', the one which differentiates them most from ancient and medieval practices, is the attempt at minimizing violence. Thus, 'most types of sport embody an element of competition. They are contests involving bodily strength or skills of a non-military type',[12] but the rules were developed in order to minimize violence and to reduce physical aggression. It was in this sense that Elias showed the existence of some degree of affinity between the parliamentary form of government and what he called sportgames.[13]

A historical perspective allows us to have a more adequate understanding of the nature and degree of transformation in patterns of sensitivity that was involved. If we think of a sport that is today considered to be violent, for example, wrestling, and if we compare it with the struggles which happened in ancient times, we can see how the change in sensitivity captured by the idea of 'civilization' has occurred. In the struggles of the pankration in ancient Greece, for example, the whole body was used (feet, elbows, knees, neck and head), and in the Spartan version, a pankratiast could also use his teeth.

(...) The pankratiasts were allowed to gouge one another's eyes out ... they were also allowed to trip their opponents, lay hold of their feet, noses and ears, dislocate their fingers and arms and apply strangle-holds. If one man succeeded in throwing the other, he was entitled to sit on him and beat him about the head, face and ears; he could also kick him and trample on him. It goes without saying that the contestants in this brutal contest sometimes received the most fearful wounds and that not infrequently men were killed![14]

Our sensitivity towards violence has now changed to such a degree that a spectacle like this could hardly be tolerated nowadays. Even wrestling has a number of limitations such as the prohibition of traumatic blows, sticking fingers in the eyes of an opponent, pinching, slashing eyes, nose, mouth and ears, pulling hair and biting.[15] One also has to consider the fact that these fights happen in delimited time and place, in the presence of referees whose acts are guaranteed and controlled by rules and institutions. In the case of football, figurational sociology has demonstrated how the versions practised today differ greatly from the ball games of the Middle Ages, such as, for example, Cornish hurling which was played in an open field or across country.[16] The game was held in the space between two or more villages without any restriction as to numbers of players and without much differentiation between them. The following description in early modern English provides a good idea of the changes that have historically occurred:

(...) When they meet, there is neyther comparing of numbers, nor matching of men: but a silver ball is cast up, and that company, which can catch, and cary it by force, or sleight, to their place assigned, gaineth the ball and victory. Whosoever getteth seizure of this ball, findeth himself generally pursued by the adverse party; neither will they leave, till (without all respects) he be layd flat on Gods deare earth.[17]

Through this description, it is possible to understand why collective games were considered dangerous by the authorities for so long. In 1314, King Edward II attempted to ban ball games in London based on the 'evils' they use to arouse. The ball came often to be regarded, because of the fury and passion involved in its dispute, as an object possessed by an evil spirit. In the same description of hurling cited above, the chronicler questions the value of the practice.

For as on the one side it makes their bodies strong, hard, and nimble, and puts courage into their hearts, to meete an enemie in the face: so on the other part, it is accompanied with many dangers, some of which do ever fall to the players share. For profe whereof, when the hurling is ended, you shall see them retying home, as from a pitched bataille, with bloody pates, bones broken, and out of joynt, and such bruses as serve to shorten their daies (...)[18]

It is our view that what figurational sociologists call 'a transformation of sensitivity' may well also be described as a transformation of morality. If we take a particular conception of morality, especially one of an emotivist type, changes in the threshold of shame, fear and disgust are the basis for the establishment of moral experience. From the standpoint of moral or ethical theory, this particular line of reasoning leads into a lot of questioning and difficulties just like any emotivist theory would have to confront, for example, the more continental type of moral philosophy. However, what it is being expressed here is not a consideration of 'civilizing process' as the development of morality in itself, but a much more simple argument: that what Elias called the 'civilizing process' can be regarded as particular type of moral theory. In other words, to understand the establishment of patterns of sociability that we call 'civilized' implies a discussion of social changing standards of morality. Below, we discuss some problems of this particular conception or what the dilemmas of a figurational sociology of morality are. Before that, it is necessary to emphasize that the great contribution made by Elias was to demonstrate how simple habits (for example, the use of forks) may be related to a complex transformation of social and moral relations.

From the perspective of morality as a concern with the 'correct' life, the importance of figurational sociology is to demonstrate how small social actions, especially those that seem natural or idiosyncratic, are actually part of a set of values that guides social dynamics. In this case, sports are another example of how this transformation took place. In fact, 'games are more than 'models' of social existence; they are microcosms of the fundamental nature of social life'[19] through which it is possible to realize the falsity of the dichotomy between individual and society and its genuine interdependence.[20] From practices that involved an extreme amount of violence (according to our 'civilized' standards) both among those who 'played' as well as among those watching, from situations that could extend to death, sports were transformed into situations marked by written rules, predetermined and controlled behaviour, where the suffering and cruelty must to a large extent be avoided.

The understanding of the civilizing process as a moral process still requires two important qualifications. First, it is important to note that the term 'civilized' does not have, for Norbert Elias, a value in itself, but is simply a term that has a meaning only in a comparative sense.[21] On referring to the thresholds of control and repression of certain acts, what is being presented is not a transformation of the species, but simply a pattern of organizing the actions of groups of individuals and one which can therefore be reversed.

Secondly, Elias did not consider the civilizing process as a development of more equitable social relations or a process of moralization (nor would sociology be up to making such judgements), but as the development of 'a double morality, a split and contradictory consciousness formation'.[22] The breach or contradiction of this morality lies in the fact that the control of and the repulsion from violence within a social group is not established in an equivalent way in the relationships between groups. The barriers and self-control that must be erected against violence within a group are constantly confronted by opposite demands due to conflicts, wars, etc. In other words, the moral rule which applies to the 'us' is not equivalent to rules that must be used for the 'other'. This idea is clarified when one considers the relationship between the old and new residents of Winston Parva[23] where the standards of moral recognition that organize and maintain internally the first group are not used in relations with the 'other'. The organization of social life between two groups, the 'us' and the 'others' in that particular case, also establishes the creation of two standards of justification and moral regulation.[24] This split, which exists in several figurations, becomes explicit in the sports world with the opposed interests that characterizes any game and its development: the desire or need to win, the ideas of shame, honour and sacrifice and the experience of supporting a team or group.

The 'Hand of God'

Figurational sociology denaturalizes our understanding of experience and lays down the basic premise of sociology – that reality is socially constructed. Regarding the study of sports, one has to emphasize their importance not only because of the place they occupy in society today, but also mainly for the way they changed socio-logical approach displacing an implicit hierarchy of activities within the social life. If there is an interest in understanding social life, figurational sociology has showed that, just like work, family and gender, for example, leisure is a fundamental part of social organization. This 'break' in a supposed hierarchy intrinsic to the spheres of social life (common in Classical Sociology) led to a fundamental methodological and epistemological rupture within the discipline.

Nevertheless, our study has a much more restricted focus: it is concerned with the relationship between game rules and moral rules. In a specific way, the question we have to answer is: what can sociological reasoning tell us about the morality of hand goals? With this question in mind, we have listed some sociological consider-ations or interpretations which could be directed at the 'Hand of God'. But before we proceed to a specific discussion of this goal, it is necessary to contextualize football relations between Argentina and England at the time it occurred. Indeed, on situating the relationship between these two countries, we confirm the idea that the match in which the 'Hand of God' occurred was a moral event. And, we take a step forward to note that this football confrontation did not become a moral event 'accidentally' but amid a clash of values or of different evaluative traditions or cultures.

Argentina vs. England in football before the 'Hand of God'

It is almost unnecessary to remember that there was a great rivalry between Argentina and England in the football world, which, according to Dave Bowler's assessment, influenced the occurrence of Maradona's 'Hand of God'.[25]

Let us remind ourselves that, until the Second World War, England refused on several occasions to participate in the World Cup organized by FIFA. The reason for this refusal was simple: in addition to inventing association football or 'soccer', the English considered themselves as being, not only the inventors of the game but also as the best footballers in the world. As such, they did not accept the idea of playing in this tournament with other nations. However, they did decide to partici-pate in the 1950 World Cup in Brazil, and the result was disastrous. England were eliminated in the first phase, including a historic defeat by the USA. Among Eng-land's players, then was Alfred Ramsey, manager of the future World Cup winning side in 1966.

According to his biographer,[26] Ramsey developed a very negative attitude towards Latin American players, particularly the ones from Uruguay and Argentina. According to him, the behaviour of players from these two countries hurt the spirit of the game, the spirit of fair play itself. Even more, he also believed that while the English played in a 'virile' and 'manly' way, nothing could compare to the cunning of the Uruguayans and Argentines.

The performance of the England team in the 1950 World Cup showed that this country was completely alienated from football developments both in continental Europe and Latin America. From then on, the English football authorities seek to play more matches against continental and Latin America sides.

In 1964, as a preparation for the 1966 World Cup Finals which were due to take place in England, Alfred Ramsey took the team to a tournament in Rio de Janeiro. During the competition, despite appreciating their beautiful technique, Ramsey's negative conception of the Argentines was further strengthened because of what he regarded as their lack of loyalty.

The next football clash between England and Argentina occurred in the quarter finals of the 1966 World Cup. According to various assessments, it was an extremely hard match which was marked by violence. To illustrate this, it is enough to realize that Antonio Rattín, the Argentine squad captain and leader, was sent off in the first half. After being sent off, he spent about 20 min discussing with the German referee Rudolf Kreitlein and after passing by a small 'Union Jack' in one corner of the field, he tore it down in a clear expression of dissatisfaction with what had happened 'and sat down on the Queen's red carpet'.[27] His explanation was that he did not understand what the referee had said. This led FIFA to introduce the yellow and red card system to symbolize this kind of warning to players from the 1970 World Cup onwards.

The sports writer, Hugh McIlvanney, defined the game 'as not so much a football match as an international incident'.[28] And Gordon Banks, the famous goalkeeper of that England squad – and also of the one in the 1970 World Cup – refers in his autobiography to the violence committed by the Argentinians, who ended up being warned by FIFA about their bad behaviour, with the following words:

> The game was only minutes old when Alan Ball was cynically felled by Silvio Marzo-lini. The referee, Rudolf Kreitlein, of West Germany, took no action except to award a free kick. The tone of the match had been set. We took the game to Argentina, a sig-nal for the body-checking and cynical fouls to gather momentum as the Argentines resorted to all manner of thuggery to keep us at bay [...] Herr Kreitlein was rapidly filling his notebook with Argentinian names and ten minutes before half time decided that the 'unofficial referee', the Argentine skipper, Antonio Rattin, who had disputed every booking, had to go.[29]

Even more, because of his allegedly negative experience playing against Argentina and other Latin American countries, Ramsey referred to Argentinian players as 'animals'.[30] The result was a diplomatic incident: the British Ambassador in Argentina was mistreated by fans and needed police protection.[31]

Another result arising from this, according to Bowler,[32] was the following:

> He [Ramsey] felt he'd suffered one way or another at the hands of the South Americans and their different attitudes since 1948 [...] though he had no idea that his use of the word 'animals' would be so provocative, having ramifications down the next four years [in the 1970 World Cup in Mexico] as a continent united against him (twenty years on, for Argentines, the 'Hand of God' seemed revenge for '66. Would even Maradona have used such spurious justification against any other team?

In short, the context of football relations between Argentina and England can be understood as a conflict of traditions or a conflict between 'imagined communities'.[33] The following considerations develop the idea of a moral dispute between communities to aid in understanding the 'Hand of God'. If one wants to understand sociologically the moral nature of this goal, we must bear in mind this historical background and how each side taking part perceived that they had a legitimate grievance, together with the resentment that it caused. One obvious argument against this historical perspective might state that passion should not be allowed to interfere with the game rules. Immediately, this attempt to displace the problem takes us into the most radical moral dilemma, such as that experienced by Antigone between following the civil law or her heart. However, if philosophy might choose from one of these positions, sociology is only concerned to reveal them.

Fair play

The 'Hand of God' goal itself was very simple:

> Five minutes into the second half, and with no goals scored, Robson's [the England manager] worst fears were confirmed. Maradona launched an attack on the English defence, beating a couple of players, before losing the move in a failed pass to Valdano. In the ensuing confusion near the English goal, Steve Hodge hooked the ball over his head, meaning it for Shilton. By then Maradona was set to recover what he had lost moments earlier, and rose to meet Shilton. The clash involved bodies and hands, some more legitimate than others. Into the net went the ball. Maradona was euphoric, racing without waiting for a verdict, to celebrate with his team mates. Shilton and the rest of the English team appealed immediately for hand ball. The English goalkeeper was so sickened by the decision that he ran out of his area signalling the infringement. It was the first time the normally cool-headed Shilton had displayed such public emotion. The linesman and the referee agreed it was a goal. For Maradona that was all that mattered.[34]

By analysing the long controversy over the 'Hand of God' and the fact that Argentineans themselves are not unanimous about the value of winning with such goal, it is possible to say that the idea of fair play has become universal. The extent of this debate cannot be credited only to the World's Cup magnitude and to media importance. It is obvious that any situation occurring in a World Cup match tends to be more discussed than regular matches. However, in this particular case, it was not the World Cup that dramatized the hand goal, but just the opposite. The way that goal dramatized the World Cup in Mexico is closely linked to the fact, not obvious, that football must be played within the parameters of justice. This figuration and its requirement for fairness (which is specific, historical and situated) can now be understood by almost all individuals on earth. If political thought in 'Late Capitalism' involves a great debate about the terms and the possibility of a transnationally applicable justice, in that particular World Cup, this problem was posed at a much more advanced level. In this particular case, differently from politics, there is an agreement about the fairness of the rules. The strong frustration emerged together with the tragic recognition of inherent game/life problems: the option of lying; promises that are not kept: a missed opportunity to establish justice. So, we have an important aspect for the questioning of the moral rules: even if morality were something related to particular cultures, the phenomenon of sportization not only spreads the understanding of a specific moral basis (the fair play that emerged from a specifically English historical figuration), but also establishes, although unintentionally, a universal standard. If, on the one hand, there is a difficulty in speaking sociologically of universal values, on the other hand, we are dealing with values that have become universal through a historical net of social processes, an ongoing debate on the notion of fairness/goodness that does not sound strange to individuals from very different cultural backgrounds.

The Falklands or Malvinas?

According to Elias, it is clear that the levels of violence between states interfere in attempts to decrease the level of violence within any given state. From this point of view, another dimension affecting the match is the war between England and Argentina over the Falklands/Malvinas Islands. In this particular aspect, we have to recognize football's extremely civilized and civilizing character. Powerful collective emotions organizing both nations' identity were allowed to be solved without physical violence.

Burns affirms that before the match, the diplomacies of the two countries were busy:

> Behind-the-scenes talks between the British and Argentine ambassadors, and a phone call to Bilardo from the Argentine President Raul Alfonsín resulted in the Argentine coach agreeing with his English counterpart Bobby Robson to depoliticize the game.[35]

Maradona himself, when pressed by John Carlin, from *The Times*, answered: 'Look, mate, I play football. About politics I know nothing'.[36]

If playing game organizes a manageable mimetic world, a little microcosm where meanings are reworked, it is really hard to avoid the fact that a certain 'real world' sense of life affects this mimetic world. Thus, the Argentines did not enter the field as mere football players; they were also responsible for healing the continuous wounds caused to the Argentinean identity. Revenge could not be accomplished through physical violence, but football enabled the symbolic and anthropological accomplishment of sacrifice.[37] In fact, at the end and unexpectedly, what was sacrificed in that match was Argentinean football which, being even more beautiful and joyful than the English game, now became suspect.[38] Argentinean football was sacrificed in the name of national identity. Sacrificing a joyful kind of football meets the ritual logic of sacrifice perfectly: the ritual's efficiency demands the purest and perfect exemplar to be taken to the altar. Thus, thinking from a radically sociological point of view, and within the logic of dispute between two communities, Maradona's act might not be considered immoral. Once we observe the facts from perspective of the community's moral organization, the sacrifice becomes necessary for its own continuity. Following this moral economy underlying the conflicts between different worlds (communities), Maradona just did what had to be done in order to repay the evil that had been inflicted on his community in the past.[39]

Maradona: a gentleman

We cannot say that the infraction committed by Maradona was in itself civilized. However, if we put it in the perspective of the historical development of ball games, we can think of the 'Hand of God' episode as actually being a genuine symbol of civilization. Taking as an example, the history of games and the level of violence that was tolerated in them, what was the 'Hand of God'? Whereas in the early twentieth-century football, it was not extraordinary for a leg to be broken during match, the indignation caused by Maradona's attitude reveals how football has internalized standards of control and fair play. The act itself was a simple touch, not seen by the referee because of Maradona's own subtlety. Ali Ben Nasser, from Tunisia, the man who refereed the match, said the following:

As far as I am concerned, I officiated perfectly. At that time there was no specialization and the linesmen were themselves referees, we were changing roles. Before the Cup debut, there was a meeting at which it was made clear that if the linesman was in a better position than the referee he had to make the case. If you watch the match, you will realize that one of the linesmen (it was the Bulgarian Bogdan Dotchev) was better located. I hesitated, but when I saw that he was running to the center, I allowed the goal. I was obliged to follow Fifa's advice [...] I called Fifa's interpreter and I asked my assistant Dotschev, who spoke neither French nor English, whether he was sure that there had been no Maradona's hand. He said no, he was convinced, he said categorically that the goal was perfectly legal ... I know Maradona said it had been the Hand of God and you know how the players are, there are things that happen and that enter into history. I saw the photo, I saw everything, but in the match I did not see anything. But again, I refereed well, even the commissioner of FIFA, who was a Scot, he congratulated me and I scored with 9.3 points [...] I am sure that my responsibility was limited in that goal.[40]

The failure of other actors involved also contributed to the act being translated into an advantage. If one stresses the traditional sociological perspective, Maradona's culpability is reduced: he alone could not orchestrate all those positions that together gave him an advantage; each player contributed to that result. It would be misleading, especially considering the constant Eliasian admonitions that there is no pure freedom or individual without society, to confer on a single player all responsibility for an action that is social.[41] Thus, when saying that the hand goal is civilized, we are not affirming that it is good and fair, but only that it is an advantage gained without violence or coercion and permitted by other actors' (failure to) act (which is sociologically valid and normal). In this sense, Maradona behaved during the match as a gentleman by establishing, despite his personal feelings, a pattern of non-violent action and respect for the referee.

Maradona himself described the moments which preceded the match and his feelings regarding his goals as follows:

... Before the match with England, we all declared that football had nothing to do with the Malvinas war. Lie! We did nothing but think about it, fucking it was going to be just another game! Our skin was all in the pain because of all the kids who had been killed like little birds over there. I played this game thinking of the Malvinas. Sentimentally, I blamed each of the English players for what had happened. I know that it sounds crazy, absurd, but that was, really, what we felt. It was stronger than us: we were defending our flag, the dead kids, the survivors. So my goal was of such a transcendent importance. In fact, they both had, they both had that feeling. The first was how to put the hand into an Englishman's pocket and get a wallet which was not his. The second covered everything ... And this was revenge, it was recuperating something from the Malvinas.[42]

He further added, 'It was a totally legitimate goal, because the referee allowed it. And I am not the one who is going to doubt the referee's honesty'.[43]

If this were a dispute among honoured gentlemen taking place many years ago and in which there was no film camera, it could be an insult to distrust Maradona's goal.[44]

Maradona 1, Sociology 0

For the development of our argument, it is necessary that, at some point earlier, the reader started experiencing changes in her/his threshold of anger or contempt. As moral subjects, we agree on some general ideas and want them to be confirmed, and the above argument frustrated this assumption as the hand goal was not condemned. One might question our analysis by asking: how does sociology deal with the fact that football fans' feel that victory is not the only thing that matters? The most fundamental question about the goal scored with the 'Hand of God' is whether it is right or wrong. And given that it is wrong, a crucial question should be asked: which person, in the same situation, would have acted differently from Maradona? We have to think of an honoured enough football player to tell the truth and deliberately miss a decisive World Cup goal. If only a few would do this, how can we charge Maradona? The fact that very few would act differently would not give validity to Maradona's action? That is what Maradona wants to demonstrate when he challenges Shilton in the documentary (passage already quoted above).

More recently, when Maradona was appointed as the new manager of Argentina, his very first match was against Scotland at Hampden Park. On hearing that Terry Butcher – the assistant manager to the Scotland team who played against him in Mexico 1986 – was not willing to shake hands with him, Maradona put forward the same argument, but this time with a concrete example as reported in *The Guardian*:

> 'I can reply [...] that when England won the World Cup, it was with a goal that everybody could see never crossed the line,' he said. As he held his hands two feet apart to indicate the distance between the bounce of Geoff Hurst's shot and the goal line at Wembley in 1966, the Scottish and Argentinian media contingents convulsed with laughter.[45]

However, following the spirit of football and its rules, the answer to the questions we put forward above is very simple. The same can be stated in terms of the game's moral logic: the 'Hand of God' goal is dishonest, and it insults the very foundation of the game. If there is a spirit (in the Hegelian sense) in football, a hand goal is its reification. If football is considered to be an expressive action (again in the Hegelian sense), then a hand goal alienates all players from football's meaning. If we use the situation or the difficulties of acting otherwise in order to justify Maradona's attitude, we use a case-by-case pattern that opposes morality's very nature. How can one judge every situation, every moment, without general patterns? From this perspective, we believe that game rules are like moral rules and, therefore, need to be universalizing. Otherwise, there is no (non-violent) basis for conflict resolution.

In our analysis, we attempted to demonstrate how the sense of right or wrong, just and unjust, seems to have no place in sociology. Even if we are able to understand how justice standards spread, we cannot say in a sociologically informed way that such a pattern is 'really just' or that it is 'good in itself'. Different historical periods will have different standards for understanding and judging the same action. Despite the fact that the understanding of the rules of football is widespread, and despite the possibilities found by actors for comparing football and life more generally, it does not entail the possibility of us accepting its universality or the validity of its rules as an example of justice. From a sociological standpoint, we can see that in football, as well as in other sports, other ways of judging particular actions have been developing.

When Maradona attributed his hand goal to God, he defined precisely the nature of those values that sociology cannot understand: that is, those which refer to transcendental structures. We do not believe this to be a particular problem of figurational sociology. However, this approach shows very well the dilemmas that arise when this kind of value is not thematized. This is not to claim that sociology should incorporate into its body the problem of the transcendental, but it is important to realize that there is a dimension of social experience (moral sentiments) that needs to be better understood within the discipline.

From a sociological point of view, there is a theoretical model of equalization between game rules and moral rules which interprets them and transforms them into rules of coercion. But the attachment of individuals to moral rules has a more extensive character than the internalization of fear or embarrassment, and therefore cannot be understood simply as a relationship with the socially accepted conventions. The *meaning* that animates the revolt against a hand goal or admiration in the face of displays of fair play is, from the standpoint of moral philosophy, completely different from other social conventions. However, even if sociology cannot fully incorporate this dimension at risk of contradicting its own epistemological basis, it is necessary to recognize how these moral meanings play a role that is different from the agency of social actors.

Final

In this paper, we have sought, through an interpretation of the hand goal scored by Maradona in the 1986 World Cup in Mexico, to discuss the relationship between game rules and moral rules in figurational sociology. We have tried to show how the idea of a civilizing process contributes not only to the understanding of sports, but also provides the foundation for a sociological understanding of morality. We hope we have made it clear that the most fundamental answer about the nature of the goal scored with the 'Hand of God' cannot be given on the basis of sociological knowledge. Our purpose is not to choose between a sociological or philosophical perspective, but just to demonstrate how the second one has a 'meaning' experienced by actors that can be thematized by sociological analysis.

Acknowledgements

The authors thank Eric Dunning, an Englishman, and Pablo Alabarces and Cesar Torres, both of them from Argentina, for their comments on an earlier version of this paper.

Notes

1. Albert Camus, *France Football*, 1957, quoted by Perryman, *Philosophy Football*, 1.
2. Sir Alfred Ramsey quoted by Burns, *Hand of God*, viii.
3. Indeed, the goal was scored by William Gallas. Henry held the ball and gave the pass which resulted in the goal. For short, we refer to it as a goal by Henry.
4. Alexander, 'On the Construction of Moral Universals' and 'Toward a Theory of Cultural Trauma'.
5. In a DVD collection entitled *The History of Soccer: A Magic Game* (Third Episode: South American Superpowers), there are references to the episode, which we transcribe below with our own description: Maradona (looking very seriously at the camera and with his finger upraised): 'Shilton, you think you are the hero, the phenomenon! [Maradona then changes his face and shows an ironic mode]. Shilton, if a ball goes through the line a little bit like this [he shows with his own hands what 'a bit' would be], and you hold it without the referee seeing it, would you say to him that was a goal?' [Maradona remains silent and stares at the camera with a very serious and challenging look].
6. In 2008, Tom Wells, writing in the English tabloid *The Sun* (31 January 2008, 14–5), in a report titled 'I hold my hands up', published an alleged repentance by Maradona. After he showed the distortion made by the reporter, the newspaper renamed the event the

'hand of the devil' (*El Porvenir*, 2009). In the wake of his alleged excuses, *El Clarín* from Buenos Aires published a poll which showed that 66.6% out of 12,426 surveyed Argentineans disapproved of Maradona, saying 'sorry' to the English (*El Clarín*, 2008).

7. For a philosophical discussion of the moral value of hand goals, see Torres and Campos. *La Pelota no Dobla?*
8. Elias, *The Civilizing Process*, x.
9. Idem, x.
10. Elias and Dunning, *Quest for Excitement*, 5.
11. Elias and Dunning, *Quest for Excitement*, 9.
12. Idem, 3.
13. Idem, 11.
14. Mezoe quoted by Elias and Dunning, *Quest for Excitement*, 117.
15. See Federação Luta Livre Submission do Rio de Janeiro, n/d.
16. Elias and Dunning, *Quest for Excitement*, 183–6.
17. Carew quoted by Elias and Dunning, *Quest for Excitement*, 185.
18. Idem, ibdem, 185–6.
19. Giulianotti, 'Civilizing Games', 147.
20. See Elias and Dunning, 'Dynamics of Group Sports …' and *Quest for Excitement*.
21. See Elias and Dunning, *Quest for Excitement*, 125.
22. Idem. 114.
23. Elias and Scotson, *The Established and the Outsiders*.
24. We assume as a presupposition of two ideas about the argument advanced by Elias and Scotson, *The Established and Outsiders*, (1) The development of power relations as presented in the community studied is also the building of a morality and (2) the imbalance between the two groups shows a sociological version of the theme of the Hegelian dialectic between master and servant.
25. Bowler, *Winning Isn't Everything*.
26. Idem, ibdem.
27. Fernández Moores, 'Hand of God or God Knows', 4.
28. Quoted by Bowler, *Winning Isn't Everything*, 210.
29. Banks, *Bansky*, 256.
30. It is worth quoting a letter to the Editor published by *The Times* immediately after that match: 'From Lord Lovat. Sir, – May I suggest that before England's manager, Mr. Alfred Ramsey, publicly insults a small but friendly nation represented by a visiting football team, he might remember that, quite apart from Latin temperament, language difficulties and the different way a game is played in South America, his own side were penalized no less than 33 times against the 19 fouls perpetrated by Argentina' (*The Times*, 26 July 1966).
31. Bowler, *Winning Isn't Everything*, 214.
32. Idem, 213.
33. Anderson, *Imagined Communities*.
34. Burns, *Hand of God*, 159–60.
35. Burns, *Winning isn't Everything*, 157–8.
36. Idem, 157.
37. See Mauss and Hubert, *Sacrifice*.
38. We acknowledge the sociological problem of this statement.
39. In the documentary on DVD already mentioned, Jorge Valdano stated the following: 'In Argentina, the illegal (malo) goal was more celebrated than the legitimate (bueno) goal, because it was against the English, and they seemed to deserve it'.
40. Todos Los Mundiales: México 1986.
41. See also Collins, *Interaction Ritual Chains*.
42. Todos los Mundiales: México 1986.
43. Idem. Of course, we realize Maradona's irony. Therefore, we are not accepting his words *prima facie*.
44. Eric Dunning reminded us that 'you should look at the late 19th century Corinthians who, when the modern penalty rule was introduced, used to kick the ball wide, because, they argued, no gentleman would commit a foul deliberately' (Personal message).
45. Williams, 'Glasgow Hails the Hand of God'.

References

Alexander, J. 'On the Social Construction of Moral Universals: The 'Holocaust' from War Crime to Trauma Drama'. *European Journal of Social Theory* 5, no. 1 (2002): 5–82.

Alexander, J. 'Toward a Theory of Cultural Trauma'. In *Cultural Trauma and Collective Identity*, eds. J. Alexander et al., 1–30. Los Angeles, CA: University of California Press, 2004.

Anderson, B. *Imagined Communities: Reflections on the Origin and Spread of Nationalism*. Revised ed. London: Verso, 2003.

Banks, G. *Banksy: My Autobiography*. London: Penguin, 2003.

Bowler, D. *Winning Isn't Everything ...: A Biography of Sir Alfred Ramsey*. London: Orion, 1998.

Burns, J. *Hand of God: The Life of Diego Maradona*. London: Bloomsbury, 2002.

Collins, R. *Interaction Ritual Chains*. Princeton, NJ: Princeton University Press, 2004.

El Clarín 'Maradona y "La Mano de Dios": "Se Pudiera Cambiar La Historia, lo Haría"' [Maradona and 'The Hand of God': 'If I Could Change History, I would Make it'], 2008. http://www.clarin.com/diario/2008/01/31/um/m-01597524.htm (accessed December 2009).

El Porvenir 'La Mano de Dios y el Gol del Siglo' [The Hand of God and the Goal of the Century], 2009. http://www.elporvenir.com.mx/notas.asp?nota_id=317824 (accessed December 2009).

Elias, N. *The Civilizing Process*. Oxford: Blackwell, 2004.

Elias, N., and E. Dunning. 'Dynamics of Group Sports with Special Reference to Football'. *British Journal of Sociology* 17, no. 4 (1966): 388–402.

Elias, N., and E. Dunning. *Quest for Excitement: Sport and Leisure in the Civilising Process*. Dublin: University College Dublin Press, 2008.

Elias, N., and J. Scotson. *The Established and the Outsiders*. London: Sage, 1994.

Federação Luta Livre Submission do Rio de Janeiro. 'Regras da Federação Para Torneios de Luta-Livre Submission' [Rules of the Federation for Wrestling], n/d. http://lutalivresubmission.com.br/?fx=pagina1 (accessed September 2009).

Fernández Moores, E. 'Hand of God or God Knows?', n/d. http://www.playthegame.org/uploads/media/EzequielMoores-ThehandofGod.pdf (accessed February 2010).

Giulianotti, R. 'Civilizing Games: Norbert Elias and the Sociology of Sports'. In *Sport and Modern Social Theorists*, ed. R. Giulianotti, 145–60. Basingstoke: Palgrave Macmillan, 2004.

Mauss, M., and H. Hubert. *Sacrifice. Its Nature and Function*. Chicago, IL: University of Chicago Press, 1981.

Perryman, M. *Philosophy Football: Eleven Great Thinkers Play it Deep*. London: Penguin, 1997.

Todos Los Mundiales: México 1986 [All World Cup Finals: Mexico 1986], n/d. http://todoslosmundiales.com.ar/mundiales/1986mexico/historias/0028-la-mano-de-dias-version-arbitral.htm (accessed December 2009).

Torres, C.R., and D.G. Campos, eds. *La Pelota no Dobla?: Ensayos Filosóficos en Torno al Fútbol* [Does the Ball not Bend?: Philosophical Essays on Football]. Buenos Ayres: Libros de Zorzal, 2006.

Wells, T. 'I Hold My Hands Up'. *The Sun*, January 31, 2008, 14–5.

Williams, R. 'Glasgow Hails the hand of God'. *The Guardian*, November 19, 2008. http://www.guardian.co.uk/football/2008/nov/19/diego-maradona-argentina-scotland-football (accessed February 2010).

DVDs

(1) History of Football – the Beautiful Game (7 DVDs)Fremantle Home Entertainment, 2004.

(2) Emir Kusturica – Maradona – Optimum Home.

Zinedine Zidane's return to the land of his ancestors: politics, diplomacy or something else?

Yvan Gastaut[a] and Steven Apostolov[b]

[a]Unité de Recherches Migrations et Société, Université de Nice Sophia Antipolis, Nice, France; [b]Department of Political Science, University of Massachusetts, Lowell, MA, USA

Zinedine Zidane was one of the best players of the late 1990s and the early 2000s. His achievements as a soccer player are well known and are documented in a few well-written biographies. Therefore, this essay will focus on lesser-known aspects of his life, such as charity, humanitarian work and, to some degree, diplomacy. During his short and historic visit to Algeria in 2006, he was successful in improving Franco–Algerian relations considerably, something that many politicians had failed to achieve in previous decades.

Introduction

Zinedine Zidane's 'official' visit to Algeria, which took place between 11 and 16 December 2006, was important not only because 'the prodigal son' visited the land of his ancestors as a world champion but also because the trip was important in terms of Franco–Algerian foreign relations and diplomacy. The return to Algeria of this extraordinary son of Algerian immigrants, much popularized by the media, created an enormous popular following and enthusiasm that improved Franco–Algerian foreign relations considerably. The visibility and impact of Zinane's trip to Algeria was compared to Jacques Chirac's official visit to the country, which took place between 2 and 4 March 2003. Chirac's visit was historic: the French president and his Algerian counterpart signed a treaty that buttressed political and economic cooperation between the two countries. It also strengthened Franco–Algerian cultural and scientific exchanges.[1]

When former socialist Spanish prime minister, Jose-Luis Rodriquez Zapatero, came to Algeria to negotiate sensitive issues such the price of natural gas, illegal immigration and the West Saharan dispute, he was greeted warmly by the Algerian people. Jacques Chirac was welcomed enthusiastically in Oran and Algiers by hundreds of thousands of people. So was his minister of economy, Thierry Breton, who visited Algeria between 10 and 11 December 2003. The official visits of the French leaders and the Spanish prime minister, however, were overshadowed by the welcome that Algerians reserved for Zinedine Zidane three years later.[2]

A week before his 'official' visit to Algeria, Zidane issued a statement on TF1, one of the main French TV channels. The statement was rather emotional: 'I would like to rediscover my origins, rediscover the land of my parents. I have to do it, and I am very excited'. This 'official' visit had multiple sides. It interconnected the personal desire of a famous athlete to rediscover his origins with politics and

Franco–Algerian international relations. More importantly, the visit of a French world champion, born to Algerian parents, created a very positive image for Algeria. Zinedine Zidane's visit was used to a great extent by the Algerian government, too. Promoted more than the visits of some politicians and heads of state, Zidane's voyage to Algeria created media expose unprecedented in the North African nation since the country's independence. Zidane, who was one of the best soccer players of the late 1990s and the early 2000s, received a warmer welcome and better visibility, and achieved only in a few days what some politicians failed to accomplish over the course of decades. His visit clearly demonstrates how soccer could be used off the pitch for political, intercultural and foreign relation purposes. This essay will focus on these aspects of Zidane's trip, rather than on writing a comprehensive biography on Zinedine Zidane.

An Algerian past transmitted via oral and family history

Shortly before he hung up his boots, Zinedine Zidane[3] told a journalist from the most popular French sports newspaper that he 'has always considered himself as Algerian and Berber'.[4] This statement, issued by a son of immigrants, showed his passion and desire to rediscover the origins of his ancestors.[5]

Zidane's family is originally from Aguemoune, a small village located in the Béjaia province of Kabylie. Zidane's father, Smail, worked as a young man cultivating the family's land and selling fruits and vegetables at local markets. In 1953, at the age of only 17, Smail Zidane left his homeland before the war of independence erupted. His departure was against the will of his parents. Smail became part of the first generation of young and impoverished Algerians who preferred an industrial job in a French metropolis to the life of a small farmer in his native land.[6] He spent his first two weeks in northern Paris in a small room with minimal comforts. Chased away by his landlord, Smail moved further north to the Parisian suburb of Saint Denis, where he supported himself as a construction worker. Like so many other Algerian immigrants, Smail shared a small apartment with three other countrymen from his native village; he was also sending half of his salary home to his parents.[7]

In 1962, exhausted from hard labour and frustrated from sharing overcrowded apartments, Smail Zidane, was on the verge of returning to Algeria. Before boarding the boat to go back home, he spent a few weeks in Marseille. It was there, while staying with relatives, that he met his future wife, Malika.[8] In January 1963, the young couple was married. They decided to stay in southern France and settled in the small town of Canet, about 80 km west of Marseille. There, the Zidanes had their first child, Madjid. The following year, they moved back to a housing project, called *La Cité Bassens*, situated not too far away from the commercial port of Marseille. From 1963 until 1969, Smail and Malika had another three children: Farid, Nourredine and Lilla. All of the children were born in this tough neighbourhood, populated almost entirely by immigrants and stricken by poverty and human congestion. In 1969, the Zidanes moved to an equally tough neighbourhood, *La Cité de la Castellane*, but to a much better and larger apartment. Zinedine Zidane was born there on 23 June 1972. He had a happy childhood, although it was affected by relative poverty. Smail and Malika transmitted their love and cultural attachments to Algeria, especially to the region of Kabylie, to young Zinedine from his early childhood. In 1986, when Zinedine was only 14 years old, the family members crossed the Mediterranean on a boat packed with many other immigrants and spent a short summer vacation in the village of their ancestors. Zinedine Zidane would not go back to Algeria until 2006.

In 1994, after the beginning of his professional career – a few years at AS Cannes and a successful transfer to FC Girondins de Bordeaux – the coach of the Algerian national team refused to select him. In the eyes of Abdelhamid Kermali, Zinedine was not quick enough. Shortly after that, Zidane received his first call for international duty from the French national team. His first official match with a French shirt would tie him for ever with France as an athlete representing the adoptive country of his parents. Little by little, Zidane would become one of the key players of *les Bleus* – the French national team. The two goals that he scored during the final of the World Cup in 1998 transformed him into a French national hero: *Zidane président* sang the ecstatic crowds after the French victory over Brazil, and the same slogan was even displayed in illuminated letters at the *Arc de Triomphe* in Paris, one of the most famous and venerated monuments in the French capital. Zinedine Zidane was also one of the most important actors for creating of the metaphor *blanc – black – beur* (*blanc* means white and black means *noir* in French slang, and *beur* –literally butter – means Arab). Reflecting its ethnic diversity, this metaphor became a description of the French national team. It united the team in a unique way and created a special relationship with the fans. It also attracted people who had not followed soccer up to that point to cherish *les Bleus* and feel patriotic after their victories.

Zidane has never claimed any credit for that. He has always been humble, if not shy. He has never tried to pass any political message about cultural assimilation, nor has he talked about sensitive issues in France, such as immigration, Islam or the difficulties that second generation young people of North African origin experience in tough ethnic neighbourhoods and housing projects. The respect that most French people have for him is largely due to the calm way in which he has often described his modest family background. A couple of times, when interviewed, he was annoyed by the question what he owed to France. 'I am what I am thanks to my mother and my father. They deserve credit for raising me and for teaching me since a very young age to work hard and to respect others', he said.[9]

An Algerian self-awareness in progress

Without any doubt, Zinedine Zidane is a product of the troubled history of the Franco–Algerian relationship. After his extraordinary accomplishments as a soccer player and world champion, his Algerian origins were constantly evoked. One of the most striking examples was during the friendly game between France and Algeria in 2001, when a predominantly immigrant or second-generation North African crowd booed the French national anthem. Even though he was completely out of shape, Zidane was the most solicited player by the media before and after the game. Journalists asked more questions about his origins and national identity than about the game. At first, he appeared annoyed by these questions and refused to grant any interviews.[10] Afterward, however, the then Real Madrid midfielder spoke to journalists from the daily newspaper *Le Figaro*. 'I am the only player of Algerian origin in our national team, and I am proud of it. But I do not understand why you are interested in talking to me more than to the other players. I would appreciate if we could keep the conversation just about sports'.[11] Later, Zidane spoke to a journalist from *Le Monde* as well: 'This match was somehow historic and special for me. For the first time in my life, I would not be disappointed if the French national team does not win'.[12] In another interview, granted from Madrid to the French radio station RTL, he explained more precisely his emotions: 'I met a few Algerians on the street here and they asked me to take it easy during the game. My wish is a draw. Hopefully it will be a nice and entertaining game and both French and Algerians will be proud of it'.[13] A day before the match, Zidane stated that he would have very strong feelings about both countries at the moment he stepped on the pitch. 'I think a lot about the Algerian people. It is the country of my parents. My origins are there, and I still have a family [there]. They are courageous people who know how to face problems and resolve them. They are proud people and deserve our admiration'.

These revelations in the French media created some contradictive follow ups in both French public opinion and in immigrant communities. Malek Bouith, the president of *SOS Racisme*, a French non-governmental organization aimed at fighting against racial discrimination, declared that 'if Zidane pretends to be more French than Algerian and is only grateful to France, I could not care less about his strong feelings about both countries'.[14] Ivan Rioufol from *Le Figaro* criticized the player from another angle: 'We would like that Zinedine Zidane, who does not hide his fondness for Algeria and his ancestors, picks a side and sticks to it. And that side should be France'.[15]

The outcome of this game was peculiar in many ways, if not catastrophic.[16] Not only was *La Marseillaise* booed by the majority of the spectators, but the play was also interrupted by a few French-born Algerian supporters who invaded the pitch. Jacques Chirac, president of France at the time, threatened to suspend the match. These troubled Franco–Algerian conflicts made Zinedine Zidane feel uneasy.[17]

Despite his statements and the events of the match, Zidane was one of France's most venerated stars. Since 1998, his popularity has not stopped growing; his popularity was neither affected by his premature retirement from *les Bleus* and his sudden return to national duty in 2006 nor by the infamous *coup de tête* which most likely cost France its second World Cup title.[18] His popularity is the same, if not bigger, in Algeria and his father's native Kabylie.[19]

Toward the end of his career, and being conscious of his growing popularity in Algeria, Zidane became more and more interested in the country of his ancestors. Interestingly, his father had never broken ties with the mother country and his native region.[20] Little by little, Zidane developed new interests. He grew up without learning how to speak Berber. Despite this handicap, he promised to learn the language. He regularly donated large shipments of clothing to Algeria, most of the time to schools in his father's native Aguemoune. He also signed and sent to Algeria, with the help of his father, hundreds of posters and cards to his Algerian fans. In 2004, he and teammate Laurent Blanc aided the charitable association *Les Enfants du Sahara*. The goal of this association was to provide internet access and computers to children from southern Algeria. The same year, Zidane signed an endorsement deal with Kuwaiti mobile network operator *Wataniya*.[21] He announced during a commercial broadcast on Algerian national television that all the funds from that endorsement would be donated to charities in Algeria.

Originally, the 'official' visit of Zidane to Algeria was scheduled to take place between 22 and 27 March 2005. It was organized with the help of a network of many Berber associations from the region of Zidane's family in Kabylie. After rumours of the visit were spread, the event was generating so much interest that it appeared to outshine the official visit of the French President, Jacques Chirac,[22] which had taken place few years earlier. At the moment when everything was ready and the hosts were reviewing final details, Zidane cancelled his trip, providing as an excuse the disappointing performance of his Spanish club team, Real Madrid in the Champions League competition.[23]

During the peak of the 2006 World Cup, which coincided with the 44th anniversary of Algerian independence, Algerian President Abdelaziz Bouteflika took an interesting and controversial position. While criticizing vigorously France for the colonial oppression and atrocities during the war of independence,[24] the Algerian head of state publicly admired the efforts and performance of the captain of the *les Bleus*. He even said that Zidane's head-butt against Marco Materazzi was justified as a result of the insults and blatant racism of the Italian player. Abdelaziz Bouteflika even decided to send a letter to Zidane 'from [the president] and the Algerian people' to express his sympathy for the incident that deprived Zidane of the ultimate joy of being at the top of world soccer once again and to congratulate him for the accomplishment of a brilliant career. President Bouteflika justified this unusual act of a head of state who congratulates an athlete from another country by emphasizing Zidane's Algerian origin, saying 'We support him because he is Algerian and he is the best player in the world'.[25]

Enthusiastic crowds and a humanitarian message

The origins of Zidane's 'official' visit go back to 6 October 2003 when a friendly game was organized between the victorious French national team of 1998 and Olympique de Marseille. The funds that were generated by the match – approximately 935,000 Euros – were used to help the victims of the earthquake that ravaged the city of Boumerdès in northern Algeria on 21 May 2003. The funds were allocated to *La Fondation de France*, which collected almost 5 million Euros to assist the victims of this natural disaster. The official purpose of the visit was to supervise humanitarian efforts and to inaugurate the medical outlets that were opened with the funds collected by the foundation.

After the aborted visit in 2005, another visit was scheduled the following year. On 11 December 2006, the Algerian presidential aeroplane was chartered to bring the Zidane family to Boumediene Airport in Algiers. The landing of the star caused enormous chaos, which prevented the authorities from conducting a proper official greeting for the important guest. Law enforcement, mobilized to handle the event, panicked and could hardly maintain order among the gathering people. The Algerian ministers of solidarity, Djamel Ould Abbes, and his colleague, the minister of youth and sports, Yahia Guidoum, could hardly make their way through the crowd to greet the official guest. Zinedine Zidane appeared on the tarmac by the aeroplane with a shy smile on his face and was instantly surrounded by bodyguards, officials and police officers. The way to the VIP's lodging was congested by many photographers and journalists. The captain of the French national team finally disappeared into a limousine under a hail of flashbulbs.

The first stage of the itinerary was a visit to the region of the city Boumerdès, located 70 km east of Algiers. The first place that the soccer player visited was the primary school at Sidi Daoud, which was reconstructed with the funds generated by *La Fondation de France*. After that, Zidane visited the mobile medical facilities in the same town, as well as the infrastructure built to rescue and assist people in Beni Amrane, Corso and Boumerdès. The atmosphere caused by this visit was electric.

It was similar to the joy most Algerians experienced in 1962 after the country was liberated from the French. Zidane was profoundly touched by the events and expressed his surprise and enormous satisfaction: 'It is the country of my parents, and I am proud to be Algerian. I am very happy to be here among all these good people'.[26] The former midfielder, however, was protected like a head of state: the police cordon was so thick so that it was almost impossible to approach him or talk to him.

Throughout his itinerary, the former captain of *les Bleus* was greeted with the slogans 'Yahia Zizou!' (which means Vive Zizou!) and 'Vive Zidane, Vive l' Algérie'! According to Algerian authorities, several million Algerians gathered along Zidane's route to greet and see their idol. Some people climbed on the roofs and fences of the surrounding buildings; others went up on the branches of olive trees around the roads. Zinedine Zidane was accompanied by his father, mother and younger brother, who could hardly hold back their tears from experiencing such a warm welcome.

The following day, Zidane inaugurated the opening of the paediatric department of the hospital of Thiénia – the city where the epicentre of the earthquake was located. It was also erected with funds donated by *La Fondation de France*. After a chat with the medical staff about their duties and personal lives, the star took the liberty to kick a few balls at the hospital's yard with a few orphans who were admitted at the paediatric services for treatments. This took place under the scrutiny of the reporters and photographers and was followed by another hail of flashbulbs and camera clicks.

The next stop was the inauguration of the training centre of the Algerian national team at Sidi Moussa, where Zidane was accompanied by the Algerian minister of the youth and sports as well as by many youngsters and prominent local athletes. After visiting the premises, Zidane stepped on the pitch for a series of dribbles, passes and spectacular juggling with the ball. The young athletes gave him a joyful ovation, which was followed by a photograph session and a signing of autographs. At first, the minister of youth and sports hardly managed to address the crowd. Afterwards, he delivered an emotional and thought-provoking speech: 'The Algerian youth should be inspired by the success of Zidane as an athlete, as a star, as well as a father of a family. Zidane is a legend, is an example to follow for our youth in order to realize their dreams and achieve their goals [...] Algeria is fortunate to have Zidane just as Zidane is fortunate to have Algeria'.[27]

The next place of visit during the second day was the hospital Mustapha Pasha in Algiers. Zidane stopped there to visit cancer victims. Most of them were young children and were treated by Dr Bouzid – a famous Algerian physician. This visit was followed by Zidane's first official press conference. It took place at hotel El-Djazair. Local and foreign media outlets sent more than 300 journalists to cover the event. The opening statement of Zidane was: 'I am very happy to be in my country of origin and to share this happy moment with all Algerians'. After that, he focused on the humanitarian aspects of his visit. In his closing statements, he attempted to stay neutral on the highly political and controversial issues in Algeria surrounding the region of Kabylie, the Berber language and the political strife of some Berberophones.[28]

The official side of the visit and diplomacy

After the first two days unfolded, the focus of the visit switched from charity and humanitarian aspects to official ceremonies and diplomacy. Wednesday, 13

December 2006, started with a meeting between President Bouteflika and Zinedine Zidane.[29] The conversation was about Zidane's future and potential involvements in Algeria. The one-hour meeting was followed by an official lunch at the presidential palace, El-Mouradia. Among the dignitaries were the iconic Algerian soccer player Rachid Mekloufi, players from the Algerian national team that defeated Germany during the World Cup in 1982, and the Olympic gold medallist of 1992, Hassiba Boulmerka.

During lunch, the elegantly dressed Zidane was awarded by the head of state the Al-Athir medal – the highest national honour. For his part, the player gave to President Bouteflika one of his shirts, worn during an official game between France and Spain, and the boots that he wore during the final in 1998. After he gave this token of appreciation to the Algerian president, Zidane stated: 'I am happy to be in Algeria and to spend a moment with you, Mister President'. The Olympic gold medallist in the 1500 m at Sydney, Nouria Bnida-Merah, told the media that, 'It was a colossal reception. I was about to go back to France, but I had to reschedule my return. Zidane was certainly born in France, but for us he is really Algerian. We feel that he has in his blood the love of this country and our land'.[30] In the evening, Zidane attended an official dinner hosted by the French Ambassador, Bernard Bajolet. He called Zidane 'a great Frenchman', underlining that he represents a 'bridge between the peoples of Algeria and France'.

All of Algeria woke up on the following day to articles on the front page of all major newspapers with photographs of President Bouteflika decorating Zidane with the Al-Athir medal. *La Liberté* came up with the following title: 'Zidane elevated to the rank of a national hero',[31] whereas *El Watan* published a story titled: 'Zidane honored by his own people'.[32] In the morning of this final day before his departure, Zidane visited field hospitals in the Béjaia province, located not too far away from his father's place of birth. These facilities were built with funds donated by his own parents. A huge crowd gathered around the facilities to greet the player. Flown back to Algiers, Zidane gave the official kick off the match opposing *Union Sportive de la Médina d'Alger* (USMA) and *Jeunesse Sportive de la Médina de Béjaia* (JSMB). Zidane did not stay for the end of the game. He attended instead a cocktail reception, organized by the mobile phone operator, *Wataniya*, with which he had an endorsement deal.

The return to Aguemoune: nostalgia and huge crowds

Friday, 15 December, was scheduled as the last day of Zidane's visit in Algeria. On the final day of his visit, the player was scheduled to visit the birthplace of his parents, Aguemoune. It is a small village of about hundred inhabitants, located in the Babros Mountains. The small village has hardly changed since the departure of Smail Zidane in the 1950s. However, since the visit was announced and confirmed, the village had been preparing carefully to greet its famous visitor: the streets were cleaned; the facades of most houses were repainted and decorated. Most importantly, the main road was improved. The mayor of the small village saw a perfect window of opportunity in this visit to use it to improve the living conditions of his constituents, who were not only forgotten by the central government in Algiers but also by the local regional and authorities.

A few days before the arrival of the soccer star, the small village was already packed by local and foreign journalists. The village had never seen such an influx of people. Before sunrise, cars with enthusiastic and cheering people started arriving from all around Kabylie. Despite heavy rain, the residents and all the visitors gathered to give a warm welcome to the 'prodigal son'. But the star was late. It was announced that the army helicopter could not land in proximity because of the bad weather. The landing was to take place 50 km away. The star was running even later because on his way to Aguemoune he stopped to pay a quick visit to one of his aunts, who was seriously ill and could not make it to the official ceremony.

Zidane finally arrived at the village around noon. He could hardly get out of his armoured limousine and approach the house. Once inside, he was greeted by traditional Berber singers and musicians. His distant family and the other villagers prepared a monumental couscous: two lambs been slaughtered the day before for the enormous meal. The women baked the traditional bread Kaddour and fixed salads with local chelita peppers and olive oil. Skipping the meal, Zidane isolated himself for 15 min at the house where his father was born. On his way out, he shook the hands of a few distant cousins. To the complete surprise and disappointment of his hosts, he headed back to his limousine on his way back the helicopter, which took him back to Algiers, where his official visit was scheduled to finish.

Political exploitation?

Several observers, in France as well as in Algeria, characterized Zinedine Zidane's visit as a highly political tool used by the Algerian authorities for their own agendas. The huge posters displayed around most Algerian cities during the visit of Zidane, on which the soccer legend appeared with President Buteflika, supported to some degree that sentiment. There were two posters. On one of the versions, both men appeared with a background of the Algerian flag with the slogan, 'Men of peace and solidarity'. On the other, the pictures and background were the same, but the slogan was different: 'Algeria is proud of you'.

In France, it was stated officially that Zidane was the 'personal invitee' of President Buteflika. Zidane himself stated that 'being invited by the president was the same thing as being invited by the Algerian people', and he was proud of that invitation. As a result of this statement, several French newspapers, right-wing as well as left-wing, criticized the retired soccer player. Le Parisien published an article in which the journalist underlined that the 'the trip was too political'.[33] Liberation was equally critical but also sarcastic; it published a story saying that Zidane was 'Boutefliked'.[34] Another major French newspaper, Le Figaro, affirmed that the Algerian head of state 'tried to prevent Berbers from drafting Zidane to be a militant and spokesperson for their continual contestation of the Algerian authorities'.[35] The Algerian head of state, in fact, could have only benefited from the visit of the renowned soccer player. Aside from his health issues, President Bouteflika was losing ground in a debate in which we was trying to amend the constitution in order to run for re-election a third time in 2008.

In Algeria, several militants for the Berber cause, which the central government has always neglected, warned the soccer star in an open letter: 'You [Zidane] so far have avoided political machinations and attempts to be used for political agendas [...] The honors and welcome that you have received here by the government are not completely sincere, based just on your athletic achievements and contributions for charities'.[36] Berber militants accused Zidane of unwillingness to get involved more actively in recognizing Berber strife and promoting liberties for Berbers. The militants' doubts were confirmed during the press conference at the hotel Al-Djazair in Algiers: the soccer star did not express any support at all for the political battle for recognition of the Berberophone minority in Algeria.

Said Sadi, president of *Rassemblement pour la Culture et la Démocratie* (RCD), an Algerian political party traditionally hostile to the government, criticized the soccer player: 'It is quite understandable that Zidane wants to discover his origins and visit the place of birth of his parents. But this trip was a big mistake because it was orchestrated by President Bouteflika'. The political leader totally disapproved of the controversial welcome that a head of state set up for this 'foreign' athlete and the fact that that the highest national honour was awarded to him. He extended further his critique by denouncing the hypocrisy of the Algerian president, who had recently criticized binational children of Algerian immigrants in France, referring to them as 'bad patriots'. The journalist Mohamed Benchicou, for his part, brought up the pertinent question: 'Would Zidane help Bouteflika to redeem his image?'.[37]

El Watan, an Algerian newspaper catering to the interest of the government, responded to the wide criticism in the following way: 'Putting the whole heavy dossier of Berber political strife for recognition on Zizou's shoulders is not fair, and it is also an insult for such a humble man'.[38] Idir, a famous Berber singer, supported the soccer player, too. This ambassador of Kabyle music and culture, who was at first very critical of the attempts of the Algerian government to use Zizou's image for a political agenda, stated that, '[Zidane] is a noble person who has many good qualities. He just came to visit the land of his ancestors. As far as politics are concerned, he is far from being involved [...] He invited neither Khaled nor Faudel[39] to join him on this trip, but invited me instead. And that says a lot, because he did not make this choice by accident. It is symbolic, and he did it on purpose'.[40]

Zinedine Zidane received some support in France, too. The president of *La Coordinaiton des Berbères de France* (CBF), Lyazid Ikdoumi, annoyed about all the buzz surrounding Zinedine Zidane's visit to Algeria, disagreed with the accusations of any political implications. According to Idhoumi, Zidane's visit to Algeria 'was important to many young Frenchmen of North African origin. It would help them build a bridge with their roots and origins'. Chérif Benbouriche, another activist opposing the Algerian government and the president of *l'Association Culturelle Berbère* (ACB), found that Zidane did not do the voyage for 'Bouteflika but for his parents'.[41]

Smail Zidane, who has never hidden his admiration for President Bouteflika, personally defended his son and denied any political involvement. In an interesting article published in the right-wing French daily newspaper *Le Figaro*, the journalist concluded that the Zidane family, excited and profoundly touched by the warm welcome and festive atmosphere and at the same time concerned with humanitarian actions and charity, did not fully understand the true intentions of the Algerian authorities to use this visit for political purposes.[42]

Despite contradicting interpretations and criticism, which gradually diminished, Zinedine Zidane's visit to Algeria was a real success: personal for Zidane; political for President Bouteflika, diplomatic and cultural for the Franco–Algerian foreign relations. After his return to France, the ex-captain of *les Bleus* issued a personal thanksgiving statement addressed to the Algerian head of state.[43] The visit also clearly showed the significant role of soccer and the part that this legendary athlete played in the improvement of foreign relations between France and Algeria. Finally, 'the return to the land of his ancestors', as leading publication *France Football* described the event, was perceived as a good thing on both sides of the Mediterranean.[44] It showed the complex identity of some immigrants and their French-born children and their relationships with the land of their ancestors. Zinedine Zidane, a legendary soccer player, a true Frenchman and a beloved son of Algeria, had the extraordinary and unique ability to gather enthusiastic cheering crowds off the pitch, without being too preoccupied by the political, diplomatic and media outcomes that such an 'official visit' could engender.

Acknowledgements

The authors would like to convey their special thanks to Dr. Lindsay Krasnoff for her invaluable suggestions.

Notes

1. *Le Monde*, March 4 and 5, 2003.
2. *L'Equipe,* December 12, 2006.
3. Fort, *Zidane, de Yazid à Zizou.*
4. *L'Equipe*, December 13, 2006.
5. See *L'Equipe Magazine*, April 2, 2005. The entire issue was dedicated to Zinedine Zidane.
6. Sayad, *L'immigration ou les paradoxes de l'altérité.*
7. cf. Simon, *L'immigration algérienne en France*; Stora, *Et ils venaient d'Algérie, histoire de l'immigration algérienne (1912–1962).*
8. Malika Zidane was born in 1947. She moved to Marseille at the age of five. Her father was originally from the same village as the Zidanes. Malika's father had moved to Marseille before WWII. After the war, he moved his entire family to Marseille.
9. *Le Nouvel Observateur*, December 24, 1998.
10. *Les Cahiers du football*, October 4, 2001, article by Djamel Attal in which the author portraits Zidane with sarcasm as a 'tongue-tied symbol'.
11. *Le Figaro*, October 5, 2001.
12. *Le Monde,* October 6, 2001.
13. *L'Equipe*, October 5, 2001.
14. *Le Nouvel Observateur*, October 11, 2001.
15. *Le Figaro*, October 13–14, 2001.
16. Gastaut, 'Le sport comme révélateur des ambiguïtés du processus d'intégration des populations immigrées, le cas du match de France-Algérie, octobre 2001'.
17. cf. *L'Equipe*, December 13, 2006. Interviewed again about that notorious match while on his official visit in Algeria, Zidane stated that the negative effect was not considerable. According to him, 'It was just a game'. He also admitted that it was his duty to score but if he had scored, he would have never celebrated.
18. *Heros d'Achile à Zidane*, Exposition organisée à la Bibliothèque Nationale, October 9, 2007–April 13, 2008.
19. After 1998, before each important match of the French national team and Zinedine Zidane, journalists usually interviewed people in the native village of his father – Aguemoune.
20. *Jeune Afrique*, June 18, 2006.
21. This mobile network operator started operating in Algeria in 2004.
22. *Le Point*, March 17, 2005.
23. According to some other sources, the cancellation could have happened as a result of President Bouteflika's commitment at the Arab Summit of Algiers, which was organized at the same time as Zidane's visit was scheduled to take place. Busy at the event, Bouteflika could not have provided 'the level attention and hospitality that Zidane deserved', cf. *La Croix*, April 27, 2006.
24. *Le Monde*, July 6, 2006.
25. *Reuters*, July 11, 2006.

26. *Le Monde*, December 13, 2006.
27. *Agence France Presse*, December 14, 2006.
28. During the press conference, a journalist addressed Zidane in Berber. The soccer player replied, 'Go ahead and ask, but I am not sure if I would be able to answer'. Nevertheless, the journalist repeated the question in Berber and Zidane replied: 'Did you not just ask me what made me come to Kabylie?' which resulted in a huge ovation throughout the entire conference room.
29. Invited at the meeting were also the minister of labour and solidarity, Djamel Ould Abbes, the minister of youth and sports, Yahia Guidoum, and the president of the Algerian football association (FAF), Hamid Haddadj.
30. *Reuters*, December 14, 2006.
31. *La Liberté*, December 14, 2006.
32. *El Watan*, December 14, 2006.
33. *Le Parisien*, December 14, 2006.
34. *Libération*, December 16, 2006.
35. *Le Figaro*, December 15, 2006.
36. *Libération*, December 7, 2006.
37. *Le Soir d'Algérie*, December 14, 2006.
38. *El Watan*, December 15, 2006.
39. Both Khaled and Faudel are famous Algerian singers who live in France and sing in Arabic and in French. Both singers are Arabophones; Idir, on the other hand, is a Berberophone and sings most of the time in Berber.
40. *La Dépêche de Kabylie*, December 16, 2006.
41. *L'Equipe*, December 16, 2006. Smail Zidane said that, 'My only wish before I die is to go back with Yazid [Zinedine Zidane] to visit my place of birth'.
42. *Le Figaro*, December 13, 2006.
43. *Agence France Presse*, January 6, 2007.
44. *France Football*, December 15, 2006.

References

Fort, Patrick et Jean Philippe. *Zidane, de Yazid à Zizou* [Zidane, from Yazid to Zizou]. Paris: Archipel, 2006.

Gastaut, Yvan. 'Le sport comme révélateur de ambigüités du processus d'intégration des populations immigrées, le cas du match de France-Algérie, octobre 2001 [Sport as the Revealing Factor of the Ambiguous Process of Integration of Immigrants: The Case of the Match France vs. Algeria, October 2001].' *Sociétés Contemporaines*, no. 69 (2008).

Sayad, Abdelmalek. *L'immigration ou les paradoxes de l'altérité* [Immigration or the Paradoxes of Otherness]. Bruxelles: De Boeck, 1992.

Simon, Jacques. *L'immigration algérienne en France* [Algerian Immigration in France]. Paris: L'Harmattan, 2002.

Stora, Benjamin. *Et ils venaient d'Algérie, histoire de l'immigration algérienne (1912–1962)* [They were Coming from Algeria: History of Algerian Immigration in France, 1912–1962]. Paris: Fayard, 1992.

A tale of two Kaisers: Ballack and Beckenbauer, and the battle for legacy

Rebecca Chabot

Iliff School of Theology, University of Denver, Denver, CO, USA

While there are a number of ways a player can be remembered after his career ends, much attention is paid to two different areas: the player's successes and failures and any scandals by which the player may have been tainted. Which of these ultimately matters more? Does scandal outweigh what happens on the pitch? Or does failure speak louder than scandal? When considering the legacy of Michael Ballack, we find ourselves asking: will he be remembered for never winning the biggest trophies or for the scandals that dogged his last few years as a player? By looking at the legacy of Franz Beckenbauer, another world-class German player and former captain of the (West) German National Team whose career was repeatedly touched by scandals but whose legacy is largely positive, due to the fact that he experienced tremendous success on the pitch, we will perhaps be able to imagine how Ballack will be remembered. After considering two major scandals, and a few minor ones, that came at the end of Ballack's career and looking towards the future of his legacy, the career and legacy of Franz Beckenbauer, the only player to have won four German Player of the Year awards, will be examined to see what clues it can offer us in regards to Ballack's legacy. Given that Ballack's nickname of 'der kleine Kaiser' links him directly to Beckenbauer, 'der Kaiser', there are many connections that enable us to ask questions about Ballack's legacy.

Introduction

On 2 October 2012, Michael Ballack officially retired from professional football.[1] And on Wednesday 5 June 2013, Ballack played his farewell match in Leipzig, alongside many of the game's brightest stars and biggest names, drawing praise and celebration from many corners. With 98 caps for Germany, Ballack leaves the game as one of the best German midfielders of all time and as a UNAIDS Ambassador.[2] His career included Bundesliga titles with Kaiserslautern and Bayern Munich, an English Premier League title with Chelsea, three cup wins in both the FA[3] Cup (with Chelsea) and the DFB Pokal[4] (with Bayern Munich), and 42 international goals for Germany. As a three-time German Player of the Year, Ballack's career certainly contained many highs, but for every high, there was always something just beyond his reach or something that stood in his way. 'In Germany, he has been described as a 'perennial nearly-man',[5] an unvollendeter, an unfulfilled person'.[6] Despite making the Champions League final with both Leverkusen and Chelsea, he never won one. He missed major games (the 2002 World Cup Final) and major international tournaments (the 2010 World Cup in South Africa) due to suspension or injury. And his departure from the German national team was clouded by a controversy about the captaincy.

While there are a number of ways a player can be remembered after his career ends, much attention is paid to two different areas: the player's successes and failures and any scandals by which the player may have been tainted. Which of these ultimately matters more? Does scandal outweigh what happens on the pitch? Or does failure speak louder than scandal? When considering the legacy of Michael Ballack, we find ourselves asking: will he be remembered for never winning the biggest trophies or for the scandals that dogged his last few years as a player? By looking at the legacy of Franz Beckenbauer, another world-class German player and former captain of the (West) German national team whose career was repeatedly touched by scandals but whose legacy is largely positive, due to the fact that he experienced tremendous success on the pitch, we will perhaps be able to imagine how Ballack will be remembered. After considering two major scandals, and a few minor ones, that came at the end of Ballack's career and looking towards the future of his legacy, the career and legacy of Franz Beckenbauer, the only player to have won four German Player of the Year awards, will be examined to see what clues it can offer us in regards to Ballack's legacy. Though both men captained their national side and both played for FC Bayern München, it is important to look at them in their own contexts. As Beckenbauer was child of the second World War and Ballack a child of the cold war, shifts in German culture and identity mean that some things that may have seemed scandalous while Beckenbauer was player are non-issues now and that shifts in how leadership is understood also play a role in the differences between these two men. However, given that Ballack's nickname of 'der kleine Kaiser' links him directly to Beckenbauer, 'der Kaiser', there are many connections that enable us to ask questions about Ballack's legacy.[7]

So how will Ballack be remembered? Will his legacy be a litany of accolades and praise for 'der kleine Kaiser'? Or will it be a study in what might have been, of missed opportunities? The essay tries to address these questions.

Der kleine Kaiser: Michael Ballack

Born in Görlitz in East Germany on 26 September 1976, Michael Ballack grew up in Chemnitz (formerly Karl-Marx-Stadt).[8] He started playing football at the age of six with a local club and, in 1992, came back from what should have been a career-ending knee surgery and made his professional debut for Chemnitz FC. After scoring his first professional goal on 1 October 1996, for Chemnitz FC, he went on to make his Bundesliga debut a few years later with the newly promoted side, FC Kaiserslautern.[9] Kaiserslautern won the league that year, giving the young Ballack a taste of success. He scored his first Bundesliga goal for Kaiserslautern on 30 October 1998 on a free kick to bring Kaiserslautern level with Hansa Rostock.[10] While playing with Kaiserslautern, he received his first call up for the German national team and making his international debut for Germany against Scotland on 28 April 1999, when he was brought on as a substitute in the 60th minute of the match.

He then signed with Bayer Leverkusen 04 because then-manager Rudi Voller was impressed with his performance. He netted his first international goal for Germany against Greece on 28 March 2001 on a penalty kick. After playing for three seasons with Bayer Leverkusen, a time period that saw the team end a single season as triple runners-up (Bundesliga, DFB Pokal, and Champions League) in

2002, Ballack moved to FC Bayern München, Germany's biggest team. In four years with FC Bayern München, Ballack again experienced great triumphs. Though he was not part of the FC Bayern München squad that won the Champions League in 2001, he did win several German cups and again experienced the thrill of wining the Bundesliga. His ability to control the ball well both offensively and defensively, coupled with his tenaciousness, led to Chelsea FC signing him in 2006.

In the four years Ballack spent with Chelsea FC, he came close to winning the Champions League, but lost twice in the Final, including to Manchester United on penalties. Under manager Jose Mourinho, Ballack had strong seasons while with Chelsea, helping them to both an FA Cup title and then the Premiere League title in 2010. Despite his happiness at Chelsea and the fact that he was playing well, an injury and his advancing age caused the hierarchy at the club to essentially push him out after the 2009–2010 season, offering him a one-year contract that they knew he would turn down, in order to sign younger players. Bayer Leverkusen 04, however, was happy to offer Ballack a two-year contract. However, his time there was plagued by injury and the realization that he was no longer the most important player on the team. 'In 2010, Ballack returned to Leverkusen but back at the club where he shot to fame, he struggled. "As you know I had worked with a lot of great managers and have got on really well with them," he told 11Freunde. "They gave me the feeling they were building a team around me. And that is why I was surprised this was no longer the case at Leverkusen"'.[11]

South Africa 2010

While playing in an FA Cup match against Portsmouth FC before the start of the 2010 World Cup in South Africa, Ballack was on the receiving end of a harsh challenge from Ghanaian midfielder Kevin-Prince Boateng. The resulting injury to his ankle ruled the German captain out for several months, which meant he would miss the World Cup. After missing the 2002 World Cup Final due to suspension, and the heartache of losing to Italy in the semi-finals at home in 2006, Ballack's streak of bad luck seemed destined, given that he was 33 in 2010, to prevent him from ever lifting the coveted trophy with his teammates. In addition to losing one of their key players, Germany's national team and its coach were now also missing their captain and leader. Coach Joachim Löwe took his time selecting a new captain; Ballack made it clear that he wanted Bayern Munich midfielder Bastian Schweinsteiger to wear the armband in his stead. When Löwe finally made his decision, it was not Schweinsteiger who was named captain but his Bayern Munich teammate, fullback Philipp Lahm. By the time the German team arrived in South Africa, Ballack had been reduced to mascot and spectator, much like David Beckham for the English side. Germany fielded one of their youngest teams ever and one of the youngest in the tournament; Ballack's replacement next to Schweinsteiger in midfield, Sami Khedira, was 23, a full decade younger than Ballack. Lahm was only 26 at the time when he took over as captain.

Lahm was a very different kind of captain. Ballack had been more of a leader from the front, a hard worker who pushed his teammates:

> He began acting out his leadership role. He shouted and threw fits on the field, and he argued with team manager Oliver Bierhoff and fellow player Lukas Podolski. He

continued to fight and score important goals, but at times he came across as an old bull reminding younger players that things weren't that bad in the old days.[12]

Some argue, however, that Ballack only became that type of leader because it was what he felt was expected of him. Germans were used to seeing a certain kind of leadership, one exemplified by former captains of the Nationalmannschaft like Oliver Kahn and Franz Beckenbauer. As one writer put it:

> Even as trophies eluded him, Ballack's fight for a functioning collective for Germany was met with scorn across numerous quarters. Everyone was obsessed with this leader of men, a player who would dominate dressing-rooms and call out orders to united a struggling Nationalmannschaft. For many Ballack was that man, for many others he wasn't. Ballack fought tooth and nail to establish his view, but in the end he gave up to the masses and gave the public what they really wanted: an arrogant alpha-male with a hierarchical view of his team. And the irony is that it was at that point the public decided that it was not really want they wanted at all.[13]

However, whether Ballack became that kind of leader or naturally was that kind of leader, there is no question that there were major issues towards the end of his tenure as captain of the national team. During a match against Wales in 2009, team-mate Lukas Podolski slapped Ballack, in the face. Podolski, largely viewed as one of the nicest and most easy-going players on the German national team, lost his temper with Ballack during the match. If Bild's account is to be believed, before Podolski slapped Ballack he told him to 'Shut your trap! Run, you arsehole'![14] While Podolski denied having used those words, the fact that a player had reacted in such a manner to his captain says much about the tension within the team at that time. Things were much different under their new captain.

When Lahm was selected as captain, he chose to create what is called the Mannschaftrat, a council of elders on the team (Miroslav Klose, Schweinsteiger, Arne Friedrich, and Per Mertesacker) that helped him lead the team of mostly younger players.[15] Under Lahm, vice captain Schweinsteiger, and the Mannschaftrat, the German team got off to a brilliant start in group play, beating Australia 4-0 in their opening match in Durban. Despite dropping their first group stage match in years, the German team topped their group and entered the knockout stages in excellent form. Victories over England and Argentina found the Germans facing Spain in one of the two semi-finals. During the match against Argentina,

> Ballack sat in the stands next to Bierhoff, like some VIP guest of the DFB top brass. He cheered whenever the German team scored a goal, but once, between Germany's third and fourth goal, a stadium camera zoomed in on his face, and he looked very serious.[16]

The German team's ease in that match led many to wonder if Ballack's time had passed.

> Fans got a sense of what was to come when they saw Thomas Müller in the thick of it, wearing Ballacks jersey number and scoring a goal. At a press conference after the match, someone asked him why he had picked the number 13, of all numbers.

> 'It happened to be available', Müller said, and laughed. Then he said that he was completely aware of the tradition he had become part of, and that it was naturally a great honor for him. But he was referring to Gerd Müller, the legendary striker of the 1960s and 1970s, not Michael Ballack. He had never seen Gerd Müller play live, he said, but he thought he was pretty good. Müller is 20. Only two weeks later, in the match

against England, the new number 13 scored twice and was voted player of the match. By that point, it seemed clear that the team was doing just fine without Ballack.[17]

When asked about the captaincy, Lahm made it clear that he was not planning on surrendering the armband or the captaincy to Ballack or anyone else:

> It is clear I would like to retain the captaincy. The job is a lot of fun for me. Why should I then voluntarily give up the role?! … If you do your job on the pitch and have it under control, as I do in my position, then you want more. And you want more responsibility. Then you want to take care of it all. And this is now the case with me.[18]

Lahm's statement did not sit well with Ballack. In a sense, Lahm's comments had added insult to injury. Though Lahm had never been afraid to be outspoken, his comments about the captaincy came at a time when Ballack had to be feeling particularly frustrated and vulnerable: his team was playing in the biggest tournament in the world, about to play for a spot in the finals, and he was forced to sit on the sidelines and watch helplessly as events unfolded around and before him. Germany lost the match to Spain 1-0 and went on to win the third place match against Uruguay 3-2. Ballack actually left South Africa two days before the match, returning to Germany in order to continue his rehabilitation.

Der Kaiser weighed in on the controversy in an editorial he penned for Bild. In it, the former West German captain said:

> Regarding Ballack's future in the national team, there can be no final decision for a long time. The changing of the guard is of course a lucky break, and Ballack is not getting any younger … The question will be asked: Don't we need Michael Ballack after all? Yes, we need him. Assuming he is 100 per cent fit and in top form. Whether he is captain or not is unimportant. Great players also show their personality when they do not wear a piece of cloth on their arm. Great players do not need armbands.[19]

And Schweinsteiger acknowledged that Ballack's presence with the team was important, 'but they just did not have much time for him, he added, given that they were in the middle of a tournament'.[20]

At his first press conference after joining Bayer Leverkusen during the summer of 2010, Ballack said:

> I am still the captain of the national team. Philipp Lahm made a claim at a time I thought was inappropriate … It is not a Wünschkonzert [literally 'wish concert', by which he means you can't always get what you want], where every player can choose where he plays – and so it is with the question of the captaincy … I will be having a word or more with Philipp.[21]

For months after the World Cup, speculation as to what, if any, role Ballack would play in the German squad ran rampant. Coach Jogi Löwe was largely silent on the matter, saying, 'I heard the wish of Philipp Lahm. I also heard and read what Michael Ballack said. Ultimately it is a decision for the coach. It's up to me. I haven't given it any final thought yet. I will also only give my decision personally first'.[22] Eventually, it became clear that Lahm was going to remain captain: throughout the friendlies and European Championship qualifiers that followed on the heels of the World Cup, Ballack's name was repeatedly omitted from the German squad. It was only after Germany had qualified for the 2012 European Championships in Poland and the Ukraine that Löwe offered Ballack a chance to rejoin the team for a farewell match in a friendly against Azerbaijan, which Ballack declined. After his injury at the legs of Kevin-Prince Boateng, Ballack never again captained the team or wore a German kit on the pitch.

Manager controversy

As if the pain of losing the captaincy and his spot on the team were not painful enough, Ballack also found himself embroiled in a controversy over his manager in the immediate aftermath of the World Cup. His manager, Michael Becker, said the following about Germany's defeat in the World Cup in an interview with journalist Alexander Osang:

> He talked a lot about people who were envious of his client, because they were supposedly mediocre, ugly, untalented, bureaucratic, provincial, unmanly or gay. He told me some unbelievable stories, which I wrote down on my pad of paper. A few days later, on the sidelines of a farewell match for footballer Bernd Schneider at Bayer Leverkusen, Becker told a group of agents and journalists in the Bayer clubhouse that there was a former player on the national team who was about to go public with the names of 'the gay combo.' I expected my fellow journalists to be all ears, but they seemed relatively blasé about Becker's remark.[23]

Becker's comments demonstrate both crassness in their attempted defense of Ballack and exemplify the worst of what people assume about football. While strides have been made in recent years to combat the racism inherent in the game, FIFA as a whole has been reticent to address homophobia in soccer. In a game where players are routinely subjected to homophobic and sexist slurs from fans regularly, Becker's comments were especially poorly conceived and spoken.

When asked if his manager's comments had changed their opinion of Ballack, many fans seemed willing to forgive and forget, excusing the incident because 'it was not him, it was his agent, and he should be free from responsibility'. But those who find it easy to say that are those who have the luxury of being someone for whom those types of insults are not something personal and harmful. If it does not really impact your life, it is far easier to excuse this kind of behaviour. For others, especially members of the LGBT community, Ballack's failure to distance himself from Becker, his failure to fire Becker, and his failure to publicly denounce Becker's comments caused many to change their opinion of Ballack.

Minor scandals

In his last two seasons as a professional player with Bayer Leverkusen, Ballack was again plagued by injuries and issues off the pitch. Once again, he failed to win any hardware. In fact, one of Bayer Leverkusen's nicknames is 'Neverkusen' given their failure to ever win the league. In September of 2011, Ballack missed a mandatory drug test due to illness. 'He initially agreed to appear before the National Anti-Doping Agency but then decided against doing so'.[24] As a result of the missed drug test, Leverkusen was forced to pay a £20,000 fine.[25] The club is currently contesting the fine, arguing that they followed the proper procedures, but it added another level of scandal to Ballack's career. Though he has not been accused of using performance-enhancing drugs, a missed drug test does not help Ballack's standing in the eyes of his countrymen and women.

In March of 2012, after Bayer Leverkusen's 2-0 win over Schalke, Ballack approached the fans with a megaphone and led the crowd in several cheers. One of those cheers used expletives to poke at Cologne, one of Leverkusen's rivals (despite the fact that the match had nothing to do with Cologne). Reaction was such that Ballack was forced to publicly apologize on the Bayer Leverkusen website: 'It was certainly not clever of me to shout the comments about Cologne. This can happen in the euphoria of victory, but it should not. Therefore I have no problem apologising to the fans of Cologne and to the club'.[26] It should be noted that, in his apology, he never actually apologizes. And in October of 2012, Ballack was pulled over for severely exceeding the speed limit while on vacation in Spain.[27] Spanish police pulled him over after he was caught driving 131 mph was fined £5400. He was also banned from driving for 18 months, as the posted speed limit was 75 mph. Ballack chose to take the case to trial rather than simply paying the fine by 'saying he is "out of work" and "doesn't have any money coming in"'.[28] His lawyer, Jesús Gallego Rol, argued that the fee should be dropped to £8000 because 'to drive at such speed in Germany' is 'not a crime'.[29]

Ballack's legacy

Though it is still far too soon to declare definitively what Michael Ballack's legacy will be, it is interesting to note that it has already shifted a bit since 2010. Even though Ballack played for another two years, his international career ended in 2010 and, for many fans, that was when his career ended. Much of the bad blood surrounding how his captaincy of the German national team seems to have dissipated. At his farewell match in June of 2013, he was joined by several current and former internationals: Jens Lehmann, Rene Adler, Oliver Neuville, Per Mertesacker, Torsten Frings, Miroslav Klose, and, perhaps most notably, German national team captain Philipp Lahm. Vice captain of the German national team, FC Bayern München's Bastian Schweinsteiger, who missed the game due to surgery to remove bone fragments from his heel, said of Ballack to Kicker,

> He doesn't get the credit he deserves, unfortunately. He did a great deal for German football. I saw him recently in Munich and he asked me if I would be keen on playing in a benefit match. If he invited me, and my club allowed me to, then I would love to.[30]

Ballack also has found a place in television commentary for both German and English-speaking audiences. During the summer of 2012, he served as one of ESPN's analysts during the European Championships in Poland and Ukraine. His banter with former American international Alexi Lalas had fans on Twitter craving a sitcom starring the two, as their football opinions and spirited discussion were one of the highlights of the entire event.

Der Kaiser: Franz Beckenbauer

A Munich native, Franz Beckenbauer was born on 11 September 1945 and started playing football at school as a child.[31] When he was eight, he signed with SC Munich 1906, his love of the game largely inspired by West Germany's victory in the 1954 World Cup.[32] His father was a postal worker and felt that football was a waste of time and energy on the part of his son.[33] Despite his father's disapproval, the young Beckenbauer pursued his passion.

The club of his youth, SC Munich 1906, was facing serious financial problems, but despite having grown up as a rabid fan of 1860 Munich, then the bigger club in Munich, Beckenbauer chose to play for FC Bayern München after having experienced first-hand the chippiness of the 1860 defense, as 'the 1860 centre-half hit Beckenbauer in the face'.[34] After joining FC Bayern München and beginning to find fame, Beckenbauer soon found himself facing his first major scandal: 'He got his girlfriend pregnant when he was barely 18 – and then shockingly refused to marry her. This was 1963, and the DFB immediately banned Beckenbauer from the national youth team'.[35] It was only after the direct intervention of then-coach Dettmar Cramer that Beckenbauer was allowed back on the team, but he was forced to room with Cramer during all trips.[36]

The whole of Germany was somewhat suspicious of cults of personality and this carried over to sports stars, too. Despite the fact that he was incredibly talented and a natural leader of his team, 'Beckenbauer was not exactly loved. (When he returned to Germany after three years at New York Cosmos, he said: "As soon as I heard the catcalls, I knew I was home.")'.[37] Beckenbauer was at once demonized and idolized.

As his career carried on, Beckenbauer was no stranger to controversy. '"Beckenbauer was encumbered with the attribute of being vain and arrogant" … It goes without saying that Beckenbauer's nickname didn't help. "The Kaiser" suggested aloofness and conservatism'.[38] And, as Hesse-Lichtenberger points out, his nickname 'had nothing to do with football. The name was first attached to him by a magazine that said he looked like the eccentric Bavarian sovereign Ludwig II … and he did indeed have that rapt, altar-boy look'.[39] The two-time Ballon D'or winner earned 103 caps for West Germany, scoring 14 goals, an impressive amount for a defender.[40] In fact, Beckenbauer was so central to German football in the late 1960s and 1970s that he was the sole soccer player to be included in Germany's starting 11 in Monty Python's 'Philosopher's World Cup', much to the surprise of Beckenbauer in the sketch.

Leadership and controversy

As Simon Kuper says in Soccer Men, 'It is hard for non-Germans to fathom the extent to which Beckenbauer towers over German soccer'.[41] Beckenbauer came of age in a world recovering from war. While others of his generation were taking to the streets, Beckenbauer and others, like Johan Cruijff, chose a different venue:

> On the soccer field, too, they made a power grab. Cruijff and Beckenbauer did not only take responsibility for their own performances, but did so for everybody else's as well. They were coaches on the pitch, forever pointing and telling teammates where to move. They helped the nominal coaches make the lineups. They did not do deference. They demanded a greater share of the game's profits.[42]

One of the major controversies of Beckenbauer's career came during the run up to the 1974 World Cup. In the wake of the devastation to the game caused by the war, soccer had to rebuild at both the club and international levels. This meant a new level of professionalism in the game and it meant that players like Beckenbauer viewed themselves as players who deserved to be compensated appropriately for their service not only to club, but also to country.

Beckenbauer was named captain of the West German squad in 1971, prior to the European Championships in 1972, which West Germany won. At this time, the pre-vailing sentiment was that 'footballers were not supposed to represent their country for money'.[43] In 1974, the German team learned that several other countries were paying their teams a set bonus amount, should the team win the World Cup. While most countries had a bonus system in place for their teams, this was the first that numbers had been made public before a tournament. 'However, the squad had learned that the Italians had been promised DM 120,000 per head for winning the World Cup. The Dutch would be paid DM 100,000'.[44] This led the German squad to demand equal treatment and compensation from the German football association.

The mood in the German training camp was already pretty grim. 'The West Germans, peeved at having been locked away in this gulag in Malente, started talk-ing money to while the time away'.[45] The conditions in which the Germans found themselves while training for the World Cup were harsh and thus, a few nights before the first match, Beckenbauer found himself on the phone with Hermann Neuberger, who was, at the time, the Vice President of both the DFB and FIFA, and the person responsible for the 1974 World Cup.[46] After haggling, the DFB agreed to a sum of DM 70,000 per player. After it was presented to the players for a vote, a vote which deadlocked 11-11, 'Beckenbauer decided the course of the 1974 World Cup for the first but not the last time'.[47] The players accepted the deal and began group play five days later with a 1–0 win over Chile but 'with a performance which drew catcalls from the Berlin crowd'.[48]

Beckenbauer was the unquestioned leader of the team, which was evident in his behaviour when the West German squad faced the East German squad in the third match of the group stage. 'Slowly and irreversibly, the West German game came apart. Beckenbauer cursed his teammates, yelled at them, began to call for every ball … everybody was playing for and by himself'.[49] East Germany went on to win the match 1-0 and a defeated West German side had to do some serious re-grouping. In light of the defeat at the hands of the East Germans, West German coach Schön had a near-breakdown and Beckenbauer was called upon to assist the coach at a press conference. Beckenbauer was not just the team captain, but also a coach who hap-pened to still be playing on, with, and for the team he was coaching.

Though West Germany would go on to win the World Cup, a cloud hung over the entire experience for many of those involved. One can only imagine that had social media existed then, as it does now, that popular opinion about many of the players, Beckenbauer especially, would have been severely impacted by the details of the negotiations becoming public, as he was charged with helping to negotiate on the part of the team. Even his staunchest critics and his biggest detractors were swept up in the celebrations; der Kaiser was a national hero just as surely as he was the target of people's frustrations with the increasing professionalism of the game.

From FC Hollywood to the Cosmos

Beckenbauer was a member of the most successful squads in the history of FC Bayern München prior to the record-shattering 2012–2013 season, wherein FC Bayern München became the first German team to achieve the coveted 'treble' and win the Bundesliga, the DFB Pokal, and the UEFA Champions League all in the same season. Along with players like Gerd Müller and Sepp Maier, FC Bayern München won the European Cup final three consecutive years (1974, 1975 and

1976). The club's star shone brightly and Beckenbauer, already captain of the West German side, was its brightest star. In 1977, Beckenbauer left FC Bayern München for the bright lights of New York City as a member of the New York Cosmos. Playing alongside players like Pele, he spent a total of five season with the US side (1977–1980, 1983), winning three Soccer Bowls in the process. He retired from club football in 1983, but he was unable to step away from the game entirely.

Der Kaiser as Teamchef

After retiring as a player, Beckenbauer continued to make a name for himself as a coach, manager, commentator and executive. The game that he had fallen in love with as a youth continued to be the most important part of his life. After several failed marriages, it was clear that Beckenbauer's longest relationship was, and would always be, with football. When German national team was facing uncertainty and needing new leadership, Beckenbauer made it clear that he was not going to be convinced to take the reigns of the team.

> Alas the Kaiser had left everyone in no doubt he was not interested in coaching. In fact, after following the 1982 World Cup with the media, Beckenbauer had told everybody willing to listen: 'One of the things I realised was that I would never make a good coach'.[50]

However, despite his protestations, Beckenbauer would eventually take the reins of the West German national team, taking over as manager in time to guide the West Germans to another World Cup final; this time in 1986, the team went on to lose the final to the Argentinians. In 1990, he led the team to victory in Rome and West Germany's third World Cup, this team beating the Argentinians 1-0 in the final. His club managerial career was not as successful as his tenure with the national team, as all of his positions were short-lived, but he did earn additional hardware, most notably during his two stints with FC Bayern München (28 December 1993–30 June 1994 and 29 April–30 June 1996). During these short periods, he added another Bundesliga title and a UEFA Cup to his already impressive collection as player and manager.

Beckenbauer's legacy

Since ending his managerial career, Beckenbauer has continued to be heavily involved in soccer in his native Germany. He spent nearly 15 years serving as the president of FC Bayern München and since 2009 has served in an honourary capacity as X. He helped to secure the 2006 World Cup for Germany and his visibility because of that landed him on TIME Magazine's list of the 100 most influential people of 1996. Former US Secretary of State Henry Kissinger said of him:

> During the month of June, no sportsman will be able to rival the attention focused on Franz Beckenbauer. Widely considered the best soccer player ever produced by Germany, he will preside over a tournament of 32 teams, including one from the US, the survivors of an elimination process involving 194 teams, that has gone on for more than two years. Being president of the organizing committee of the World Cup is a particularly delicate and complicated job. He must satisfy 32 national passions, all but one of which will be disappointed. Fortunately for Germany, Beckenbauer, 60, is of a stature beyond the reach of those passions. No other soccer figure, except possibly

Pele, has ever reached the mythic status of Beckenbauer ... Not for nothing is Beckenbauer's nickname in Germany 'der Kaiser' –the Emperor.[51]

Whether because of his success on the pitch or merely the stature of his name, Beckenbauer's legacy is one of huge triumphs, unprecedented name recognition (he currently serves as a commentator for Bild, a German newspaper) and international acclaim. His name is consistently mentioned amongst the greats of the sport and he has developed a bit of a reputation as one of Germany's elder statesmen, despite never having held elected office. His leadership style is still widely regarded as effective and the scandals that touched his career (including a child out of wedlock) would hardly qualify as scandals today.

Conclusion

As Ballack himself says, 'Many footballers are being admired, especially by young people. That's why they have the position of a role model'.[52] Whether a player wants to simply play the game he or she loves or actively courts fame, when one captains the national team in a country as soccer-obsessed as Germany, one is in the public eye. This means that actions are scrutinized, comments are overanalysed, and in the world of social media and a 24-h news cycle, a player's behaviour, on or off the pitch, can travel the world in an instant. Perhaps Ballack will be remembered as tenacious and dedicated, a player who made things happen. Perhaps he will be remembered as someone who never quite managed to see his full dreams come true. And perhaps Ballack will be largely remembered as a footnote in history, as some-one who came and played and left, like many of the other German captains before him.

Regardless of what his legacy is five years from now (or 20 years from now or even 50 years from now), it will help observers of the game to examine the role that failing to win the biggest trophies on the pitch coupled with scandal plays in a player's place in history. Beckenbauer has proved that scandals can be overcome, both through performance on the pitch and continued involvement with the game at its highest levels. Given the success of the Ballack/Lalas pairing during the 2012 Euros and the fact that Ballack is still sought out to provide commentary on the game for television, it may be fair to say that he has a chance to erase some of the sting of the scandals and his near misses on the pitch. Judging by the reception of his farewell match, his continued presence in the public eye has already helped to heal some of those wounds.

Acknowledgements

Special thanks to Samantha Villella, Jeff Culver, Charyse Diaz, and Matthew Spotts, SJ, for their assistance with this article.

Notes

1. 'Ballack Announces Retirement', *ESPN Staff*, http://soccernet.espn.go.com/news/story/_/id/1178004/michael-ballack-announces-retirement?cc=5901 (accessed June 13, 2013).
2. All statistics in this paragraph are from Ballack's ESPN profile (http://soccernet.espn.go.com/player/_/id/12641/michael-ballack?cc=5901) and from Ballack's Kicker profile (http://www.kicker.de/fussball/bundesliga/vereine/1666/vereinsspieler_michael-ballack.html).

3. The FA here is the English Football Association.
4. The DFB stands for Deutscher Fußballbund, the German Football Association. Pokal is the German word used for the Cup competition.
5. Tom Gatehouse, 'Michael Ballack: 90 min of Long-awaited, Unthreatened Triumph for German Legend-"Ciao Capitano"', *Soccerlens*, http://soccerlens.com/michael-ballack-german-legend-ciao-capitano/109009/ (accessed June 13, 2013).
6. Marcus Christenson, 'Michael Ballack: A Nearly Man or an Undisputed Midfield Genius?' in Talking Sport on *The Guardian*, http://www.guardian.co.uk/football/blog/2013/jun/05/michael-ballack-nearly-man-genius (accessed June 10, 2013).
7. Schulze-Marmeling, *Die Bayern*, 519.
8. Michael Ballack, 'Looking Back on Michael Ballack's Career- Part 1: The Dream', http://www.michael-ballack.com/?103A0A2A100A0A13325 (accessed June 13, 2013).
9. Ibid.
10. Michael Ballack, 'Personal Data', http://www.michael-ballack.com/?201A1A2.
11. Marcus Christenson, 'Michael Ballack: A Nearly Man or An Undisputed Midfield Genius?' *The Guardian*, June 5, 2013, http://www.guardian.co.uk/football/blog/2013/jun/05/michael-ballack-nearly-man-genius (accessed June 10, 2013).
12. Alexander Osang, 'The "Mannschaft" at The World Cup: Ambassadors of a New Germany', *Spiegel Online International*, http://www.spiegel.de/international/zeitgeist/the-mannschaft-at-the-world-cup-ambassadors-of-a-new-germany-a-706012.html (accessed June 13, 2013).
13. Quazi Zulquarnain, 'A Tribute to Michael Ballack', *Bundesliga Fanatic*, http://bundesligafanatic.com/a-tribute-to-michael-ballack/ (accessed June 13, 2013).
14. 'Scandal Erupts in Germany after Lukas Podolski Slaps Michael Ballack in the Face', *The Spoiler*, March 3, 2009, http://www.thespoiler.co.uk/2009/04/03/scandal-erupts-in-germany-after-lukas-podolski-slaps-michael-ballack-in-the-face/ (accessed June 13, 2013).
15. The German press has continually asserted that neither Philipp Lahm nor Bastian Schweinsteiger are true leaders, given that their leadership style differs from that of previous German captains and vice captains like Ballack and Oliver Kahn. 'For many of the country's football traditionalists, the two of them were not big and brash enough, and the lack of international trophies – with Bayern and Germany – was blamed on their perceived lack of leadership quality'. Neither Lahm nor Schweinsteiger are the kind of leaders who berate their teammates or believe that they should be front and center in all situations. Because of the tradition of strong, hierarchical leadership exhibited by players like Ballack, Kahn and even Beckenbauer, it will perhaps take time for Germans to come to appreciate new styles of leadership. After FC Bayern München won their historic treble in 2013, German international and offensive midfielder for FC Bayern München, Thomas Müller said to the press, '"Here are your Führungsspieler [leading players] who [you said] aren't Führungsspieler", Müller shouted defiantly at reporters in the mixed zone, when the two captains were passing through'. Raphael Honigstein, 'Bayern Munich's Five-star London Bash Dominated by Feelings of Relief', *The Guardian*, May 26, 2013, http://www.guardian.co.uk/football/blog/2013/may/26/bayern-munich-champions-league-party (accessed June 13, 2013).
16. Osang, 'The "Mannschaft" at The World Cup'.
17. Ibid.
18. 'Power Struggle: Lahm vs. Ballack – I Wont't Give the Captains Armband Band Voluntarily', *Bild*, http://www.bild.de/news/bild-english/news/i-wont-give-captains-armband-back-voluntarily-13201070.bild.html (accessed June 13, 2013).
19. Franz Beckenbauer, 'Der Kaiser: Great Players do not Need Armbands', *Bild*, http://www.bild.de/news/bild-english/news/great-players-donot-need-armbands13215494.bild.html (accessed June 13, 2013).
20. Osang, 'The "Mannschaft" at The World Cup'.
21. 'At Bayer Leverkusen Unveiling Ballack Attacks Lahm: "I'm Still the captain"'! *Bild*, http://www.bild.de/news/bild-english/news/bayer-leverkusen-unveiling-im-still-captain-13306792.bild.html (accessed June 13, 2013).
22. 'Germany Coach: '"It's My Decision" Will Jogi Löwe Now Dump Michael Ballack?' *Bild*, http://www.bild.de/news/bild-english/news/will-germany-coach-now-dump-michael-ballack-13374446.bild.html (accessed June 13, 2013).

23. Osang, 'The "Mannschaft" at The World Cup'.
24. Mohammed Ali, 'Leverkusen Face £20,000 Fine Over Ballack Missed Doping Test', *Goal.com*, http://www.goal.com/en-gb/news/3275/bundesliga/2012/11/04/3501165/leverkusen-face-25000-fine-after-ballack-misses-doping-test?source=breakingnews (accessed June 13, 2013).
25. Ibid.
26. 'Bundesliga-Ballack Sorry for Cologne Insults', http://uk.eurosport.yahoo.com/22032011/58/bundesliga-ballack-sorry-cologne-insults.html (accessed June 13, 2013).
27. David Kent, 'Ballack Banned From Driving after Former Chelsea Midfielder is Caught Speeding at 131 mph', *The Daily Mail*, http://www.dailymail.co.uk/sport/football/article-2229868/Michael-Ballack-banned-driving-caught-speeding.html (accessed June 13, 2013).
28. Lee Moran, 'I Can't Pay Speeding Fine as I'm Out of Work and Have No Money Coming in, Insists Former £120 k-a-week Chelsea star Michael Ballack', *The Daily Mail*, http://www.dailymail.co.uk/sport/football/article-2225767/Ex-Chelsea-star-Michael-Ballack-I-pay-speeding-fine-Im-work-money-coming-in.html (accessed June 13, 2013).
29. Ibid.
30. Amerta, 'One Final Fling with Michael Ballack – It's Time to Say Goodbye!' *Sportskeeda*, http://www.sportskeeda.com/2013/06/05/one-final-fling-with-michael-ballack-its-time-to-say-goodbye/ (accessed June 13, 2013).
31. Schulze-Marmeling, *Die Bayern*, 523.
32. Hesse-Lichtenberger, *Tor!*, 163.
33. Ibid., 162.
34. Ibid., 163.
35. Ibid., 171.
36. Ibid.
37. Ibid., 119.
38. Ibid., 171.
39. Ibid., 173.
40. All statistics concerning Beckenbauer's career are from his Fussballdaten profile (http://www.fussballdaten.de/spieler/beckenbauerfranz/1996/) and from his official FIFA profile (http://www.fifa.com/classicfootball/players/player=25113/bio.html).
41. Kuper, *Soccer Men*, 28.
42. Ibid., xvii–xviii.
43. Hesse-Lichtenberger, *Tor!*, 190.
44. Ibid., 90.
45. Ibid.
46. Ibid.
47. Ibid., 191.
48. Ibid., 91.
49. Ibid., 92–3.
50. Ibid., 254.
51. Henry Kissinger, 'Franz Beckenbauer', *TIME*, http://www.time.com/time/specials/packages/article/0,28804,1975813_1976769_1976779,00.html (accessed June 13, 2013).
52. Michael Ballack, 'Personal Data'.

References

Hesse-Lichtenberger, Ulriche. *Tor! The Story of German Football*. London: WSC Books, 2003.
Kuper, Simon. *Soccer Men: Profiles of the Rogues, Geniuses, and Neurotics Who Dominate the World's Most Popular Sport*. New York: Nation Books, 2011.
Schulze-Marmeling, Dietrich. *Die Bayern: Die Geschichte des Rekordmeisters* [Bayern: The History of the Record Champions]. Göttingen: Verlag Die Werkstatt, 2007.

Spanish football: from underachievers to world beaters

Shakya Mitra

MSc. Sports Management, Stirling University, Stirling, UK

Spain, for long considered the glorious underachievers of world football, have in the last five years made a spectacular transition. From having a solitary European Championship win in 1964, they have won the last three major international tournaments they have appeared in. This achievement has evoked comparisons with some of the world's greatest teams. Yet, it was not always so good for Spain; ravaged by the civil war and with infighting amongst different regions, Spain struggled on the international arena despite two immense clubs in Barcelona and Real Madrid. In recent years, the football team has risen above these divisions and ironically, given the long-standing tensions between Catalonia and Spain, the core of their success has been through players from FC Barcelona, the Catalan-based powerhouse. A major catalyst in Spain's stunning rejuvenation as an international football powerhouse has been midfielder Xavi Hernandez. The interesting fact about Xavi is that not only is he a fabulous player who would have surely won more accolades if he were not in the shadow of Lionel Messi, but also that he is a born and bred Catalan. It is of great interest that the region, with which Spain has had its most bitter relationship, has provided Spain the core of players that has driven them to glory for the last five years.

Introduction

Four minutes short of the 2010 World Cup Final in Johannesburg going to penalties, Andres Iniesta's goal gave Spain what was certainly a decisively one goal lead. The players were in a joyous celebration for it put the country on the verge of winning, the holy grail of football for the first time in their history. It was to become the country's second major success in the space of two years following their win at Euro 2008.[1] The claim of Spain as one of the greatest teams of all time was made following their World Cup victory, which was reinforced following their victory in the 2012 European Championships.[2] Home to two of the greatest football club sides of all time in Real Madrid and Barcelona, it is puzzling why it took Spain such a long time to find the success at international level, having only had the 1964 Euro Cup win to show in the past?

Throughout their history, Spain has produced some outstanding footballers like 1960 Ballon D'Or Winner Luis Suarez, Emilio Butragueno, Michel, Raul and Fernando Hierro; although this has never translated into team success. Jimmy Burns in his book *La Roja* says as much when he argues that 'Spain's soccer had for much of its history also mirrored its politics, touched as it was with its tales of individual brilliance, occasional collective effort, but ultimate underachievement of the national squad in contrast to the international success of rival clubs'.[3] Spain, though a nation state in its own right, has often come across as a divided house. The centre is at the capital Madrid, but there are diverse identities in the country like Catalans, Basques, Galicians, Asturians and Andaulsians. Though there is no concrete evidence to suggest this, a reason often proffered to explain Spain's continued underachievement at the international level has been the lack of team cohesion resulting from the coming together of players of different regions from across the country at the time of international tournaments.

The Euro 2008 triumph might have ended the country's long wait for a trophy (it wasn't their first Euro victory as mentioned in the first paragraph), however it was the World Cup with all its history, hallowed status and the participation of teams from all continents, which has come to symbolize the more special victory. Burns wrote that World Cup 2010 had a special unifying force on the country, where even the most nationalistic anti-Spanish neighbourhoods such as those in the Basque region as well as in Catalonia celebrated the victory. All political, cultural and social prejudices that had separated Spaniards from different regions were set aside for this special moment in their history.[4]

The Real Madrid-Barcelona rivalry has not only been the most celebrated club rivalries in Spain but perhaps across the world. These two teams have provided the majority of players for the Spanish national team in major tournaments like the European Championships and the World Cup. They are also amongst the two most successful teams in European club history with 13 European Cups/Champions League titles between them. However, this rivalry, though tinged with great footballing history and some of the most memorable encounters in club football, has strong political and regional undertones which have been a part of Spain and their football ever since the game started there. While Real Madrid is the club from the Capital, Barcelona is the most prominent club from the region of Catalonia which has had tense relations with the centre for years. Thus, FC Barcelona has in some ways become more than a football club, because for a lot of their supporters, particularly the local ones, the club stands as a symbol of Catalan nationalism.

Spain, often considered to be one of the most talented but divided football teams to have played, have ironically had a golden phase in their football history which coincides with the success of FC Barcelona as a club football powerhouse. It is remarkable given the past political and regional differences between Catalonia and the Centre, that the core of the Spain team that won the 2010 World Cup as well as the European Championships in 2008 and 2012 are players who are either playing for FC Barcelona or who are born in Catalonia. At the same time, FC Barcelona have gone on to establish themselves as one of the finest football clubs to have ever played the game, having won the league title three years in a row between 2009 and 2011, as well as winning the Champions League in 2009 and 2011.

While most of this essay will discuss Spanish football, the period under General Franco, the Catalonia–Spain divide and the El Classico rivalry, the opportunity will also be used to discuss an individual player as well. A lot of names could have been chosen, like Andres Iniesta, David Villa or Iker Casillas who have all contributed to Spain's success as a national team. However, it is midfielder Xavi Hernandez whom I wish to write about as a pivot, not just for his abilities as one of the finest midfielders to have played the game, but also because he is a Catalan. Xavi is a proud Catalan who has achieved enormous success with his hometown club Barcelona. Despite the differences between Catalonia and Spain, on the football ground Xavi's performance as a member of the Spanish football team has been exemplary.

The impact of General Franco on Spanish football

Between 1939 and 1975, Spain was famously under the dictatorship of General Francisco Franco. The impact of the dictatorship was clearly discernible from the state of Spanish football. Football in Spain under Franco has been compared to football in Adolf Hitler's Germany and Benito Mussolini's Italy – how it was used to shape public opinion, inculcate mythical nationalist values and develop the country's standing in the international arena. At the height of Franco's regime, Spain was seen as a country politically divided; but football presented the dictatorship an opportunity to cover this up. It was a difficult phase for Spain with the United Nations having imposed sanctions on the country in 1946, and with the United States and the United Kingdom having withdrawn their ambassadors.

Spain's performance in the 1950 World Cup, where they reached the second group stage, began to act as bridge to the outside world. Their performance was judged to have enough significance to transform them from a diplomatic outcast into a full member of the international soccer community. With General Franco concentrating most of his energies on the Centre located in Madrid, there was a growing perception of Real Madrid being associated with him. It was described by certain sections as 'Franco's team'. On top of this, his attitudes towards the other prominent regions of Spain, the Basque region as well as Catalonia, were considered discriminatory. At the height of the civil war, General Franco went on to strip both the regions of their rights and freedoms. Catalonia's FC Barcelona is believed to have stood for everything that was opposed to Franco's regime and principles.

An example of this tension came about in 1943, in the midst of two volatile games that were played between Real Madrid and Barcelona in the semi-finals of the La Copa Del Generalissmo. The first leg of the clash which was played in Barcelona was won 3–0 by the home team. Following the game, a major national newspaper accused the Catalans of a deliberate conspiracy against the state. A few minutes prior to the start of the second leg to be played at Real Madrid's home, General Franco's director of state security entered the locker room to tell the Barcelona team 'Do not forget that some of you are playing only because of the generosity of the regime in forgiving you your lack of patriotism'. This was believed to be a threat to at least three members of the Barcelona team who fled Spain during the civil war, and though they returned to the country they were believed to be secretly opposed to General Franco's regime. The Barcelona players were at the receiving end of much verbal abuse from the crowd and eventually went on to suffer a massive 11–1 defeat.

Following General Franco's death, the Catalan and Basque community who had their rights and freedoms suppressed under his rule, started expressing themselves. During a match between FC Barcelona (Catalonia) and Athletic Bilbao (Basque) in 1977, the stadium was bathed in the colours of the Catalan and Basque nationalist flags, as the stadium united in giving the players a standing ovation. In 1975, less than a month after the death of Franco, the captains of the two prominent Basque sides Athletic Bilbao and Real Sociedad walked into the stadium holding the banned Basque flag. Iribar, the captain of Athletic Bilbao in the match against Barcelona, said when they were welcomed to a sea of Basque and Catalan flags: 'The dictatorship had ended, and we were in a transition towards democracy and there was a general expression of joy in the stadium that day, a hunger for liberty on both sides so that the game became a mirror of what a reflection of all that was happening'.

Even after Franco's death, the relative lack of popular support for Spain's national team reflected in the absence of an agreed national identity. Given the continuing and unresolved political tensions between Madrid and the regions, there were inevitable consequences on the national squad leading to its poor performance. The footballing aspect of this divide was manifest in certain teams' complaints about favourable decisions going Real Madrid's way helping them win matches and subsequently league titles. Most of these claims tended to be unfounded because Real Madrid had very good teams most of the time. However, the anger against referees within the stadium seemed an escape from the political suppression outside it.[5]

Relationship between Catalonia and the Centre

Jimmy Burns in his book *Barca: A People's Passion* says 'much of Catalonia's history is a story of humiliation and frustration, its aspirations as a regional power curbed and stamped upon by the centralizing tendencies of Madrid'. The formation of FC Barcelona was the perfect vehicle for galvanizing local Catalan pride. Barcelona's identity was forged by persecution, its competitive edge by the obsession of proving itself better than Madrid on the playing fields, whether by winning or simply by stopping them from winning. Since the restoration of democracy after Franco's rule, Catalonia has achieved a greater degree of autonomy than Northern Ireland, Scotland, Corsica and the South of Italy. The reason why FC Barcelona means so much to Catalans is as much for footballing reasons as it is for the persecution and frustration they have suffered at the hands of the Spanish state. But yet, some part of the support that Barcelona garners does come from their sporting success as well. For a lot of people who migrated to Catalonia from the poorer parts of Spain, FC Barcelona was feeling part of something that went above the mediocrity of life. Former Barcelona striker Jose Maria Fuste who played for the club between 1953 and 1972 said about the club thus, 'Barca is easily the best club in the world because it represents a country, Catalonia, and this is something that gives it its extraordinary potential'. He added that he played for a club which represented its people during Franco's dictatorship and it was at the Nou Camp – FC Barcelona's grounds – where they could take their anger out on the regime if they wanted to. The rivalry against Real Madrid was almost like a political expression capable of restoring the Catalan's sense of pride. Through Franco's dictatorship, the rivalry had attained intense political dimensions. For Barca fans Real Madrid represented everything about Franco, while for Real Madrid fans Barcelona was seen as a separatist club.[6]

The bitter relationship between the Spanish Centre and Catalonia has become even more tense in recent times, with the Catalan Parliament passing a referendum for independence from the Spanish centre in 2014.[7] Though this move is regarded to be symbolic, it is also said that with Spain in a massive economic crisis, Catalonia by gaining independent status can flourish as a separate country.[8] The move has understandably irked the Spanish Parliament based in Madrid, which has said that it will block any move for Catalan independence in the courts.[9] The Catalan–Spain divide, though political, and to an extent symbolic, has deep undertones for the country's football future. If indeed, Catalonia becomes an independent country, then the entire backbone of the current Spanish team which has many Catalan-born players in their ranks including Xavi Hernandez (who we shall discuss in this essay) will break down. The current Spanish team, which has already set very high benchmarks for themselves by winning two European Championships and a World Cup, may not be the same strong team that they are, without their Catalan contingent.

The move for Catalan independence could have very strong ramifications for Spanish domestic football because it could mean FC Barcelona, arguably amongst the greatest football teams ever, having to step out from playing in the Spanish Primera Division. There is a Catalonia national football team which first came into existence in 1904, but isn't affiliated to FIFA and UEFA. The Catalonia football team regularly plays friendly international internationals[10] and as recently as January of 2013 against Nigeria, had five members of their team who have been part of the all-conquering Spanish team between 2008 and 2012.[11] It is still unclear that in the event of independence for Catalonia, what would be the future of FC Barcelona. In Britain, for example, though the prominent football league is called the English Premier League, it has for many years opened the doors for teams from Wales to participate. Though Wales competes as a separate country in many sporting events including football, it is still a part of the United Kingdom. Catalonia, however, does not compete as a separate country in any sporting event, and the difference between them and Wales is that an independent Catalonia would become a separate country altogether. It will be interesting to see in that scenario, whether FC Barcelona will continue to be a part of the Spanish Primera Division or not?

The FC Barcelona–Real Madrid rivalry

The Spanish centre has had tense relations with several regions in the country, but its relationship with Catalonia has always been highlighted from a footballing context. To a large extent, this has to do with the tremendous success of the Catalan region's most successful club FC Barcelona. Like any major rivalry in football, examples of which abound (in England, Manchester United vs. Liverpool; in Scotland, Glasgow Rangers vs. Glasgow Celtic; in Argentina, River Plate vs. Boca Juniors), the rivalries are defined not just by the political, regional or in case of Scotland, religious differences, but also by their competitive nature. In each such instance, there is as much a case of two clubs fighting for one-upmanship as they are for proving points which have ramifications off the field. In the last 20 years, since a more liberal policy was adopted towards the inclusion of more foreign players in European Football Clubs, Real Madrid and Barcelona, more than any other clubs in the world, have become a breeding ground for the best in the world.

One statistic will show the dominance of the two clubs in world football: of the World Player of the Year award winners since 1993 (FIFA Ballon D'Or since 2010–2011); only two have not played for Real Madrid or Barcelona at some point in their career.[12] No other clubs in the world in any league have the pulling power that these two possess in unison, and though there are often claims that Spanish football is becoming too monotonous because of the dominance of these two clubs, their rivalry and particularly the El Classico encounters arguably remain amongst football's showpiece events. With such depth of world-class talent on display, contests between the two sides have become engrossing encounters attracting massive audiences both on-field as well as on television. At many times, personal rivalries take centre stage with the star player of either club being pitted against the other, with fans of either club out to prove that their star is bigger than the other.

Perhaps, the most prominent rivalry in recent times has been that between Barcelona's Lionel Messi and Real Madrid's Cristiano Ronaldo. With so much of wealth of talent on display in both the teams and with the Spanish La Liga title on most occasions coming down to both these teams, an El Classico encounter is often like the season decider. It is though, also as much about Catalonia vs. Spain, an occasion, a platform where a country seeking autonomy takes on the big country of which it is still a part.[13]

While the rivalry between these two football giants has existed for years, it is really only since Barcelona started matching Real Madrid's early domination on the world stage that it became really intense. That Real Madrid was General Franco's favourite team was known to most in Spain. But it was only a coincidence that the greatest phase of their history came during Franco's dictatorship. Real Madrid won the European Cup on six occasions before 1970 including the first five that took place between 1955 and 1959. Barcelona won the tournament for the first time only in 1992. Real Madrid were Spain's pre-eminent club renowned for international superstars like Alfredo Di Stefano, Ferenc Puskas and Raymond Kopa.[14] Barcelona countered that domination somewhat in the 1970s, with the signing of Dutchman Johan Cruyff, arguably the world's most creative player at the time. Cruyff was not just a great player but he was also someone who understood what the Barcelona shirt meant to the people of Catalonia. During his tenure at the club he became an icon to the Catalan people. For a short time in the 1980s, FC Barcelona also had Diego Maradona, possibly the greatest footballer ever. Unlike Cruyff who spent the best part of his career at the Nou Camp, Maradona spent only his formative years there and then moved to Napoli in Italy. Barcelona was without any doubt a symbol of Catalan nationalism, but at the same time it was also a very successful football club which was battling Real Madrid head-on for Spanish football supremacy.[15] This enabled Barcelona to attract the best footballing talent in the world, some of whom then went on to join the Catalan nationalist rhetoric. An example of this was the mercurial Bulgarian striker Hristo Stoichkov[16] who was also the leading goalscorer in the 1994 Football World Cup as well as the European Footballer of the Year.

Though the rivalry between the two clubs has always been intense, it has acquired an interesting dimension in the last four to five years. This could in many ways be to do with the success the Spanish national team has had. With Real Madrid and Barcelona providing the lion's share of players for the national team, the spotlight has always been on on-field battles between individuals who are otherwise teammates in national colours. With Jose Mourinho taking over as Real Madrid coach, the rivalry has gained a sharper edge and often the desperation to win, particularly for Real Madrid, who have – until very recently – been at the receiving end more than Barcelona in the last five years, has been pretty big. This desperation to win has often led to unsavoury scenes during El Classico clashes and the duel between Spanish national teammates. An example of such an incident was when Carlos Puyol, the Barcelona captain as well as someone who has spoken proudly of his Catalan roots, had a violent clash with his Spanish international teammate from Real Madrid Sergio Ramos at the end of a particularly heated El Classico encounter in 2010.[17] This happened only a few months after they played together in Spain's historic World Cup triumph. There are other aspects to this rivalry as well, with some of the main players such as Real Madrid goalkeeper and captain Iker Casillas and Barcelona midfielder and vice-captain Xavi Hernandez sharing a cherished friendship from their days in the Spain Youth team. Though the two players continue to share a good friendship, the rivalry between Barcelona and Real Madrid has led to a certain degree of tension between the players.[18] There was talk of Jose Mourinho being unhappy with Casillas for his close friendship with Xavi.[19]

Since the 2008–2009 season, FC Barcelona has not only been the best team in Spain but also the world and have laid claim to being one of the best football teams to have ever graced the game. In El Classico encounters between the two sides since 2008–2009, Barcelona has come out overwhelmingly the better side. In the history of clashes between the two sides, two of the most convincing victories ever by Barcelona have come since the 2008–2009 season: the first was a 6–2 demolition in May 2009 at Madrid's home ground at the Bernabeau stadium and the second was a brilliant 5–0 victory in November 2010 at the Nou Camp. Barcelona appeared to be running away with the bragging rights in this rivalry, but Real Madrid did get a certain measure of revenge in 2011–2012 by ending Barcelona's streak of three consecutive league titles.

Despite the rivalry between the two clubs has been intense in the last four years, and despite Catalonia's aspiration to become an independent country, this has had little impact on the Spanish national team in recent years. The core of the Spanish national team comprises almost entirely of players from these two clubs; Barcelona (Gerard Pique, Carlos Puyol, Jordi Alba, Sergio Busquets, Cesc Fabregas, Xavi, Pedro, Andres Iniesta and David Villa[20]) with a good number of them being Catalan as well and Real Madrid (Iker Casillas, Sergio Ramos, Alvaro Arbeloa and Xabi Alonso). Despite the rivalry, there seemingly appears to be no difficulty for the players to put it aside when they don the national team shirt. It is ironical that the Spanish national team which was not always loved by the different regions in the country, especially Catalonia, was dominated in the two Euro Cup and one World Cup victories by players from the Catalan region's most famous football club.

Xavi Hernandez and the revival of Spanish football in the new millennium

Xavier Hernandez better known as 'Xavi' has had an illustrious career. Few football players in the history of the game have made the kind of impact that Xavi has in his prime, in terms of influencing trophy-winning teams. There have been many more successful and enthralling players like Pele, Franz Beckenbauer, Michel Platini, Diego Maradona, Ronaldo, Zinedine Zidane and Lionel Messi, but have not had the sustained success with their club and national side as Xavi has had. Since June 2008, Xavi has won the Spanish La Liga title on three occasions, the UEFA Champions League twice, and won every major competition in which he has represented Spain – the European Championships (twice) and the World Cup in 2010.

But the other interesting side to Xavi's dual achievements with Spain and Barcelona is that he is a born and bred Catalan. Following Spain's victory in the 2010 World Cup, Xavi was seen brandishing the Catalan flag.[21] Although much water has flown under the bridge from the footballing perspective between Catalonia and Spain, it was still seen as interesting that one of the major architects of Spain's World Cup triumph was holding his Catalan identity dear to him, and that too at a tense phase in the country's history when Catalonia was in the process of seeking independence. Though Xavi is a proud Catalan and a one-club man having represented Barcelona, the club he supported while growing up, throughout his life, a time did come in his early 20s when he contemplated leaving Barcelona for the English powerhouse, Manchester United. He did not make the move and the rest, as they say, is history. But there were other issues at the start of his career. Xavi, a central midfielder par excellence who is rated among the greatest to have played in that position, was during the regime of Louis Van Gaal played as a defensive midfielder in Barcelona, a player who was sitting right in front of the back four. It was the arrival of Frank Rijkaard at Barcelona midway through the 2003–2004 season that not only heralded a turn of fortunes for the club but also Xavi's as a footballer. Having played for close to six years in a position that did not appear to suit him, Rijkaard convinced Xavi to move into a more attacking role. It was in this first half season of Rijkaard's arrival that Xavi made one of the most important contributions of his career. In the El Classico encounter against Real Madrid, Madrid were comfortably leading the league standings while boasting of their full array of superstars – Zinedine Zidane, Luis Figo, David Beckham, Ronaldo, Roberto Carlos and Raul. Barcelona, which had lost at home in the corresponding fixture, got their revenge over their rival and it was Xavi who struck the decisive blow, scoring a well-worked goal following a 1–2 with Brazilian superstar Ronaldinho.[22]

Though he was a markedly improved player under the coaching of Frank Rijkaard, Xavi truly came into his own from the 2008 season onwards when Josep Guardiola took over as coach of Barcelona. There is a little bit of irony here in that Guardiola was the club's incumbent central midfielder and iconic figure during Xavi's formative days in the senior team. It was Guardiola who kept Xavi out of the playing XI initially, but as luck would have it, it was under his management that Xavi metamorphosed into the world-class footballer he has become.[23] That said, even before the 2008–2009 season had begun for Barcelona, Xavi had a particularly sweet moment in the summer of 2008. Spain, winless in international tournaments since 1964, broke that losing record as they proceeded to glory in the European Championships held in Austria and Switzerland. In what might have been a precursor of his growing influence as a footballer for both FC Barcelona and the country, Xavi was named Player of the Tournament.[24] Though he did not score a goal during the tournament, as the leader of Spain's dynamic midfield he had controlled games superbly. The final in Vienna, where Spain beat three time champions Germany, saw Xavi make his defining contribution, his pass to Fernando Torres leading to a goal was the match's decisive moment.[25]

The arrival of Guardiola heralded Xavi's growing reputation as one of football's finest midfielders of all time. The great French midfielder and current UEFA President Michel Platini acknowledged as much when he asked for Xavi's shirt following the 2010 World Cup Final. The great thing with Xavi is his ability to perform at the same level for both his club and his country, despite the long cultural divide between Catalonia and the Spanish Centre. If 2008 was Xavi's breakthrough as an international footballer, then 2009 was arguably when he set the tone at the domestic level. In 2004, Xavi had made huge strides in Barcelona's El Classico triumph, five years later he was surely to have the game of all games at the Bernebeau Stadium. Xavi supplied four assists as Barcelona went on to crush Real Madrid 6–2 at Real's own stadium. A few weeks later at the Champions League Final against Manchester United, it was Xavi's cross which was headed in by Lionel Messi to seal the 2–0 victory that guided the club to their third title.[26] In 2010 and 2011 as well, Xavi has played a starring role in the triumphs of both his club and country. At the 2010 World Cup, Xavi added to his burgeoning reputation, as he was nominated for the 'Golden Ball', the award given to the tournament's best player. Though Xavi did not win the award, he played a decisive role in Spain's first ever World Cup title.

He was named Man of the Match for his performance in the semi-final where Spain beat one of the tournament's heavyweights and three-time Champions Germany.

Xavi's performance at club level during the 2010–2011 season, a time when Barcelona's performances made people ask if this was the 'greatest football club of all time', was very good as well. In November of 2010, in the first of the six meetings between the two clubs during the season, Xavi opened the scoring for Barcelona in their crushing 5–0 victory over Real Madrid. Xavi also played a key role in the club's 3–1 victory over Manchester United in the Champions League Final in May 2011. Not only did he captain Barcelona that night, in the absence of Carlos Puyol, it was his exquisite through ball that cut open the Manchester United defence for Pedro to score, and help his club take a 1–0 lead.[27]

Xavi has lived in Lionel Messi's shadow for most of the last four years in FC Barcelona. Yet to put into perspective how good Xavi has been, is to compare his performance with that of the Argentine maestro at the international level. Since 2008, Xavi has won almost all significant competitions at both club as well as international levels, while Messi, a titan playing for Barcelona, has had a distinctly below average career while playing for Argentina. Xavi has been a galvanizing effect on almost all attacking players around him, and it's perhaps significant that without Xavi's assists, Messi has struggled while playing for Argentina. This in itself tells you why Xavi should be rated as one of the finest midfielders to have ever played the game.

However, in the context of the discussion here, Xavi has come to symbolize what may be described as the rise of a new integrated Spanish national football team – a fierce Catalan himself, Xavi has showed exemplary commitment while playing for the national side and has been a key instrument in its international victories. There was a time, especially during General Franco's dictatorship and in its aftermath, when strong regional sentiments appeared to have acted as a centripetal force to the grave detriment of the national side, leading to its chronic underachievement. That appears to have changed since 2008. Xavi, and the contingent from FC Barcelona playing fluid football in the national side, possibly signal a new inclusiveness in the team now – both in style and spirit – which may be responsible for Spain's emphatic and dominating arrival on the global football stage.

Conclusion

Spain finds itself in a golden period of their footballing history in recent times. Few nations have achieved the kind of success over a defined period of time like Spain has between 2008 and 2012. Some other footballing nations could be put in the same bracket, such as the Brazilian team that won three World Cups between 1958 and 1970 as well as the West German team of the 1970s which had a strong run in the World Cup and the Euros, but the aura and prowess of this current Spanish team has been something very special. While as a team, it might lack the ruthless goal-scoring touch of the celebrated Brazilian team, Spain has shown time and again that they can turn on the magic when it really matters. The 4–0 victory over Italy in the 2012 European Championship Final was as good a team performance that has ever been seen in a big game. While the debate will linger about whether the current Spanish side is better than the Brazilian team of 1958–1970, the core of the Spain team that played between 2008 and 2012 is likely to play in the 2014 World Cup, and a few may even play in the 2016 European Championships, raising the possibility of Spain extending their astonishing winning streak in major football events in years to come. If that happens, Spain may well be regarded as the greatest international football side of all time.

The dominating arrival of Spain, and its exhibition of magical football, raises the question: what took Spain so long to become a football giant it is today? Was it the divided loyalties of the various regions in the aftermath of the Spanish Civil War or was it for footballing reasons? It makes one wonder why with such great club teams, Spain could not ever succeed at the international level for so long. The unavoidable conclusion one has to draw for an answer is the obvious fact that Spain is today gifted with an extraordinarily talented bunch of footballers, who have managed to put regional and club loyalties and rivalries aside to create one of the most astonishingly remarkable and successful football teams of all time. Some might find irony in that the core of the Spain team today is from FC Barcelona, a club that symbolizes everything about Catalan nationalism, and a long-time and bitter rival club of Real Madrid, the club from the capital and one which for many years has been identified as the club which General Franco supported. Spain's success as a national team has coincided with that of FC Barcelona at the club level, whose performances over the last five years has made many regard them as one of the best or if not the best club side in the history of football.

Xavi Hernandez, a catalyst for Spain and Barcelona's tremendous performances over the last five years, is also a Catalan who proudly wears his Catalan identity on and off the football field. His extraordinary performances, as detailed in this essay, certainly force us to acknowledge that Xavi be rated as one of the finest midfielders to have ever played the game. When an estimate will be done of Xavi at the end of his career, the fact that he has been a winner at both club and international levels, and has been a champion midfielder should make Xavi recognized as one of the greatest Spanish players of all time.

Notes

1. Burns, *La Roja*.
2. 'Are Spain the Best Team of All Time', *BBC Sport*, July 2, 2012, http://www.bbc.co.uk/sport/0/football/18669029.
3. Burns, *La Roja*.
4. Ibid.
5. Ibid.
6. Ibid.
7. 'Catalan Parliament Paves Way for Referendum on Independence', *Associated Press*, January 23, 2013, http://www.guardian.co.uk/world/2013/jan/23/catalonian-parliament-referendum-independence-spain.
8. 'Viewpoints: Independence for Catalonia', *BBC News*, November 21, 2012, http://www.bbc.co.uk/news/world-europe-20407873.
9. 'Catalan Parliament Paves Way for Referendum on Independence'.
10. 'Barca a Catalyst for Catalonia's Independent Streak', *Eurosport*, September 26, 2012, http://uk.eurosport.yahoo.com/blogs/pitchside-europe/barca-catalyst-catalonia-independent-streak-165604732.html.
11. FC Barcelona Website, 'Catalonia with 9 FC Barcelona Players Tie Nigeria 1–1', http://www.fcbarcelona.com/football/first-team/detail/article/catalonia-with-9-fc-barcelona-players-tie-nigeria-1-1 (accessed January 2, 2013).
12. FIFA Website, 'FIFA World Player of the Year', http://www.fifa.com/classicfootball/awards/playeroftheyear/winnermen.html.
13. Fitzpatrick, *El Clasico*.

14. Burns, *La Roja*.
15. Burns, *Barca*.
16. Fitzpatrick, *El Clasico*.
17. 'Carlos Puyol says "What Happens on the Pitch Stays There" after Sergio Ramos Clash', *The Daily Telegraph*, November 30, 2010, http://www.telegraph.co.uk/sport/ football/competitions/la-liga/8170017/Barcelona-v-Real-Madrid-Carlos-Puyol-says-what-happens-on-the-pitch-stays-there-after-Sergio-Ramos-clash.html.
18. Hunter, *Barca*.
19. 'Xavi's Father Reveals Spain Tensions', ESPN, July 4, 2012, http://espnfc.com/news/ story/_/id/1122592/xavi%27s-father-claims-mourinho-objected-to-iker-casillas-friendship? cc=4716.
20. With the exception of Pedro, Iniesta and Villa, all the players mentioned are Catalan as well.
21. Simon Kuper, 'Spain's Football Unity Shows Regions the Way', *Financial Times*, June 17, 2012, http://www.ft.com/intl/cms/s/0/b1a368a6-b89b-11e1-a2d6-00144feabdc0. html#axzz2NRHE1FQ7.
22. Hunter, *Barca*.
23. Ibid.
24. Barney Ronay, 'Xavi Takes Top Player Award', *The Guardian*, June 30, 2008, http:// www.guardian.co.uk/football/2008/jun/30/spain.euro20082.
25. Hunter, *Barca*.
26. Ibid.
27. Ibid.

References

Burns, Jimmy. *Barca: A People's Passion*. London: Bloomsbury, 2009.
Burns, Jimmy. *La Roja: How Soccer Conquered Spain and How Spanish Soccer Conquered the World*. New York: Nation Books, 2012.
Fitzpatrick, Richard. *El Clasico: Barcelona vs. Real Madrid: Football's Greatest Rivalry*. London: Bloomsbury, 2012.
Hunter, Graham. *Barca: The Making of the Greatest Team in the World*. Glasgow: Backpage Press, 2012.

Looking at the extraordinary success of the 'Clockwork Orange': examining the brilliance of total football played by the Netherlands

Ric Jensen

Department of Marketing, Montclair State University, Montclair, NJ, USA

This essay describes some of the legendary accomplishments of the Netherlands football team in the World Cup and other international tournaments. It focuses on the Dutch teams led by Johan Cruyff and affectionately known as 'The Clockwork Orange' because they introduced a modern style of play with precision passing that was referred to as 'total football'. The Netherlands advanced to the World Cup final in 1974 and 1978, only to lose the championship each time. The study also explores the role of the Dutch coach Rinus Michels and some of Cruyff's teammates such as Johan Neeskens and Rob Rensenbrink. Looking at the Netherlands' performances in the European championships and World Cups in the last three decades, the essay attempts to bring out the transformations in Dutch football in post-Cruyff age. Finally, it discusses the team's rabid and energized fan base, and the ambush marketing scandal that took place during the 2010 World Cup.

Introduction

Since 1905, the Netherlands has fielded a national football team and they have provided some of the most exciting and inspiring matches played anywhere in the world. The team is adored and venerated by their fans as the 'Oranje', in honour of the House of William I of the House of Orange who led the Netherlands fight for independence against Spain in 1568.[1] Even though the Netherlands is geographically a small nation with a population of only roughly 17 million, the fact is that the Oranje have overachieved on football's largest stages – the FIFA World Cup and the European Championships. The Dutch have been at the doorstep of winning soccer's grandest prize – The World Cup – more than any other nation in the history of the competition, but they have never won the title. The Netherlands lost in the World Cup final to West Germany in 1974, to Argentina in 1978 and to Spain in 2010. Despite the lack of a World Cup championship, the Netherlands has achieved many other successes in international football. They won the European Championship in 1988 and, despite finishing as runner-up in the 2010 World Cup, they still topped the FIFA global football rankings in 2011. Professional football clubs from the Netherlands have also excelled in international competitions; since its inception in 1955, clubs from the Netherlands have won the European Cup five times (Ajax in 1970, 1971, 1972 and 1995, and PSV Eindhoven in 1988).

Perhaps as much as anything, the Netherlands has captured the imagination of football fans worldwide because of their inventive and creative style of play that is widely known as 'total football', a fluid system in which any player (other than the goalie) can assume any role on the team, be it an attacker, a midfielder or a defender. It has been described as 'paradigmatic examples of beautiful football'.[2] In fact, the coaches, players and fans of the Netherlands are so convinced that total football is the only way football should be played one writer suggests they have developed a 'national superiority complex' that other football strategies and tactics are simply inferior.[3] Winner described the style of football played by the Netherlands as 'Clockwork Orange'[4] (Orange because the team usually wears orange jerseys and clockwork because the individual members of the team play with the mechanical perfection of the world's best timepieces).

In a broad perspective, the way in which football has evolved in the Netherlands is a construct of processes within politics, culture and sport that have been evolving throughout Europe in the twentieth century. Tracing the genealogy of total football is daunting if not impossible, but Winner suggests it might be heavily influenced by the style of play of professional club Ajax, which began utilizing an intelligent and attacking strategy as early as World War II.[5] Missiroli suggests that the character and legacy of the Netherlands' national team have been based on some degree to their epic struggles against Germany and regional rivals such as Belgium.[6] The collective style of play the Netherlands employs, which emphasizes the ability of every player to quickly make critical decisions in a limited physical space, has been seen by some experts as a reflection of the Dutch character and culture. Lechner goes so far as to suggest that the self-image of the nation of the Netherlands is in large part a reflection of how the national team plays its exciting style of total football.[7] In fact, the Netherlands national team at the 2006 European championship was criticized by the media when they failed to show the distinctive flair and grace that fans had come to expect even though the team won enough games to advance to the semi-final of the tournament. It has also been suggested that the Netherlands national soccer team exhibits a playful and innovative style that epitomizes traits of the famous artists, explorers and creative thinkers that the country has produced over centuries,[8] while another theory proposes that the concept of total football might be instead attributed to the traditions of Dutch architecture which emphasizes designing buildings that efficiently use physical space while, at the same time, being aesthetically pleasing and playful.[9] Perhaps no other nation has had to come to terms with the challenge of creating more land than the Netherlands; the country has developed an ambitious programme to build dikes and reclaim areas that once were underwater and today roughly 27% of the population lives in lands that are below sea level.[10]

The most famous player in Netherlands' football history, Johan Cruyff, said:

> There is no better medal than being acclaimed for your style. For the good of football, we need a team of invention, attacking ideas and style to emerge. Even if it doesn't win it will inspire footballers of all ages everywhere. That is the greatest reward.[11]

Merkel described the concept of total football this way:

> This new and revolutionary approach [total football] meant the end of a traditional and rigid division of labour between attackers and defenders, and gave all players a creative role. The Dutch players were very comfortable with the ball and the aim was to keep possession by continually passing and moving.[12]

The early years – Netherlands football before the 1970s

The Dutch national football team played its first international game against Belgium in 1905, winning on 4–1 with three goals from Eddy de Neve. The Netherlands appeared in the 1934 and 1938 World Cup tournaments. In the 1934 World Cup played in Italy, the Dutch were seeded fifth entering the tournament but lost 3–2 in the opening round and were eliminated by Switzerland. When France hosted the 1938 World Cup, the Netherlands were eliminated in the opening round after being shut out by Czechoslovakia, 3–0. It would not be until the 1970s that the Netherlands reappeared on the global stage as one of the world's elite football programmes.

The beginnings of 'Total Football' – Dutch soccer in the 1970s

In the 1970s, the Dutch shocked the world by introducing the idea of 'Total Football'. The concept of total football was developed and pioneered by two of the most successful professional football teams in the Netherlands – club teams Feyenrood Rotterdam and AFC Ajax of Amsterdam. Yet, it is still unclear exactly who should be given the credit for inventing total football. Winner describes how Ajax had exhibited 'intelligent attacking football' since the First World War, traits that were foundational for total football.[13] Others believe total football was developed by legendary coach Rinus Michels, who coached Ajax from 1965 to 1971, where he won the European Cup championship.[14] In 1971, Michels left Ajax to coach FC Barcelona from 1971 to 1974 and led the club to the Spanish national championship. Michels began coaching the Netherlands national team in 1974 and promptly led the team to the finals of the 1974 FIFA World Cup, where they lost to host West Germany. In 1988, he coached the Dutch national team in the European Championships, where they defeated West Germany in the semifinals in Germany, gaining a little vengeance for the 1974 World Cup final; they won the championship by defeating the USSR, 2–0. Michels is so respected he was named the Coach of the Century by FIFA in 1999.

If Michels is credited as the genius who created the concept of total football, the player who was the exemplar of how the concept should be implemented on the pitch was superstar Johan Cruyff, who was honoured with the European Football Player of the Year award (the Ballon d'Or) three times and is widely recognized as one of the greatest players in the history of the game. From 1964 to 1974, Cruyff (who was born in Amsterdam) played for Ajax and he guided the club to six Netherlands Football League (Eredivisie) championships and three European Club titles (in 1971, 1972 and 1973). Cruyff left Ajax for FC Barcelona in 1973 where he played until 1978, leading Barca to the La Liga championship (its first in two decades) and being awarded his second Ballon d'Or title as European Footballer of the Year. Cruyff received this prestigious award a third time (the first player ever to do so) in 1974, while he was still with Barcelona. At the twilight of his career, Cruyff briefly played for Los Angeles and Washington, DC, in the North American Soccer League. After his playing career ended, Cruyff went on to coach Ajax (1987), FC Barcelona (1988–1998) and the Catalonia national team (1999).

Just what is total football and why did it make such an impact on how football is played, not only in the Netherlands and Europe and throughout the world? 'Total Football' might be best described as a football strategy in which any player can take over the role of any of his teammates. In this fluid system, any player can be successively become an attacker, a midfielder or a defender. In order to succeed, total football depends on ability of each player to quickly recognize and adapt to changing conditions on the pitch. The concept was pioneered by Dutch professional clubs Feyenrood and Ajax and became famous when it was implemented by the Netherlands national teams of the 1970s. Carlos Alberto, who played for Brazil against the Netherlands in the 1974 World Cup, referred to the style of play as a 'carousel'.[15]

Two heartbreaking near misses – losses in the 1974 and 1978 World Cup Finals

To many of their most loyal and avid fans, the World Cups of 1974 and 1978 represent the biggest emotional highs and the lowest lows. The Netherlands holds the dubious distinction of being the only team to lose World Cup finals to the host nation in back-to-back tournaments. In the 1974 World Cup in Germany, the Netherlands won their group stage in the first round, defeating Uruguay 2–0 and Bulgaria 4–1, before reaching a scoreless draw against Sweden. In the second round, the Netherlands overwhelmed Argentina 4–0, with two goals coming from Cruyff. In the third round, the Netherlands defeated East Germany 2–0. In the semi-final, they beat Brazil 2–0 based on goals from Johan Neeskens and Cruyff. The Netherlands played against host West Germany in Munich in the World Cup championship game. The Dutch took an early 1–0 lead before the Germans even had a chance to touch the ball; Johan Neeskens' converted a penalty kick that was awarded after Cruyff had been fouled. But West Germany rallied for a 2–1 victory; Paul Breitner converted a penalty kick in the 26th minute and Gerd Müller scored the game winner in the 45th minute. In the tournament, Neeskens led the Netherlands with five goals while Cruyff scored three times. This critical game has been dissected at many levels; one analysis suggests the Netherlands lost because 'Holland started to bugger about in an attempt to humiliate the Germans for the crimes of World War Two' by taunting their opponents, instead of merely focusing on winning the game.[16] Just how devastating was the loss in the 1974 World Cup final? Winner quotes playwright Johan Timmers as saying, 'The defeat of 1974 is the biggest trauma that has happened to Holland in the twentieth Century, apart from the floods of 1953 and the Second World War'.[17] Van Houtum and van Dam describe this loss to West Germany as 'the mother of all defeats' for Netherlands fans, in large part because it reminded them of how brutally Germany had treated the Dutch in the Second World War.[18] The horrors of the Second World War haunt the residents of the Netherlands today, in large part because 105,000 Dutch Jews – an astonishing 80% of the Jews in the country – were murdered by the Nazis.[19] As late as the 1990s, the loss to Germany still haunted fans of the Netherlands. Dutch novelist Anna Enquist wrote, the loss is 'A very living pain, like an unpunished crime ... It matters very much ... There is still deep unresolved trauma about 1974'.[20]

In the 1978 World Cup hosted by Argentina, the Netherlands again reached the championship game only to lose to the hosts. The Netherlands were handicapped by playing without Cruyff who retired in 1977 and boycotted the tournament because Argentina was governed by a ruthless military dictator, General Jorge Rafael Videla; during the tournament the Videla regime was accused of torturing and killing dissidents. On the pitch, the Netherlands struggled in the opening round where they defeated Iran 3–0, settled for a scoreless draw with Peru and lost 3–2 to Scotland;

even with this mediocre result the Netherlands still advanced as the runner-up their group. In the second round, the Dutch began regaining their form, overwhelming Austria 5–1, tying with West Germany 2–2 and coming from behind to edge Italy 2–1 on a late goal by Arie Hann. In the championship game against Argentina in front of a hostile crowd in Buenos Aires, the Netherlands fell behind 1–0 only to the tie game on a goal in the 82nd minute by Dick Nanninga. The Dutch missed a golden opportunity to win the game in stoppage time when Rob Rensenbrink's shot on goal bounced off the post; the Argentines scored two goals in overtime to win 3–1. Rensenbrink scored 5 goals in the tournament, tying him for second place. Between the two World Cup finals, the Netherlands reached the semi-final of the 1976 European Championships only to lose 3–1 to eventual champion Czechoslovakia.

The end of 'Total Football' and a decade of decline

After the 1978 World Cup loss, Dutch football entered a decade of failure, which represented a marked drop-off from the glory of the years of total football. In 1980, the Netherlands qualified for the 1980 European Championships only to fail to advance beyond the first round; the Dutch defeated Greece 1–0, lost to West Germany 3–2 and tied Czechoslovakia 1–0. Soon after the tournament, Rensenbrink and Ruud Krol retired, signalling the end of the total football era. In 1982, the Netherlands failed to qualify for the World Cup, finishing next to last in their qualifying group that included Belgium, France and Ireland. In 1984, the Netherlands failed to qualify for the European Championship; despite having the same record in qualifying as Spain, the Dutch lost a tiebreaker because Spain had scored more goals. In 1986, the Netherlands were eliminated from qualifying for the World Cup, when they split a two-game series with Belgium, losing because the Belgians had scored more goals away from its home pitch.

Redemption in 1988 – the Netherlands win the European championship

Perhaps it's a coincidence, but when Rinus Michels returned to coach the Netherlands national team in 1988, the squad once again began to perform superbly. In the first round, the Netherlands lost its opening match against the Soviet Union, 1–0; crushed England 3–1; and outlasted Ireland 1–0. The win over England was especially noteworthy because Marco van Basten scored all three goals; van Basten would go on to score 5 goals in the tournament (more than any other player). Although one might think that the championship game of a tournament represents the pinnacle of a competition, the match Dutch fans most anticipated was the semi-final against hosts West Germany; fans of the Oranje desperately wanted revenge for their loss to the Germans in the 1974 World Cup final in Munich. One estimate suggests that 9 million Netherlands fans (more than half the nation's population) gathered in public places to watch the match.[21] West Germany scored first on a penalty kick by Lothar Matthaus in the 55th minute after the Netherlands fouled Jurgen Klinsmann, but the Dutch tied the game 20 min later on a penalty kick by Ronald Koeman after the Germans fouled van Basten. Van Basten scored the game-winning goal in the 88th minute on an extraordinary volley from an impossible angle. The game was highly emotional on many levels; immediately after the victory, members of the Oranje 'went totally, utterly, entirely out of their minds with joy';[22] more than half the population of the Netherlands began singing, dancing, drinking and setting off fireworks in celebration. The victory was marred by an incident following the game in which Koeman wiped his backside with the Olaf Thon's German's shirt as if it were toilet paper; Koeman later apologized.[23] The match was important for several reasons. It marked the first time the Netherlands had defeated Germany in a major international competition and the victory advanced the Oranje to their first-ever European Championship game. In the final, the Netherlands beat the USSR 2–0 on goals by Ruud Gullit and van Basten.

Netherlands football in the 1990s – mixed results

Throughout the 1990s, the Netherlands played solid football but could not meet the high expectations of their rabid fans. In the 1990 World Cup, the Netherlands entered the tournament as one of the favourites; however, the Oranje could only achieve draws in the opening round (against England, Ireland and Egypt). The Netherlands lost to long-time nemesis West Germany 2–1 in the round of 16; the game was so intense that Frank Rijkaard of the Netherlands spit at West Germany's Rudi Völler.[24]

In 1992, the Netherlands advanced to the semi-finals of the European Championship, defeating Scotland 1–0, tying with Russia (then known as the Confederation of Independent States) and beating Germany 3–1. In the semi-finals, the Netherlands were upset by Denmark, who went on to win the championship, by penalty kicks after the game ended 2–2 after regular time. In some respects, the tournament signalled the decline of older players and the emergence of future stars; young Dennis Bergkamp led the Dutch by scoring 3 goals; this was one of van Basten's last appearances in major international tournaments because he suffered a serious ankle injury shortly afterwards. After the tournament, Dick Advocate replaced Rinus Michels as the manager of the national team. Bergkamp, on the other hand, became the leader of the Netherlands in the 1994 World Cup; he again led the team in scoring with 3 goals. In the opening round, the Netherlands defeated Saudi Arabia 2–1, lost to Belgium 1–0, and beat Morocco 2–1. The Netherlands beat Ireland in the round of 16 by a score of 2–0, but were eliminated by a 3–2 loss to eventual champions Brazil in the quarter-finals. In that game, Bergkamp and Aron Winter scored for the Dutch.

In the 1996 European Championship, the Oranje made news when allegations of racial friction within the team emerged in the media. Black players such as Edgar Davids, Clarence Seedorf, Patrick Kluivert, Michael Reiziger and Winston Bogarde squabbled against white members of the club about the amount they were paid and how they were being treated.[25] On the pitch, the Netherlands advanced to the quarter-finals only to lose to France on penalty kicks after playing to a scoreless draw in regular time. The tournament is best remembered for a late goal by Patrick Kluivert in a 4–1 loss to England that advanced the Netherlands based on goal differential.

In the 1998 World Cup, the Netherlands defeated Argentina in the quarter-final 2–1, after Dennis Bergkamp scored a remarkable goal in the 89th minute. Bergkamp chased down a long pass from Frank de Boer, played it off Argentine defender Roberto Ayala and volleyed it into the net. A sportswriter described the goal as defying the laws of physics.[26] In the semi-finals, the Netherlands lost to Brazil in penalty kicks after a 1–1 draw in regular time; former coach Rinus Michels suffered a heart attack while watching the game.[27] After the tournament, Netherlands manager Guus Hiddink resigned and was replaced by Frank Rijkaard.

The dawn of a new century – Netherlands football in the 2000s

In 2000, the Netherlands and Belgium hosted the European Championship. The Netherlands swept the opening round, shutting out the Czech Republic and Denmark before edging France 3–2. The Dutch overwhelmed Yugoslavia, wining 6–1 in the quarter-finals, but lost in the semi-finals to Italy in penalty kicks after a scoreless draw in regular time. In the match against Italy, the Dutch played against a short-handed squad for most of the game and failed to convert two penalty kicks.[28] Netherlands coach Frank Rijkaard was criticized by the media, and resigned after the tournament, being replaced by Louis van Gaal. Despite not winning the championship, the people of the Netherlands were happier than normal simply because they hosted the tournament.[29] However, in a shocking disappointment, the Oranje failed to qualify for the 2002 World Cup. In qualifying matches, the Netherlands failed to advance in a group that included Ireland and Portugal. Ireland eliminated the Dutch 1–0 despite being down to 10-man in a decisive match in Dublin.[30] After failing to qualify for the World Cup, van Gaal was replaced as the Netherlands manager by Dick Advocaat, who had previously coached the national team in the 1990s. In the 2004 European Championships, the Netherlands had an uneven opening round, earning a 1–1 draw against Germany, losing 3–2 to the Czech Republic, and defeating Latvia 3–0. In the second round, the Oranje defeated Sweden in penalty kicks following a scoreless draw, but were then eliminated by host Portugal 2–1 in the semifinals.[31] This was the last major international tournament for many of Netherlands' World Cup veterans.

In 2006, the Netherlands qualified for the World Cup and advanced to the second round before losing to Portugal in a bizarre match characterized by an extraordinary number of penalties. The Netherlands qualified for the World Cup by winning a group that included the Czech Republic, Romania, Finland, Macedonia, Armenia and Andorra. In the opening round of the World Cup, the Netherlands defeated Serbia & Montenegro (1–0) and the Côte d'Ivoire (2–1), while earning a scoreless draw against Argentina. In an infamous match against Portugal in Nuremburg, the Dutch lost 1–0 to Portugal in a game that produced 16 yellow cards and four red cards, forcing each side to finish the game with only nine players. One sportswriter described the game as 'an evening of mayhem and spite, sometimes synchronized cheating and complaining',[32] while another reporter dubbed the penalty-filled match 'The Battle of Nuremburg'.[33] The loss eliminated the Netherlands from the tournament.

Coached by Marco van Basten and employing a new 4-2-3-1 formation, the Netherlands qualified for the 2008 European Championship with victories against Luxembourg, Bulgaria, Albania and Slovenia. Unluckily, the Netherlands were paired in what the media described as the 'Group of Death', where they had to face perennial powers France and Italy. In their opening game, the Oranje earned their first victory over Italy since 1978 winning by 3–0 on goals by Ruud van Nistelrooy, Wesley Sneijder and Giovanni van Bronckhorst. In their second match, the Netherlands convincingly beat France 4–1 and in their final opening round game they defeated Romania 2–0. Ironically, the Oranje lost 3–1 in the quarter-finals to a Russian team coached by former Netherlands manager Guus Hiddink, eliminating them from the tournament.[34]

The 2010 World Cup: another loss in the final and abandoning 'Total Football'

In the 2010 World Cup, the Dutch once again reached the precipice of the championship only to lose in the final. Led by new coach, Bert van Marwijk, the Netherlands won their first round group stage by defeated Denmark 2–0, Japan 1–0 and Cameroon 2–1. In the second round, the Oranje defeated Slovakia 2–1 with goals from Arjen Robben and Wesley Sneijder. In the third round, the Netherlands won a hard-fought 2–1 victory against Brazil, a team favoured by many experts to win the tournament. The Oranje came back from a 0–1 half-time deficit on an own goal by Brazil that was eventually credited to Sneijder and a Sneijder-header in the 68th minute.[35] The Netherlands defeated Uruguay 3–2 to advance to the championship game, but lost to Spain 1–0 after Andres Iniesta scored in extra time. At least one sportswriter criticized the Dutch for playing an ugly style,[36] while another reporter suggested that since the Netherlands had waited so long to win the World Cup, they were entitled to triumph while not playing an artistic game.[37] Ironically, Spain's style of play was heavily influenced by the Netherlands' own Johan Cruyff and Rinus Michels, who introduced 'total football' to FC Barcelona.[38] Off-the-pitch, fans of the Netherlands were linked to an 'ambush marketing' campaign, where a bunch of beautiful young women were dressed in bright orange dresses that were sponsored by a beer company, which was not an official sponsor of the event.[39] These fans were shown frequently on televised matches before broadcasters became aware they were working for the brewery.

Other issues: hooliganism, racism and anti-semitism

An examination of Netherlands football would not be complete without touching on other off-the-pitch issues. Racism, hooliganism and anti-semitism are all part of the uglier side of global football, even in the Netherlands. Despite the fact that the Netherlands has reached the pinnacle of the football universe since they began playing large numbers of blacks from Surinam as early as the 1970s, tensions about race are an ongoing concern. Some fans and members of the media question the extent to which the team should be made up of whites from the Netherlands and blacks from Surinam and other former Netherlands colonies.[40] Dealing with racism has been an ongoing challenge for everyone involved with the Netherlands national football team for many years: players, coaches, fans and the media.[41] In the 2012 European Championship, fans in Poland taunted the black players on the Netherlands team, calling them 'monkeys'.[42] There have also been instances of racial infighting within the Dutch national team, most notably when Surinamese players felt they were being discriminated against in the 1996 European Championship.[43] It's not just blacks who are the victims of racism in the Netherlands, Muslims have also been targetted.[44]

From the perspective of hooliganism, the attitudes and behaviours of Dutch fans that follow the national team have also evoked controversy. When Feyenrood hosted Tottenham Hotspurs in 1974 in the UEFA Cup, more than 200 people were injured when fans of the two sides attacked one another.[45] How can one explain why hooliganism occurs in Netherlands football? One research study found that fans of the Oranje are more psychopathic and anti-social than the general public thus being more prone to act out.[46] Another investigation suggests that the attitude and possibly violent behaviour of some Netherlands fans are influenced in part by how they feel about mortality and death.[47]

Anti-semitism has long been a concern in all of Dutch society, including football. During the Second World War, the Nazis killed a large number of Jewish athletes and destroyed the viability of sports organizations that fostered the participation of Jews in sports in the country.[48] In contrast, the Germans did little to interfere with professional soccer in the Netherlands that was run and played by non-Jews.[49] Fans of the Amsterdam club Ajax have been greeted with songs about gas ovens and Auschwitz by some supporters of rival clubs such as Feyenrood[50] and ADO,[51] in large part because Amsterdam has a rich Jewish heritage and culture.

What lies in the future for football in the Netherlands? For professional clubs, there is increased fan interest and corporate support. In fact, many soccer stadiums in the Netherlands are being expanded and made more fan- and corporate-friendly to accommodate growing demands.[52] And the prospects are good that the Netherlands will continue to be a global football power. Despite losing in the 2010 World Cup final, the Dutch national team was ranked best in the world by FIFA in 2011.[53]

Summary

Despite being a small nation with a relatively small population, one might argue that the Netherlands has exerted a powerful influence on global football. Much of the influence of the Oranje can be traced to the development and implementation of 'Total Football', an exciting style of play featuring the concept that all players should quickly assume interchangeable roles. Total Football is no longer just a phenomenon in the Netherlands only; instead, it has been adopted by Spain, Germany, Portugal and many other of the top-ranked football playing countries in the world. Perhaps, another reason people root for Holland is that the Oranje is a loveable underdog; it says something special when a team has reached the World Cup finals twice only to lose to the host country. Perhaps as much as anything, the Dutch have forever changed the way in which football is played around the world. Because of the creative innovations developed, implemented and exported by the Oranje, many of the world's best teams are imitating that glorious style of total football that features an ever-attacking, rapidly-adapting style that so many football fans have come to love.

Notes

1. van Houtum and van Dam, 'Topophilia or Topoporno?'
2. Richards, *Soccer and Philosophy*.
3. Kuper and Szymanksi, *Soccernomics*.
4. Winner, *Brilliant Orange*.
5. Ibid.
6. Missiroli, 'European Football Cultures and Their Integration'.
7. Lechner, 'Imagined Communities in the Global Game'.
8. Hilvoorde, Vorstenbosch, and Devisch, 'Philosophy of Sport in Belgium and the Netherlands'.
9. Winner, *Brilliant Orange*.
10. John Tagliabue, 'The Dutch Seek to Claim More Land from the Sea', *The New York Times*, November 7, 2008, http://www.nytimes.com/2008/11/07/world/europe/07iht-journal.1.17618884.html?_r=0.
11. David Ornstein, 'Dutch Substance Over Style', The British Broadcasting Corporation, June 4, 2008, http://news.bbc.co.uk/sport2/hi/football/euro_2008/netherlands/74154 57.stm.

12. Merkel, 'The 1974 and 2006 World Cups in Germany'.
13. Winner, *Brilliant Orange*.
14. John MacLeary, 'Rinus Michels: The Originator of Total Football', *The Telegraph* (UK), October 25, 2008, http://www.telegraph.co.uk/sport/football/teams/england/3,258,800/Rinus-Michels-The-originator-of-Total-Football-Football.html.
15. Tom Williams, 'Tactics: Were Holland 1974 the Last True Innovators?' *Football Further*, October 15, 2010, http://www.tomwfootball.com/2010/10/15/tactics-were-holland-1974-the-last-true-innovators/.
16. Scott Murray, 'On Second Thoughts: the 1974 World Cup Final', *The Guardian* (UK), September 19, 2008, http://www.guardian.co.uk/sport/blog/2008/sep/19/germanyfootball team.holland.
17. Winner, *Brilliant Orange*.
18. van Houtum and van Dam, 'Topophilia or Topoporno?'
19. Croes, 'The Holocaust in the Netherlands and the Rate of Jewish Survival'.
20. Winner, *Brilliant Orange*.
21. van Houtum and van Dam, 'Topophilia or Topoporno?'
22. Winner, *Brilliant Orange*.
23. Rick Joshua, 'Classic Euro Performances – Germany vs. Netherlands, the 1988 Horror in Hamburg', *Bundesliga Fanatic*, June 12, 2012, http://bundesligafanatic.com/classic-euro-performances-germany-vs-netherlands-1988-horror-in-hamburg/.
24. Steve Wilson, 'The Top-10 Worst Spitting Incidents in Football', *The Daily Telegraph* (UK), March 18, 2009, http://www.telegraph.co.uk/sport/football/competitions/premier-league/5010546/Top-10-Worst-spitting-incidents-in-football.html.
25. Jamie Jackson, 'Holland Row Was More about Money than Divide over Racism', *The Guardian* (UK), February 27, 2012, http://www.guardian.co.uk/football/blog/2012/feb/27/holland-euro-96-racism-england.
26. Ernst Bouwes, 'Tribute to the Iceman'. ESPN, July 19, 2006. http://soccernet.espn.go.com/columns/story?id=374050&root=europe&cc=5901.
27. Winner, *Brilliant Orange*.
28. Richard Williams, 'Holland Pay the Penalties', *The Guardian* (UK), June 29, 2000, http://www.guardian.co.uk/football/2000/jun/30/match.sport.
29. Kuper and Szymanksi, *Soccernomics*.
30. Ian Whittell, 'Superb Ireland Pull Off the Impossible Dream', *The Guardian* (UK), September 1, 2001, http://www.guardian.co.uk/football/2001/sep/02/newsstory.sport2.
31. Peter Berlin, 'Euro 2004: Portugal Breezes past Netherlands, 2–1'. *The New York Times*, July 1, 2004, http://www.nytimes.com/2004/07/01/sports/01iht-soccer_ed3_.html.
32. Michael Walker, 'Holland Exit in Acrimony as Four See Red', *The Guardian* (UK), June 25, 2006, http://www.guardian.co.uk/football/2006/jun/26/worldcup2006.match3.
33. Stefan Coerts, 'The Battle of Nuremberg: How Portugal & Netherlands Picked up 16 Cards and Set the Tone for A Very Modern Grudge Match', *Goal.com*, June 16, 2006, http://www.goal.com/en-gb/news/3284/euro-2012/2012/06/17/3180009/the-battle-of-nuremberg-how-portugal-netherlands-picked-up.
34. Roy Collins, 'Guus Hiddink's Experience and Wisdom Wins the Day as Russia beat Holland'. *The Telegraph* (UK), June 22, 2008, http://www.telegraph.co.uk/sport/football/international/2303796/Euro-2008-Guus-Hiddinks-experience-and-wisdom-wins-the-day-as-Russia-beat-Holland.html.
35. Michael Lewis, 'Powerhouse Brazil Bounced from the World Cup by Netherlands, 2–1, in Stunning Upset', *The New York Daily News*, July 2, 2010, http://www.nydailynews.com/sports/brazil-holland-powerhouse-brazil-bounced-world-cup-netherlands-2-1-stunning-upset-article-1.464685#ixzz2HJaM6Tax.
36. Raphael Honigstein, 'Underdog Dutch Nearly Pull Off World Cup Upset in Ugly Fashion', *Sports Illustrated*, July 11, 2010, http://sportsillustrated.cnn.com/2010/writers/raphael_honigstein/07/11/world.cup.final/index.html#ixzz2HJcZa0j5.
37. David Winner, 'After Years Being Total losers, Holland are Entitled to Win Ugly', *The Telegraph* (UK), July 10, 2010, http://www.telegraph.co.uk/sport/football/teams/holland/7882541/World-Cup-final-after-years-being-Total-losers-Holland-are-entitled-to-win-ugly.html.

38. Jeffrey Marcus, 'A Dutch Great Helped Transform Spain's Game'. *The New York Times*, July 10, 2010, http://www.nytimes.com/2010/07/11/sports/soccer/11cupfeature.html?_r=0.
39. Sutherden, 'Laying the Law Down on Ambush Marketing'.
40. Hermes, 'Burnt Orange'.
41. Kassimeris, 'Football and Prejudice in Belgium and the Netherlands'.
42. Rob Preece, 'Polish Thugs Attack English-speaking Fans and Hurl Racist Abuse at Holland Stars as Trouble Flares at the Start of Euro 2012', *The Daily Mail* (UK), June 8, 2012, http://www.dailymail.co.uk/news/article-2156303/Euro-2012-Polish-thugs-hurl-racist-abuse-monkey-chants-Holland-stars-Krakow.html#ixzz2HJtELRcr.
43. Jackson, 'Holland Row was More about Money than Divide Over Racism'.
44. Moller, van Zoonen, and de Roode, 'Accidental Racists'.
45. Spaaj, 'Football Hooliganism in the Netherlands'.
46. Russell and Goldstein, 'Personality Differences between Dutch Football Fans and Non-fans'.
47. Decshesne et al., 'Terror Management and the Vicissitudes of Sports Fan Affiliation'.
48. Kruger and Sanders, 'Jewish Sports in the Netherlands and the Problems of Selective Memory'.
49. Benoit, 'The Politicization of Football'.
50. Ben Findon, 'Feyenrood's Latest Clash with Ajax Peaceful Thanks to Absent Friends', *The Telegraph* (UK), February 2, 2010, http://www.telegraph.co.uk/sport/football/european/7135955/Feyenoords-latest-clash-with-Ajax-peaceful-thanks-to-absent-friends.html,
51. Gerstenfeld. 'Anti-semitism and the Dutch Soccer Fields'.
52. Van Dam, 'Refurbishment, Redevelopment or Relocation?'
53. Brian Straus, 'FIFA Moves Netherlands Up to No. 1'. *The Sporting News*, August 24, 2011, http://aol.sportingnews.com/soccer/story/2011-08-24/fifa-moves-netherlands-up-to-no-1-us-28th-in-rankings.

References

Benoit, Macon. 'The Politicization of Football: The European Game and the Approach to the Second World War'. *Soccer & Society* 9, no. 4 (2008): 532–50.

Croes, Marnix. 'The Holocaust in the Netherlands and the Rate of Jewish Survival'. *Holocaust and Genocide Studies* 20 (2006): 474–99.

van Dam, Frank. 'Refurbishment, Redevelopment or Relocation? The Changing Form and Location of Football Stadiums in the Netherlands'. *Area* 32 (2000): 133–43.

Decshesne, Mark, Jeff Greenberg, Jamie Ardnt, and Jeff Schimel. 'Terror Management and the Vicissitudes of Sports Fan Affiliation: The Effects of Mortality Salience on Optimism and Fan Identification'. *European Journal of Social Psychology* 30 (2000): 813–35.

Gerstenfeld, Manfred. 'Anti-semitism and the Dutch Soccer Fields'. *The Journal for the Study of Antisemitism* 13, no. 3 (January 16, 2012), http://www.jsantisemitism.org/essays/GerstenfeldJSA213(3).pdf.

Hermes, Joke. 'Burnt Orange: Television, Football, and the Representation of Ethnicity'. *Television & New Media* 6, no. 1 (2005): 49–69.

van Hilvoorde, Ivo, Jan Vorstenbosch, and Ignaas Devisch. 'Philosophy of Sport in Belgium and the Netherlands: History and Characteristics'. *Journal of the Philosophy of Sport* 37 (2010): 225–36.

van Houtum, Henk, and Frank Van Dam. 'Topophilia or Topoporno? Patriotic Place Attachment in International Football Derbies'. *The International Social Science Review* 3 (2002): 231–48.

Kassimeris, Christos. 'Football and Prejudice in Belgium and the Netherlands'. *Sport in Society* 12 (2009): 1327–35.

Kruger, Arnd, and Astrid Sanders. 'Jewish Sports in the Netherlands and the Problems of Selective Memory'. *The Journal of Sport History* 26 (1999): 271–86.

Kuper, Simon, and Stefan Szymanksi. *Soccernomics: Why England Loses, Why Germany and Brazil Win, and Why the U.S., Japan, Australia, Turkey and Even Iraq Are Destined to Become the Kings of the World's Most Popular Sport.* Philadelphia, PA: Perseus Books, 2009.

Lechner, Frank. 'Imagined Communities in the Global Game: Soccer and the Development of Dutch National Identity'. *Global Networks* 7 (2007): 193–229.

Merkel, Udo. 'The 1974 and 2006 World Cups in Germany: Commonalities, Continuities and Changes'. *Soccer & Society* 7, no. 1 (2006): 14–28.

Missiroli, Antonio. 'European Football Cultures and their Integration: The 'Short' Twentieth Century'. *Culture, Sport, Society* 5, no. 1 (2002): 1–20.

Moller, Floris, L. van Zoonen, and L. de Roode. 'Accidental Racists: Experiences and Contradictions of Racism in Local Amsterdam Soccer Fan Culture'. *Soccer & Society* 8, nos. 2–3 (2007): 335–50.

Richards, Ted. *Soccer and Philosophy: Beautiful Thoughts on the Beautiful Game.* Chicago, IL: Carus, 2010.

Russell, Gordon, and Jeffrey Goldstein. 'Personality Differences Between Dutch Football Fans and Nonfans'. *The Journal of Social Behavior and Personality* 23 (1995): 199–204.

Spaaj, Ramon. 'Football Hooliganism in the Netherlands: Patterns of Continuity and Change'. *Soccer & Society* 8, nos. 2–3 (2007): 316–34.

Sutherden, Andy. 'Laying the Law Down on Ambush Marketing'. *The Journal of Sponsorship* 4 (2010): 311–13.

Winner, David. *Brilliant Orange: The Neurotic Genius of Dutch Soccer.* Woodstock, NY: Overlook Press, 2008.

Hristo the 'Terrible', Stoitchkov the misunderstood: a biographical sketch of Bulgaria's most famous athlete

Steven Apostolov

Department of Political Science, University of Massachusetts, Lowell, MA, USA

Several scholars, journalists and players have described Hristo Stoitchkov as an obnoxious and racist individual. Based on interviews with him and people who have coached him and evolved as players under his mentorship, this essay will challenge those assumptions. Stoitchkov's achievements at FC Barcelona and in the World Cup are well known to many soccer historians, biographers and aficionados. Therefore, his accomplishments as a player will not be the focus of this piece. Instead, this biographical essay will focus on Stoitchkov's contribution to the development of young players and his coaching career in the US, Spain, South Africa and Bulgaria.

Introduction

The life experience of some soccer players is very similar to the way the life of Vincent Van Gogh unfolded. Manuel Francisco dos Santos, better known in Brazil as Garrincha, practised as destructive lifestyle as the famous Dutch painter. Consequently, Van Gogh and Garrincha both died before they reached middle age. Their respective arts and skills became more appreciated, perhaps even worshiped, after their deaths. Some other soccer players like David Beckham have outshined even the great Pelé, achieving idol status on and off the field worldwide. The Englishman even succeeded in doing what the most famous Brazilian failed to do in the 1970s: popularizing soccer in the country of American football. Finally, talented players such as Paul Gascoigne, who became a star too early, ended their careers in disgrace. Gascoigne fell from his pedestal of soccer star as a result of his difficult and destructive character.

To a certain extent, Hristo Stoitchkov's story is similar to that of Gazza. Both Stoitchkov and Gascoigne reached the peaks of their careers in their early 20s, playing for their national teams. They were embraced by fans of foreign clubs, with Gascoigne inducted into the Rangers Hall of Fame and Stoitchkov worshiped as a Catalan national hero. That status developed as a result of Stoitchkov's fanatical devotion to Catalan nationalism. During the World Cup in 1998, when Bulgaria played Spain, he hung a Catalan flag from the window of his hotel room. It is also documented that he promised to wear a t-shirt underneath his soccer jersey bearing a slogan in favour of Catalan secession from Spain.[1] Ironically, both Stoitchkov and Gascoigne finished their playing days in far-flung locations and were hated by many soccer fans, as well as by the general public, in their respective countries of birth. One of the very few differences between them is their coaching career and contribution to the development of young players. The Englishman's coaching career is rather insignificant, whereas the Bulgarian coached in four different countries and contributed to the development of many young players.

It would be futile to write about Stoitckov's achievements as a player for FC Barcelona and his native Bulgaria. A couple of biographies cover those topics very well.[2] In addition, many journalists have written shorter biographical articles about the famous Bulgarian and have published interviews in respected sports publications. On the other hand, some other important moments of the life of Bulgaria's most popular athlete are almost completely ignored. This essay will focus on them. It will first examine and challenge some of the literature that paints Hristo in dark colours as a racist. It will, after that, analyse his contribution to the development of young players. Finally, it will examine his recent achievements as a coach.

Hristo the 'Terrible'

Some of those who have encountered or interviewed Hristo Stoitchkov would not object to a comparison between him and Ivan the Terrible, as is suggested in the title of this essay. In historical sources, Ivan the Terrible is described as a smart and devout ruler, yet unpredictable, susceptible to rages and prone to episodic outbreaks of mental illness. His rages and inconsistent character have inspired many Russian artists to create paintings, depicting the Tsar as stern and intimidating. One of the most convincing examples is the painting by Victor Vasentsov, completed in 1897 and currently displayed at the Tretyakov Gallery in Moscow. A similar image appears later on in Soviet cinema. The famous movie director, Sergei Eisenstein, might very well have been inspired by those late nineteenth century Russian historical paintings, as his characterization of Ivan IV Vasilyevich appears equally daunting in his trilogy, *Ivan the Terrible*.[3]

Nobody has ever contested Hristo Stoitchkov's talent on the pitch: he won prestigious awards such as the European Golden Ball, the European Golden Shoe, the World Cup Golden Boot and the World Cup Bronze Ball. Very few players, not even many world champions, can boast of so many trophies. Besides his talent, he is also known for his behaviour on and off the field, which is described sometimes as intimidating and ill-tempered. One of the descriptions of an ultimately disastrous interview with Stoitchkov comes from Franklin Foer. After having attempted to interview Stoitchkov in the locker room during the player's last year in the US, when the Bulgarian served as a player and assistant coach for DC United, Foer wrote that,

> Stoitchkov made me too nervous to ask questions in Spanish. He blurts out his phrases and has perfected the tough man's look that seems menacing even in the nude. He wears a permanent coat of stubble over gaunt cheeks. His most innocuous movement looks like wind-ups to a punch.[4]

After a brief introduction of Foer's project, Stoichkov refused to grant him an interview. Frustrated by that, Foer portrayed Stoitchkov in his book as a petulant, intimidating and primitive individual, who requested a fee for the interview.[5]

Sports journalism, particularly in soccer, is sometimes of very low quality in the US. Besides the work of a few gifted sport writers, such as Frank Dell'Apa, Steven Goff and Grant Wahl, most of the soccer reporting in the US over the last couple of decades has been poor and contradictive.[6] This could be attributed largely to the fact that high level of professional soccer was absent from American sports from 1984 until 1996; and broadcasting of Champion's League games was mostly non-existent until the beginning of the last decade. Until 2003, ESPN would only broadcast the semi-finals and the final of the Europe's most prestigious competition. This lack of competitive soccer negatively affected reporting on the game. Annoyed by low-quality reporting, some of the famous European players in MLS have been reluctant to talk to reporters. According to veteran reporter Frank Dell'Apa, it took a few months to gain the confidence of Walter Zenga, while the Italian goalkeeping legend was performing for the New England Revolution.[7] Some players, having been depicted negatively in tabloids, refuse to talk to journalists. Fearing that the author was trying to dig into his personal life, George Best refused to talk to David Tossell, whereas the mighty Pelé requested a fee bigger than the entire budget of the film when he was approached by the directors of one of the greatest documentaries on the New Your Cosmos and the North American Soccer League. The resulting works, *Playing for Uncle Sam: The Brit's Story of the North American Soccer League,*[8] and *Once in a Lifetime: the Extraordinary Story of the New York Cosmos,*[9] could have been much better had Best and Pelé agreed to participate without getting paid exorbitantly.

It is not unusual for soccer players to request fees if interviews are not closely related to a particular game after which they are interviewed. The legendary Diego Maradona became notorious for requesting the most outrageous fees, which only journalists with a solid financial backing could afford. Foer's interview with Stoitchkov turned disastrous because of a few factors. First, the interviewer and interviewee communicated in a foreign language; it is, therefore, highly possible that a miscommunication occurred and that the true intention of the interviewer – notably on the question of Catalan nationalism – was lost in translation. Second, some athletes suspect interviewers of trying to learn facts about their lives in order to publish 'unauthorized' books; Grant Wahl described such a case involving David Beckham. It is not quite clear why Stoitchkov refused to grant an interview to Foer. Whatever the reason was, the author went overboard and way off topic when he dedicated three pages to Stoitchkov's ill temper in a twenty-page chapter on Catalan nationalism.

Journalists were not the only actors who dedicated space to Hristo Stoitchkov in their books. Some scholars did too. Andrey Markovits, who attempted to provide an explanation of why professional soccer in the US never caught fire, reserved in his book a long chapter focussed on the World Cup of 1994. In that chapter, among other thoughts – analytical and descriptive – he paints Stoitchkov in dark colours. 'The gruff Hristo Stoitchkov of Bulgaria whose wonderfully skilled play on the field was matched only by his ugly racism and excessive arrogance', was Markovits's description of the player.[10] Although most of Markovits's book is well documented, this statement is not supported by any explanation or quotation.

Other well-respected scholars have written about Stoitchkov, too. Interestingly, their descriptions of Stoitchkov are not that much different than those of Foer and Markovits. In his thought-provoking book on black players in the French national team and the racism that they have experienced during their careers, Laurent Dubois evokes an incident that occurred between Stoitchkov and Marcel Desailly.[11] In a fiercely disputed match between France and Bulgaria during the European Championship of 1996, the tension between Stoitchkov and Desailly built from the time the referee blew his whistle to start the game. In the opening minutes of the game, Stoitchkov stole a poor pass from the then-young midfielder Zinedine Zidane and was passing Marcel Desailly to be one-on-one with the French goalkeeper Bernard Lama. Desailly tripped him. It was a brutal foul for which the Frenchman was booked. As a result of the Frenchman's rough play, a *New York Times* correspondent compared Desailly to a 'New York cop walking the beat and working on Stoitchkov'.[12] The players clashed again later in the match and were separated by the English referee. They then clashed again and were almost involved in a brawl, only to be separated by their teammates. After the game, Desailly accused Stoitchkov of making racist comments, including, 'shitty country, shitty blacks, shitty skin'.[13] Desailly went further with his accusations, claiming that after the French scored their first goal Stoichkov approached him and said, 'hey, Desailly, do you know that little kids are dying of hunger in your country?'.[14] Kids are not dying of hunger in France. And had Stoitchov said this, he would have certainly aimed the insult at Desailly's native Ghana. But did the Bulgarian even know at that time that Desailly was born in Ghana?

Such accusations of racism are very serious. But a key issue remains unresolved: how did Desailly and Stoitchkov communicate? At that time, the Bulgarian would have only had an intermediate knowledge of spoken Spanish from his first spell with FC Barcelona, whereas in addition to his French, Desailly was most likely still limited to basic conversational Italian. Both players would learn English later on, while playing and coaching in England, the United States and South Africa. During the European Championship in 1996, though, it is highly unlikely that they were able to communicate coherently in any language that they fluently spoke in common. Dubois admitted during a talk based on his book that his sources were limited to interviews with Deasilly and to the player's autobiography. The author acknowledged that he should have enquired about additional details of this incident to clarify it better in his book.[15]

Stoitchkov's own autobiography sheds more light on the incident. Curiously, in his book, Stoitchkov speaks very highly of Desailly. The book was actually published shortly before the infamous 1996 clash occurred. In his book, Stoitchkov discusses the World Cup qualifier between France and Bulgaria in 1993. He praised Desailly for his clean play and audacity. According to Stoitchkov, during that game,

> the Frenchman prevented me from touching the ball without even kicking me or pushing me once throughout the entire 90 minutes ... after the game I took the ball and kissed it, because I could not see much of it during the game.[16]

Stoitchkov also praised Desailly for his role in defeating FC Barcelona as an AC Milan player during the 1994 UEFA Champions League Final.[17] Since he refers to him as a Frenchman, Stoitchkov likely did not know anything about Desailly's Ghanean origins and place of birth. Desailly's accusation of Stoichkov's alleged comment on kids dying of hunger in Ghana must have been either resulted from a misunderstanding or a misinterpretation. And one thing is certain: if Stoichkov had racial prejudices, he would never have spoken so highly of Desailly, and other black players, in his autobiography; also, he would have never coached either in South Africa, where most of the soccer players are black, nor mentored, as we shall see later on, young African-American players.

What really happened in the 1996 game, and why were the French so motivated to deliver such a brutal performance? According to a witness, who stood not too far away from the quarrel between Stoitchkov and Desailly, Stoitchkov did insult the Frenchman. But it was with a profanity that had nothing to do with a racial slur, and it was uttered in Bulgarian. Desailly, who does not speak Bulgarian, obviously could not have understood it.

> It was the type of insult for which a player in a junior league will have had his ear pulled by his father ... insults which professionals hear on a regular basis on the field and don't even pay attention to them, the witness said.[18]

The clash between Desailly and Stoitchkov almost certainly originated from the World Cup qualifier of 1993. Bulgaria defeated France with a last-minute goal by Emil Kostadinov, who sneaked between Desailly's partners in defence, Laurent Blanc and Didier Deschamps. The loss was not Desailly's fault: he played a perfect game, as Stoitchkov documented in his autobiography. Desailly's dream of playing in the World Cup as young player turned into a nightmare for another five years. The date of the game – November 17, 1993 – is still dark in the memories of a lot of French players and soccer aficionados. It signalled the end of the international careers of many French stars, such as Eric Cantona, Jean-Pierre Papin and David Ginola, and it is remembered by French fans as *le coup bulgare*. After the defeat of the French national team and the team's failure to qualify for the World Cup in the United States, national team players became a regular target of the daily puppet-satire show *Les Guignols de l'Info*. Some of the jokes were indeed quite demeaning. The iconic French television commentator, Thierry Roland, was so enraged by France's defeat during that World Cup qualifier that he never missed an opportunity after that game to issue derogatory statements about Bulgaria and its players. In 1996, during a game between FC Girondins de Bordeaux and FC Bayern Munich, Emil Kostadinov injured the young French defender Bixente Lizarazu. The accident was unfortunate, and Kostadinov certainly did not attempt to hurt Lizarazu. The referee did not even caution the Bayern Munich striker. Lizarazu was taken out on a stretcher and ended up in a hospital, whereas the Bulgarian scored one of the three goals that earned his German team the second-most respected European title in professional soccer at the time. Nevertheless, Thierry Roland called Kostadinov on French national television *un sal mec*, which literally means dirty bastard. For similar rants, journalist and commentators around the world have been sanctioned or dismissed. That was not the case for this one. Even the left-wing newspaper *Liberation*, which seldom covers any sporting events, published a derogatory article after Stoitchkov was awarded the most prestigious individual trophy in soccer – *le ballon d'or*.[19]

The bitter defeat of 1993 was taken way too seriously by the very few players remaining on the 1996 team. Aimé Jaquet, who experienced the defeat on the bench as an assistant coach, over-motivated his young players in 1996 as coach. 'From the lusty singing of *La Marseillaise* beforehand to the crunching foul Desailly inflicted on Stoitchkov in the third minute, it was clear that they were highly motivated', confirmed Guy Hodgson in *The Independent*.[20] Mocked in some shows on television, over-motivated in the locker room by his coach, brutal on the field and still haunted by his shattered American World Cup dream, Desailly did not hesitate to try to totally destroy his adversary by accusing him of racial abuse. And Stoitchkov was the perfect scapegoat; appearing stern and intimidating on television, he had a reputation of injuring referees, fighting with players and insulting journalists. There have been quite a few ill-tempered athletes like that in other sports, with John McEnroe being the perfect example in tennis. Being ill-mannered, however, does not automatically mean being racist. The following part of the essay will analyse Stoitchkov's contribution to the development of young players, among them some African-Americans, as well as the achievements of his coaching career in the US, Spain, South Africa and most recently in Bulgaria.

Stoitchkov the misunderstood

After the peak of his career with FC Barcelona and brief stints at Parma FC in Italy, Al Nassr FC in Saudi Arabia and Kashiwa Reysol in Japan, Stoitchkov hung up his boots in the US in 2003. His stay in the US was short but interesting: from 2000 until 2002, he spent two seasons with the Chicago Fire, followed in 2003 by his last season, which he spent as a playing assistant coach with DC United. During these three years, Stoitchkov played almost 70 games and scored more than 20 goals. He enjoyed his stay in the US and was impressed by the headway the young professional league was making and especially by the growth of youth soccer and the abundance of talented youngsters.[21] He contributed to the development of many young US players and also started his coaching career there.

As opposed to previous attempts to establish professional soccer in the US, notably Pelé's NASL of the 1970s, MLS teams in the mid-2000s did not exclusively rely on the import of expensive foreign internationals. Most of the players were young, college-educated Americans. Of course, some famous internationals were hired to buttress the quality of play, but their numbers were not as significant as in the old NASL. Besides Stoitchkov, Columbia's Carlos Valderrama, Mexico's Jorge Campos, Germany's Lothar Matthäus, Italy's Roberto Donadoni and France's Youri Djorkaeff played in the league. Some players like Valderrama had solid performances. Others, like Campos, Matthäus, Donadoni and Djorkaeff, were not convincing at all. In a similar fashion as in the 1970s, some ageing professionals came to the US to collect a few extra pay cheques before retirement. In 1998, after a few games with the Chicago Fire, Campos did not hesitate to 'desert' his American team for a better salary with a Mexican professional team. Matthäus was notorious for his extravagant demands for expensive apartments and cars during his final year as a professional player in New York. The loyalty of Djorkaeff seemed questionable when he took a break during MLS's active season, citing personal problems, but was seen on television in Germany during the World Cup in attendance of some of France's games. Most of these renowned internationals and World Cup champions stayed for a short period of time in MLS. Their role in the development of young professional players was insignificant. Stoitchkov, on the other hand, positively affected the league not only with his solid play and loyalty but also with his contribution to the development of young American players.

During his two-year spell with the Chicago Fire, Stoitchkov mentored several youngsters, including DaMarcus Beasley, Josh Wolff and Dema Kovalenko. After a couple of years playing alongside the Bulgarian veteran, most of these players impressed the scouts of foreign teams and were able to transfer overseas. Josh Wolff played for a while for TSV 1860 München, whereas Dema Kovalenko had stints with FC St. Pauli in Germany and FC Matalurgh Zaporizhya in Ukraine. Without any doubt, DaMarcus Beasley is Stoitckov's most successful protégé. By the age of 22, he was already a member of the US national team and a player for PSV Eindhoven. In 2004, The Dutch team enticed him for $2.5 million, a record transfer fee at the time for an American player. The young American player had the difficult task of replacing Arjen Robben, who had signed with Chelsea FC. Beasley excelled at his Dutch team: his record of goals scored in Europe's most prestigious club competition, the UEFA's Champions League, has not yet been matched by any other American player. From 2007 until 2011, Beasley played for other European power-houses, such as Manchester City, Glasgow Rangers and Hanover 96.

In an interview, Beasley stated that Stoitchkov was the most emblematic player for his development as a young professional. At the time of the interview, Beasley was still playing for the Chicago Fire, whereas Stoitchkov was already a playing assistant coach of DC United.

> Hristo is a very good friend of mine and we still talk on the phone very often. He was my mentor in Chicago. Every time before an important game, he would invite me to stay at his place with his family. He has a couple of spare rooms for friends.

The interview finished with a statement that if one day Beasley accomplishes an out-standing professional career it would be 'most definitely thanks to Hristo'.[22] Such a strong statement, given by a young African-American player, is very interesting in two ways: first, it shows the friendship between the veteran and the youngster, and the latter's deep gratitude; second, it makes Marcel Desailly's earlier accusation of racial abuse even more doubtful. If Stoitchkov were a racist, he would have never befriended an African-American youngster; he would have never mentored him or invited him to his home to meet his family.

Stoitchkov started his coaching career while mentoring young players in the US. As a playing assistant coach with DC United, he was able to reach the semi-final of the US Open Cup. The team was also able to end up an embarrassing four-year absence from the MLS Cup play-offs. 'Hristo is a motivator, the type of player that anybody would like to have in his team', said Ray Hudson, head coach of DC United at the time.[23] The team that was built by Ray Hudson, assisted by Hristo Stoitch-kov, captured the MLS Cup the following year. During his first tenure as a head coach, between 2004 and 2007, Stoitchkov failed to qualify his native Bulgaria for the World Cup in 2006 and started a poor campaign for the 2008 European Championship qualifiers. Consequently, he resigned. His short stint as a coach at Celta Vigo turned out to be disappointing too: the team was relegated from *La Liga* to the second division of Spanish professional soccer. His next coaching job brought him to South Africa's Mamelodi Sundowns FC, where he replaced the renowned French manager, Henry Michel. Stoitchkov was able to bring the team up from the mid-table in the South African Premier League to a remarkable second place, only a point behind the 2010 champions, SuperSport United. Since 2012, he has been coaching PFC Litex Lovetch of Bulgaria's top flight professional soccer league.

Stoitchkov still needs to prove himself as a coach. His short coaching career is interesting and indeed contradictive. He failed as a coach twice, and was arguably successful as many times. With very few exceptions, most coaches attain the level of coaching a national team after several years of success at the helms of professional teams. It was perhaps a little bit too quick and too ambitious for Stoitchkov to skip those stages and go straight to coaching at national level. Ironically, some proven coaches, notably the famous Johan Cruyff, never coached at a national level. As a national team coach, Stoitchkov was crippled by the shrinking number of top-level Bulgarian professional players. Even Stoitchkov's predecessor, Plamen Markov, was obliged to deal with that shortage by selecting players who were naturalized Yugoslavs, among them Predrag Pazin, Zoran Jankovic and Zlatomir Zagorcic. Stoitchkov tried in his own way to solidify the national team by selecting a naturalized Brazilian, Lucio Wagner. Interestingly, Lucio Wagner is black and if Stoitchkov had any racial prejudices, as previously asserted by Marcel Desailly and some scholars and journalists, he would have never called up a black player into the Bulgarian national team. As a result of the relative shortage of Bulgarian professionals playing at top-level European clubs and the mediocre performance of the domestic league, which produces very few gifted players, the task to coach the Bulgarian national team would be challenging even for specialists with the most solid credentials. In 2007, Stoitchkov was hired after the mid-season break to rescue Celta Vigo from relegation in Spain. Stoitchkov and his team finished 18th and barely missed their goal of staying in *La Liga*. Stoitchkov could have probably achieved that goal had he coached the team throughout the whole season.

While his tenures at Celta Vigo and the Bulgarian national team are considered as failed missions by many, and although he drew the anger of some fans, the supporters and players of Mamelodi Sundowns FC embraced him and certainly did not demand his resignation after the team finished a point behind the winners of the South African Premier League in 2010. The previous year, the team had fallen with Henry Michel to a mediocre ninth rank in the 16-team league. The deep racial division in sports in South Africa is widely acknowledged. Rugby is the favourite sport of the white minority, whereas more than 90% of all players and followers of soccer are black. Once again, if Stoitchkov was bothered by any racial prejudices, he would have never coached soccer in South Africa. As far as his tenure of PFC Litex Lovetch is concerned, it is still too early to judge, as he has not yet completed a whole season at the helm of the team. He was given the job after the winter break of 2012.

With very few exceptions, notably the famous Brazilian, Socrates Brasileiro Sampaio de Souza Vieira de Oliveira, and some American players, soccer players are seldom college educated. Stoitchkov has never pretended to be well educated. Like most Bulgarians of his generation, he earned a high school degree and was trained at a technical school to be an electrician. He states in his autobiography that he enjoyed being an electrician and would have practised that trade had his athletic career failed.[24] Like so many other soccer players, he is not particularly outspoken when giving interviews. He has often been involved in verbal conflicts with journalists, especially during his coaching career. As a result of that, he was often demonized in foreign as well as in domestic media outlets. In 2011, he was awarded an honorary doctoral degree by the University of Plovdiv for his financial support of the institution. Called Doctor Stoitchkov by the press, he handled the sarcasm of the journalists at the event poorly, which resulted in a misunderstanding, followed by misinterpretations and many complaints in the Bulgarian media.[25] In a similar fashion as in England, where the journalists of some tabloids are vicious and would do anything to misinterpret a quote or an act by some player, some Bulgarian journalists take advantage of Soitchkov's stern and intimidating look, sometimes stubborn behaviour and difficulties in effectively communicating with the press. He was obviously not the friendliest player on the soccer pitch and is not the most pleasant on the coaching bench. But he was often misunderstood, and some of his acts were misinterpreted. One the other hand, his real contributions to the development of the game and his legacy have thus far been underestimated at best or ignored at worst.

Conclusion

Most soccer legends, after they retire, still remain involved in soccer as ambassadors of the game, professional team administrators or television analysts. Such is the case for Pelé, Eusebio, Karl–Heinz Rummenigge, Gary Lineker and Peter Schmeichel. They usually appear before kick-offs of international tournaments, assist non-profit organizations for charitable causes or work as commentators. Some other famous players, such as Eric Cantona and Vinnie Jones, became actors after they hung up the boots. There are even a couple of politicians like George Weah.

Few are the legendary soccer players who have achieved impressive careers as coaches. Some famous players, like Maradona, Matthaus, Ruud Gullit and Roberto Donadoni, have so far had unimpressive, if not disastrous, coaching careers. There are a few exceptional players, however, who shined as coaches as well. Among them are Franz Beckenbauer, one of the two people in the world who has won the World Cup as both player and coach. Johan Cruyff never raised the World Cup trophy; in fact, it was Keizer Franz who deprived him of the ultimate joy of being at the top of world soccer. But the Dutchman's accomplishments at the helm of FC Barcelona are very much in the history books.

It was Johan Cruyff who discovered Stoitchkov and enticed him to play in his dream team. Loved by many and hated by some, Stoitchkov was already an established professional in PFC CSKA Sofia. It was, however, the transfer to FC Barcelona that elevated him to stardom and fame. Cruyff served, without any doubt, as a role model to Stoitchkov for his development as a player, and later on as a coach. As players, the Dutch mentor and his Bulgarian protégé are almost even in their legacies. They were both able to capture some of the most prestigious trophies with their professional teams. With the colours of their national teams, they were able to reach respectively a final and a semi final of the World Cup. The Dutchman and the Bulgarian have discovered many young and talented players and helped them improve as professionals. Cruyff achieved in almost 10 years of coaching what most coaches will never achieve in a lifetime. In terms of his coaching career, however, Stoitchkov hasn't been able so far to get close to the results of his mentor. Will he ever be able to achieve the same results as a coach as he did as a player and become one of the very few legendary players who have also excelled as coaches? It's only possible to speculate at this stage. But if one day he reaches that level, it will definitely help him to redeem the image of Hristo the 'Terrible', Stoitchkov the misunderstood, and simply to be remembered as Bulgaria's most popular athlete.

Notes

1. Foer, *How Soccer Explains the World*, 208.
2. Стоичков, *Сто на Сто Стоичков, Автобиорафия* [Stoitchkov, *Hundred Percent Stoitchkov, an Autobiography*].
3. *Ivan the Terrible*, directed by Sergei Eisenstein (Moscow: Mosfilm, 1944).
4. Foer, *How Soccer Explains the World*, 210.
5. Ibid., 210–1.
6. Wahl, *The Beckham's Experiment*, 18–9 and 42–3.
7. Frank Dell'Apa (former journalist from *The Boston Globe* and currently Chief Editor of the website of beIN Sport USA), in discussion with the author, November 14, 2011.
8. Tossell, *Playing for Uncle Sam*.
9. *Once in a Lifetime: The Extraordinary Story of the New York Cosmos*, directed by Paul Crowder (Los Angeles: Miramax, 2006).

10. Markovits and Hellerman, *Offside*, 223.
11. Dubois, *Soccer Empire*.
12. Ian Thomsen, 'French Take their Revenge on Bulgaria', *The New York Times*, June 19, 1996.
13. Dubois, *Soccer Empire*, 97.
14. Ibid., 99–100. Marcel Dessaily as quoted by Laurent Dubois.
15. Laurent Dubois (Professor of Romance Studies and History, Duke University), in discussion with the author, Skype conference organized by *The Football Scholars Forum*, University of Michigan, November 16, 2010.
16. Stoitchkov, *Hundred Percent Stoitchkov, an Autobiography*, 127.
17. Ibid., 145.
18. Ivo Georgiev (Former player form Debreceni VSC, PCF Spartak Varna, and the Bulgarian National Team), in Discussion with the author via Skype, January 26, 2013. Ivo Georgiev was a substitute player for the Bulgarian national team. He was a few yards away from the accident and observed and heard everything clearly.
19. Sergio Mondelo, 'Hristo Stoitchkov, ballon d'or et caractère de cochon' [Hristo Stoitchkov, golden ball and a character of a pig], *Libération*, December 20, 1994.
20. Guy Hodgson, 'France Banish the Ghost of Bulgaria to Reach the Last Eight', *The Independent*, June 19, 1996.
21. Hristo Stoitchkov (Former player from FC Barcelona and the Bulgarian national team, at the time of the interview player for the Chicago Fire), in discussion with the author, September 26, 2002a; in discussion with the author, October 2, 2002b.
22. DaMarcus Beasly (Former player from the Chicago Fire, PSV Eindhoven, Manchester City, Glasgow Rangers, Hanover 96; and, currently playing for Puebla FC), in discussion with the author, May 17, 2003.
23. Ray Hudson (Former player from Newcastle United FC and Ft. Lauderdale Strikers [NASL]; former coach of Miami Fusion [MLS] and DC United [MLS]; and currently play-by-play analyst for beIN Sport USA), in discussion with the author, March 23, 2011.
24. Stoitchkov, *Hundred Percent Stoitchkov, an Autobiography*, 15.
25. Mitko Lishev, 'Христо Стоичков стана Доктор хонорис кауза на Пловдивския университет [Hristo Stoitchkov awarded a doctoral degree by the University of Plovdiv]', *Darik News*, www.dariknews.bg (accessed March 1, 2013).

References

Dubois, Laurent. *Soccer Empire: The World Cup and the Future of France*. Berkeley: University of California Press, 2010.
Foer, Franklin. *How Soccer Explains the World: An Unlikely Theory of Globalization*. New York: Harper Collins, 2004.
Markovits, Adnrey, and Steven Hellerman. *Offside: Soccer and American Exceptionalism*. Princeton, NJ: Princeton University Press, 2001.
Стоичков, Христо. *Сто на Сто Стоичков, Автобиорафия*. София: Труд, 1995 [Stoitchkov, Hristo. Hundred Percent Stoitchkov, an Autobiography. Sofia: Trud, 1995].
Tossell, David. *Playing for Uncle Sam: The Brit's Story of the North American Soccer League*. Edinburg: Mainstream, 2003.
Wahl, Grant. *The Beckham's Experiment: How the World's Most Famous Athlete Tried to Conquer America*. New York: Crown Publishing Group, 2009.

David Beckham's re-invention of the winger

Søren Frank

Institute for the Study of Culture, Comparative Literature, University of Southern Denmark, Odense, Denmark

It seems David Beckham is destined to be judged more according to his celebrity status than to his soccer skills. Even as a soccer player occupying one of the most mythic positions on the pitch, the winger, Beckham has constantly fallen short to the inevitable (but also unfair) comparisons with Cristiano Ronaldo, Ryan Giggs, Luis Figo and even earlier prototypes such as George Best or Raymond Kopa, whose basic qualities consisted in dribbling, speed and goal line crosses. The problem with these comparisons is that Beckham, at the outset, is categorized as a winger when he in fact was, initially, a central midfielder. However, because Beckham brings along some of the virtues as a central midfielder – passing skills and combative tackling – when he migrates from the centre of the field to the right, he is able to invent a completely new type of winger. Overall speaking, Beckham fuses a Bergsonian epic quality of *durée* and accumulating presence with a Nietzschean lyric quality of unexpectedness and abruptness. More specifically, what sets Beckham apart and secures him a seat in the Pantheon of soccer's great innovators are timing ('early on and unexpectedly'), sense of spacing ('halfway') and the fusion of Euclid and Einstein ('curled crosses with extreme precision').

Introduction

It has almost turned into a cliché and sedimented into a timeless Truth in Soccer's Collective Memory: Mention the name David Beckham and you immediately come to think of phenomena such as global brand, off-field celebrity and political correctness, of metrosexuality, Galácticos and Galaxy. Los Angeles? Yes, that's it. Soccer player? Not really. One of the game's all time greatest? Certainly not. Hence, David Beckham as an icon, a legend, has – on the face of it – more to do with society than soccer. However, if we begin to actually think critically about this cliché and to think seriously about David Beckham's contribution to the game of soccer, we soon realize that behind, or, rather, under the cliché – buried under all these layers of LA glimmer and Parisian glitter – was a player who (almost by sheer coincidence) ended up re-inventing one of soccer's most mythical positions, the winger, thus reserving a seat for himself in the Pantheon of Soccer together with the likes of other innovators such as Mano Garrincha, Johan Cruyff and Andrea Pirlo. This presumption is also why this essay will devote itself more to soccer than society, that is, more to David Beckham as a soccer legend than to David Beckham as a society icon – without totally neglecting the latter dimension, though.

David Beckham's name is inextricably linked with two things when it comes to soccer abilities: his goal-assisting crosses and his goals from set pieces. The question then is if these characteristics are weighty or spectacular enough to earn him such high praise that, as I have implied, will be heaped upon him in this essay. But before we venture into the entertainment scene, let alone soccer tactics, player attributes and traditions of the winger, let us get a few facts about Beckham's career sorted out. At the end of the 1998/1999 season, which must be categorized as the best season in his career, David Beckham ended up second on FIFA's World Player of the Year list, superseded only by Rivaldo, FC Barcelona's Brazilian magician (Beckham emulated this achievement two years later when the only person to beat him was Luis Figo, his future team mate at the Santiago Bernabéu in Madrid). In 55 matches for Manchester United during that legendary Treble-winning season, Beckham scored nine goals and, more impressively, he delivered the assisting passes to 23 goals, primarily through his precise, yet curling crosses from the right wing and his dangerous corner kicks. Speaking of assists, he is currently third in the Premier League's all-time assist provider chart with 152 assists in 265 appearances, more than one goal-decisive pass in every two matches.[1] From his debut in 1992 until 2003, he played 394 matches and scored 85 goals for Manchester United, and he won six Championships, two FA Cups, one Champions League and one Intercontinental Cup during that period. In Real Madrid, LA Galaxy, AC Milan and Paris Saint Germain, Beckham continued to collect silverware, although not with the same frequency as at Old Trafford, winning one Championship with both Real Madrid, LA Galaxy and PSG.

Iconic society celebrity

The starting point of this essay, its presupposition, is the fundamental belief that Beckham, despite his impressive statistical track record, has not always received the credit he deserves as a soccer player. But why is that? One obvious reason is that his image and iconic celebrity status have overshadowed his soccer qualities – something which is no doubt partly self-inflicted and very much a consequence of his marriage with Victoria 'Posh' Adams from Spice Girls. Sir Alex Ferguson, who indeed was aware of the potentially detrimental consequences of Beckham's transformation through his marriage from shy and one-dimensionally focused soccer player to still shy, yet many-headed and many-masked post-modern fashion icon, once remarked: 'He was never a problem until he got married. He used to go into work with the academy coaches at night time, he was a fantastic young lad. Getting married into that entertainment scene was a difficult thing – from that moment, his life was never going to be the same. He is such a big celebrity, football is only a small part. The big part is his persona'.[2] Soccer is a team sport, and it is widely known how much emphasis Alex Ferguson puts on collectivism, solidarity and team spirit. In his eyes, Beckham neglected these values by elevating his persona, his I and his individuality above the club and the team.

However, Ferguson's public critique of Beckham's lifestyle – a critique that culminated in the infamous dressing room bust-up, the 'freak accident' involving a flying boot and a cut above one eye, after United's FA Cup defeat at Old Trafford to Arsenal on 15 February 2003, and the subsequent transfer of Beckham to Real Madrid – was actually preceded by someone from outside the club. In 1998, Glenn Hoddle, the England manager at the time, created quite a furore (at least for Britons) by leaving Beckham out of his team in England's first match against Tunisia at the World Cup in France:

David was not focused coming into the tournament – he was vague – and maybe his club need to look at that further. I had a chat with him and he's more focused now but I needed to have words before that sank in. I love him to bits – after all, I brought him in. But he's got to understand that football comes first. His focus was not there but now he understands what I'm looking for.[3]

One of the fiercest critics of Hoddle's decision was in fact Ferguson (other Manchester United people such as Bobby Charlton and Teddy Sheringham also expressed their support to Beckham in what could easily be called a club-versus-country struggle), but Hoddle's explanation for overlooking Beckham in his starting 11 (actually, he did not even feature as a substitute in the game) resonates closely with Ferguson's own later critique and may thus have converged with what Ferguson very early on, perhaps immediately after Beckham's involvement with 'Posh', felt inwardly, but wasn't yet at the time prepared to express outwardly (his determination to protect and never criticize his own players in media and in public is well known).

Of course, Hoddle's intuition concerning Beckham's mental condition, the player's difficulties in uniting his new many-dimensional life as a celebrity with his old much more one-dimensional life as a soccer player, proved prophetic. In the match against Argentina, the pressure got to Beckham and he retaliated against Diego Simeone and was (correctly, let us be clear about that) shown the red card by Kim Milton Nielsen. Inside Old Trafford, the reaction was to rally round their superstar, since the manager, the coaches and the directors knew they were in possession of a truly unique talent: 'He has an ability which isn't anywhere else in the team. His passing and ability to score goals, the quality of his crossing if he plays on the right side. You're looking at one of the rare players in the world. He's got fantastic ability'.[4] The words came from Bobby Charlton. Beckham's manager took another angle which had less to do with soccer quality and more to do with club ethos:

We will be looking after the player and we will protect him, because that is the way Manchester United behave. We are a great club and we will not be giving into mob rule. I admit there are sound reasons for thinking it would make sense for David to go and play abroad, but that would be the easy way out. In any case, he doesn't want to leave Old Trafford. He's Manchester United through and through.[5]

But this was back in 1998. As we have already seen, in terms of Beckham's relationship with his manager, things were very different in the summer of 2003. Beckham was still, and has been ever since, Manchester United through and through, but Alex Ferguson felt otherwise.

Beckham's escalating media exposure toward the end of his Old Trafford career made even the George Best of the late 60s and early 70s look like a media shy hermit, and one of the main reasons behind Alex Ferguson's and Manchester United's decision to sell Beckham was undoubtedly that he, as an individual brand, rivalled the brand of the club just as his many obligations outside the world of soccer resulted in disturbing reverberations in the United locker room – a room that has been, historically speaking, notoriously sealed off from the outside world of media and fans by Alex Ferguson.

There are many similarities between the George Best of around 1970 and the David Beckham of around 2000, but obvious differences also come to mind. They both inscribe themselves in the long line of players who have contributed to make Manchester United a club associated not only with free-flowing attacking soccer, vibrant youth and magical European nights, but also with glamour. Billy Meredith, who played for United between 1906 and 1921, was perhaps the first player in the history of the club who had this celebrity aura about him, and the Busby Babes were also part of this association between Manchester United and stardust. In recent years, Cristiano Ronaldo was undoubtedly the heir to Best and Beckham.

It is important to acknowledge, though, as Stephen Wagg has done it, that the difference between the Busby Babes of the 1950s and the George Best of the 1960s was as big a difference as the one between social realism and pop art.[6] When the Busby Babes died in the Munich Air Crash on 6 February 1958, they still had one leg in the old world of tradition, working class loyalty and dance hall evenings, while their other leg was only beginning to feel the new ground of the modern world. But with George Best, we fully enter the world of modernity, individualism and rock'n'roll. If Eddie Colman and David Pegg were dancing to Bill Haley and His Comets' 'Rock Around the Clock', George Best was showing (alarmingly) increasing 'sympathies for the devil' in the late 1960s–early 1970s.

The story of George Best is the story of a timid and not particularly articulate boy from Belfast, who was transformed into 'Georgie', the pop-culture icon and confident city slicker. It is the story of how the fragile and exceptionally talented apprentice was transformed into the strong but fiery-tempered professional. It is the story of how Mrs Fullaway's boarding house and Manchester's public transport were replaced with an endless series of mink-clad models, architect-designed villa and a white Jaguar. It is also the story of how snooker evenings in the company of David Sadler were turned into visits to nightclubs in the company of gorgeous women. And it is the story of how abstinence is transformed into addiction.

It was precisely the urge for alcohol and the flashlights of fame that began to eclipse Best's soccer radiance in the late 1960s and early 1970s. And the flashlights of the 60s were undeniably sharper and more dazzling than the one's pointed at the Busby Babes in the 50s. Their fame was characterized by a necessary, but at the same time also minimal distance to the common people. Some of them still lived at boarding houses or at home with their parents, and they earned no more than the ordinary skilled worker. When George Best made his debut for Manchester United in 1963, the maximum wage in English football had been abolished two years earlier. The top footballers of the mid 1960s inevitably, therefore, had quite a different status to those from an earlier decade.

During the 1960s, Best gained an image of being both arrogant and extravagant, but he was basically just a young and popular guy and based on lower middle-class standards, he was also rich. However, it was only because it was just a few years since footballers and workers earned the same money that Best and some of his contemporaries seemed so wealthy and swashbuckling. Best's extravagance was thus a relative phenomenon and partly the result of the time in which he lived. His decadent lifestyle, which began to escalate in the early 1970s, was also partly the result of the new times characterized by the dialectics between more powerful flashlights and the abolishment of the wage limit. This dialectics certainly created superstars but it also created victims. Of course these external circumstances do not explain the entire reason for Georgie's fall, but they are essential for understanding the contrast between the Busby's Babes and Busby's Best.

David Beckham stepped unto this carousel of glamour, celebrity status and global imaging inaugurated by George Best, and he made it accelerate into hitherto unknown velocities and dimensions. However, if Best and Beckham both are associated with fashion, fame and pop culture, Beckham managed to replace Best's 'pussy galore' with 'wife-in-*singularis*' (more or less, at least) and Best's alcohol with Adidas. Beckham was able to stay afloat, perhaps because he shares with Victoria the condition of being famous beyond ordinary fame and thus they have supported each other and been mutually aware of what pitfalls stardom entails. In that sense, Beckham epitomized the postmodern soccer player's ability (and right) to migrate from club to club carrying along with him his image, his brand and the whole circus of legal advisors, agents, financial experts and family, all of whom are also part and parcel of the everyday life of today's superstars.

Legendary soccer player?

However, another and even better explanation (better because soccer related) of the lack of credit is that Beckham the soccer player has often been judged on completely wrong premises. This is what the remaining part of this essay will be about: wrong premises and Beckham's exceptional soccer attributes which made it possible for him to re-invent the mythic position of the winger. In Manchester United, it was first and foremost the perhaps inevitable, but essentially unfair and deeply problematic comparison with Ryan Giggs that contributed to veil Beckham's unique qualities (qualities that were, admittedly, recognized in for example the FIFA awards, but which were nevertheless always subject to being unfavourably compared with the qualities of the traditional winger), but also the comparisons with his predecessor Andrei Kanchelskis and his successor Cristiano Ronaldo have played a part in this. In Real Madrid, it was primarily the analogies to Luis Figo that contributed to the discrediting of Beckham.

The main problem is that Beckham, at the outset, is categorized as a winger and not a midfielder, and this makes us blind to what novelty Beckham actually brings to the outside right, since we automatically judge him in relation to what we would normally expect from a traditional wide player. The comparisons with Giggs, Kanchelskis or Ronaldo – or with any other more straightforward winger in the history of Manchester United (Billy Meredith, David Pegg, Nani) or in the history of soccer in general for that matter (Stanley Matthews, Raymond Kopa, Marc Overmars) – prevent an appreciation of Beckham's distinctive contribution to the story of soccer's great innovators, and, what is more, the comparisons never tilt in his favour as they constantly point to his shortages in relation to these players. Giggs is elevated to the platonic ideal of a winger, and in comparison to this idea of 'The Winger' Beckham is merely a simulacrum, a false pretender.

But which attributes is it, then, that we associate with 'The Winger'? In the following discussion, I will attempt to characterize some of the wingers already mentioned in this essay through what I believe to be the most significant concepts defining them, and I will do so in order to reach some sort of overall qualitative picture of the typical winger. During the first decades of the twentieth century, Billy Meredith made dribbling into an art form and he also demonstrated superior technical abilities in comparison to all others at the time whenever he ventured out on one of his many touchline raids. His main attributes were his dribbling and his speed, and one other crucial component was his crosses – three major ingredients in almost every winger's profile. In addition, Meredith was in possession of an inexorable winning instinct, but unlike Charlie Roberts, his famous teammate who also had a strong will to triumph, Meredith's desire for victory was not manifested in aggression on the field but was expressed in a more subtle way.

Old film clips show Meredith's behaviour and attitude on the field to be a mixture of casualness and indifference bordering on outright dullness. But behind this fraudulent outer shell was hidden an incomparable ability to focus all his energy into cut-throat creative details – for example, his famous and often decisive back heel passes. If Roberts' influence was apparent as a continuous presence, then Meredith's felt more like a focused flash of lightning. This brings us to another conventional difference between wingers and central midfielders: the winger operates in split seconds and moments of extreme fullness, whereas the central midfielder more often works through continuities and steady accumulations of time. Philosophically put, the winger is Nietzsche (think of his propensity for the *Augenblick*, 'thunderbolts' and 'the aphoristic, abrupt quality'), while the engine room operator is Bergson (think of his emphasis on *durée* and continuity). As to Beckham, he is much like Bergson, a steady, accumulating presence, but as we shall see, he also has the Nietzschean quality of the unexpected and the abrupt.

Another philosophical or literary way to put it is to say that the central midfielder corresponds to Hegel's idea of the novelistic protagonists who 'stand opposed to [...] the prose of actuality which puts difficulties in their way on all sides'.[7] The central midfielder is also situated in the midst of a prosaic world full of obstacles, this is what the crowded engine room of the soccer field looks like for the central midfielder, and Hegel's assumption is that the novelistic hero (our central midfielder) constantly attempts 'to breach this order of things, to change the world, to improve it, or at least in spite of it to carve out of it a heaven upon earth'.[8] Most often this is a *cul de sac*, a never-ending battle, which seldom leads to any redemption. This is the epic dimension of soccer. On the other hand we have the winger, who like the central midfielder of course faces obstacles, but who is also gifted with the periphery's less crowded space and the ability to dribble. The epic dimension of the engine room along with its quality of ongoing *Stellungskrieg* is replaced with sudden surprises, constant escapes and getaways and even, sometimes at least, complete redemption in the form of goal-assisting crosses. The central midfielder deals in prose and epic (because Sisyphus-like) battles, whereas the winger deals in poetry and lyric (because escapist) redemptions. Again, Beckham has a little bit of both – but he also has something, which only he has.

David Pegg, one of the Busby Babes and a casualty of the Munich air disaster, was built in the same way as Meredith and Giggs, that is, as a lean, almost lanky player with relatively long legs. Again, like in Meredith's case as well as in Giggs's, what set Pegg apart was his ability to run with the ball at high speed and to challenge, take on and dribble past several opponents before delivering goal-assisting crosses, often from near the goal line. Compared to Eddie Colman, United's unrelenting number 4 who faced the interminable battles in central midfield with his head held high, Pegg, the floating number 11, ran, or rather flew or zigzagged, up and down the touchline providing crosses for 'The Smiling Executioner', the prolific goal poacher Tommy Taylor, until 'Munich' put an end to their lives.

Different from the likes of lanky Pegg, Meredith and Giggs are wingers such as Raymond Kopa, Marc Overmars and Nani who are more stoutly built and have low-lying centres of gravity. Kopa, who was used both as a central and wide forward, quite simply excelled in dribbling, so much so that he was often accused of slowing down the pace of matches because he held onto the ball for way too long. This problem was primarily linked with his time in Stade de Reims, whereas in Real Madrid, playing alongside soccer's greatest at the time – Ferenc Puskás, Alfredo Di

Stéfano and Francisco Gento – Kopa was among equals in terms of technical ability and soccer intelligence, and this meant he could pass the ball to his teammates knowing it would be handled very well. Kopa was, like Nani and Overmars, but unlike Giggs, Pegg and Meredith, gifted with two great feet and with a powerful, dry shot, not needing much space around him in order to shoot.

In comparison with these two types of typical wingers, the lanky type and the stout type, whose common characteristics are *dribbling*, *speed* and *goal line crosses*, Beckham falls short of a lot of things. He lacks speed and penetration; he is (more or less) unable to dribble and 'lose' an opponent; and he rarely crosses the ball from the goal line as real wingers are supposed to do. Compared to Giggs's sliding run and Ronaldo's potent penetrations, Beckham seemed just a sedentary supporting actor.

All this is not entirely wrong, but we owe it to Beckham to define him in a positive manner – that is, to use David Beckham as the starting point for passing judgments on David Beckham, and, from this starting point, to delineate the contours of his exceptional soccer profile. Let us begin by stating that Beckham the soccer player originated from the central midfield (a position he kept characterizing as his favourite position). In Manchester United's youth team, the team that won the FA Youth Cup in 1992 by defeating Crystal Palace and whose backbone was the famous 'Class of 92' (Gary Neville, Phil Neville, Nicky Butt, Paul Scholes and David Beckham), Beckham usually (and naturally) played alongside Butt in the centre of the midfield. So, during the next couple of years, on his journey from the centre to the right, Beckham actually brought with him a series of distinctive characteristics of a typical engine room operator, not least ball control, stamina and hard work. As Gwen Russell writes in *Arise Sir David Beckham* about a young David, 'Four years in a row he won the Essex 1500-metre championship, impressing everyone with his stamina and determination'.[9] Neither should we forget that he was always an excellent tackler and a supreme passer of the ball. These attributes – control, stamina, work, tackling and passing – combined with his leadership qualities (which are more related to his soccer abilities than to his personality – Beckham is no Roy Keane, no Steve Bruce either) and long shot abilities would no doubt have made Beckham into one of the world's best central midfielders if his career had unfolded in the centre of the midfield.

But on the right – a position he more or less accidentally ends up in as a result of Kanchelskis's sudden 1995 transfer – Beckham invented a completely new type of winger never before seen by the world of soccer, and this invention ought to secure not only his immortality, but also a permanent seat in the Pantheon of Great Soccer Players. What basically characterized Beckham's new type of winger was the fusion of Euclid's geometrical and Einstein's relativistic worldview together with an extraordinary sense of time and space.

Beckham's special shooting technique endowed his shots and crosses with a *geometrical ultra-precision*. A pure example of this would be his great breakthrough moment, his goal from the centreline against Wimbledon on 17 August 1996. But at the same time, this technique meant that Beckham was capable of bending space, that is, when Beckham curled a shot, space was, so to speak, wringed out of its geometrical and three-dimensional coordinate system and into a whole new fourth dimension. This happened through the *extreme curl* that Beckham was able to give the ball, and which in itself made it difficult for the opponent team to find secure anchoring points for their defensive actions, for example during a corner kick, but also when Beckham executed one of his dangerous free kicks.

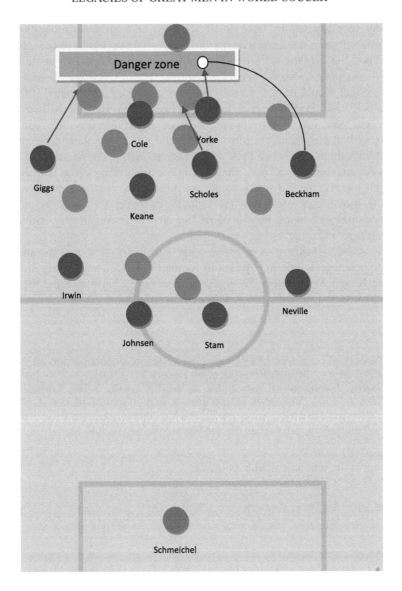

Figure 1.   Beckham's fusion of unexpectedly early on, halfway, precision and curl.

However, when the ball was in play – that is, when Beckham was a winger and not a set piece specialist – and the curled crosses were combined with Beckham's sense of time and space (or, perhaps rather, his sense of tim*ing* and spac*ing*, since there was undoubtedly a crucial element of human agency in the equation: the ability to choose the proper moment and the right spot) – that is, when the crosses were executed *halfway* between the centreline and the goal line, *early on and unexpectedly* (and, in contrast to typical wingers, without any ambition to reach the goal line before making the cross) – they were epiphanies of a new spatial dimension in which the drawing of hitherto unseen and unimaginable attacking options became possible.

Halfway (conditioned by a sense of spacing) and early on (conditioned by a sense of timing) were the key elements in Beckham's successful re-invention of the winger. When the crosses were executed halfway and with the right timing, there existed *a vulnerable space between the opponent team's goalkeeper and defensive line*, a space that would have been minimized or downright eliminated if the crosses had been delivered from the goal line. However, early on and halfway between centreline and goal line is not enough, because if the unexpectedly early crosses from halfway had only been executed with Euclid's foot, the defenders could easily have dealt with them. But when they were executed with a combination of geometrical precision and relativistic curl, they became a paralysing blow in the opponent team's solar plexus: the defenders could not meet these crosses straight on, instead they had to move backwards into the vulnerable space; the attackers, in contrast, had the advantage of being able to meet the crosses more directly and with their front towards goal (Figure 1).

In that sense, Beckham is granted what only very few players are granted, namely the privilege to add new pages to football's ABC. Those pages are all about timing ('early on and unexpectedly'), sense of spacing ('halfway') and the fusion of Euclid and Einstein ('curled crosses with extreme precision').

Notes

1. 'All Time Player Records', http://www.premiersoccerstats.com/Records.cfm?DOrderby = Ass&DYearby = All%20Seasons (accessed January 14, 2013).
2. Nick Harris, 'Ferguson will never talk to the BBC again', *The Independent* (UK), September 6, 2007. http://www.independent.co.uk/sport/football/news-and-comment/ferguson-will-never-talk-to-the-bbc-again-401487.html (accessed January 15, 2013).
3. Quoted from Russell, *Arise Sir David Beckham*, Loc 631 of 3692.
4. Ibid., Loc 608 of 3692.
5. Ibid., Loc 681 of 3692.
6. See Wagg, 'The team that wouldn't die', 25.
7. Hegel, *Aesthetics*, 593.
8. Ibid.
9. Russell, *Arise Sir David Beckham*, Loc 128 of 3692.

References

Hegel, G.W.F. *Aesthetics: Lectures on Fine Art*. Vol 1. Trans. T.M. Knox. Oxford: Clarendon Press, 1998.

Russell, Gwen. *Arise Sir David Beckham: Footballer, Celebrity, Legend – The Biography of Britain's Best Loved Sporting Icon*. Kindle ed. London: John Blake, 2007.

Wagg Stephen. 'The Team that Wouldn't Die: On the Mystique of Matt Busby and Manchester United'. In *Manchester United: A Thematic Study*, ed. L. David Andrews, 13–27. Oxfordshire: Routledge, 2004.

From local heroism to global celebrity stardom: a critical reflection of the social, cultural and political changes in British football culture from the 1950s to the formation of the premier league

Mark Turner

Faculty of Sport Business and Enterprise, FBSE, Southampton Solent University, Southampton, UK

This essay through a critical reflection of various social, cultural and political changes in British football, from the 1950s to the formation of the global premier league, explores how they facilitated the broader change in which football players have transformed from local heroes to global stars. As British football became more Europeanized, at the same time, players began to hold greater financial power and the conditions were set for an acceleration in the relationship between football and consumerism, whereby the new economics of signs and space allowed entrepreneurs to commodify the identity of the football club thus providing the foundation for the new consumption of football in the 1990s. Finally, the essay concludes that the development of 'new' football and late modern 24 h news culture supports Buckley's suggestion that new media is primarily concerned with stories of 'empty global stars, cod personalities and celebrities whose fame is largely self-referential'.

Introduction

Through a series of critical discussions of various social, cultural and political changes in the relationship between British football and society from the 1950s to the formation of the global premier league in 1992, this essay explores the conditions which have facilitated the transition of footballers from local heroes to global celebrity stars. The paper specifically notes how the emergence of post-Fordism and the early Europeanization of British football alongside the abolition of the maximum minimum wage set the context for an acceleration of late modernity, whereby through the advancement of television and sponsorship within free market hegemony, football's 'star' players and clubs have become incorporated more deeply within the wider commodification of popular culture. Finally, the paper concludes that formation of the Premier League in 1992 perhaps acting as the optimal 'commercial, economic and global entertainment miracle'[1] and the acceleration of new media have created a hyperreality in which we are now more often concerned with stories of 'empty stars, cod personalities and celebrities whose fame is largely self-referential'.

The affluent 50s and the early 'Europeanization' of British football

During the 1950's and early 1960's, British football embarked on a new journey undergoing a series of significant changes which would alter its social, cultural and political landscape for ever. The economic and technological changes in society such as the rise of television, transport, wealth and living standards helped produce a growing division between the larger and smaller clubs and significantly altered the nature of football support and allegiances.[2]

In his historicising of the transformation of English Football in the 1990s, Anthony King discusses the influence of the post-war consensus and the later emergence of British post-Fordism which played a significant role in how society was to become more affluent, thus aiding such economic and technological advancements. King explains that, 'partly as a result of Keynesian economics and Beveridgean social policies but more particularly, because of Fordism, there was something of a revolution in affluence from the late 1950s'.[3] Carter also highlights the role of the 'cradle to the grave' welfare state which 'spawned a more egalitarian ethos and permeated the public consciousness', as a significant part of what was a, greater prosperous and more 'consumer based, affluent society' throughout the 50s, relating this to a developing liberated society and burgeoning youth culture, which allowed wider access to contraception.[4]

One of the most significant aspects of the post-war economic revival, however, was the establishment of the EEC by the Treaty of Rome in 1957, which allowed greater social 'political and economic' integration amongst European countries and a 'determination to eliminate the all-too-recent national antagonisms'.[5] As 'Europeanization' developed, so too did the 'Europeanization' of British football, representing an 'acceleration of established trends, rather than a radical break from the past'.[6]

The establishment of the European Cup in the 1955–1956 season which provided club football with a European structure, was a significant step towards greater integration amongst leading European football clubs, yet the idea was still met with some hostility in Britain.

However, as Taylor notes, that by 1958 and after the significance of the Munich air crash, European football and competition became more recognized and centralized by British clubs, players and supporters and accepted as the main goal of the best clubs.[7] So, by the late 1950s, the traditional colonial and imperial view of the British could 'no longer ignore football in the wider world' and so British football was transformed by the 'lure of European competition and financial rewards'.[8]

The early 'Europeanization' of British football during this affluent period of social change is significant because it set the context for the acceleration of 'European' modernity during the 1990s and early twenty first century, specifically laying the foundations for the social, cultural and political developments which led to the creation of the UEFA Champions League and Bosman transfer ruling.

Jimmy Hill and the paradox of Keynesianism

In historicizing the significance of the late 1950s intermediate modern period and its specific relationship with football, it is important to recognize the origins of the football leagues labour regulations and rules in order to critically discuss the abolition of the maximum minimum wage and its significance for football economics and culture during late modernity.

King provides a critical historicizing of the rationale behind the maximum wage suggesting that the 'leagues rules were originally forged, like the US Constitution, in historical conditions completely different from those in which they were subsequently employed',[9] for example, in 1888 when the league was inaugurated, there were only 12 clubs.

Around this time, the Keynesian national economic framework and consensus 'prioritized economic and social universality'[10] and thus the football league attempted to 'sustain all the clubs in the league through the redistribution of revenues, the suppression of wages and restriction of transfers'. The relationship with Keynesian economics was thus that as the economy attempted to sustain 'full employment through methods of demand management', the football league attempted to 'restrain economic activity in order to ensure the continued economic viability of the smaller clubs'.[11]

Walvin discusses the effects of such economics and restrictions on players earnings noting that British footballers, in particular were the 'poor relations shackled to an industry which was characterized by appalling labour relations and by an attitude towards labour which had disappeared in all but football and the domestic trades'.[12] Furthermore, the influence of Keynesian economics on the working class and the belief that workers should be encouraged to consume led to an inevitable rise in workers' wages, which in turn, left professional footballers underpaid.

As relationships between the players Union; the PFA and the football league worsened during the late 1950s, it became evident that some players and representatives would no longer accept the 'illegal restraints on trade'.[13] At this time, Jimmy Hill succeeded Jimmie Guthrie as the players' representative and 'successfully highlighted the anomalous character of the maximum wage in the context of the increasing affluence of Keynsian society',[14] and thus in 1961 the maximum wage was finally abolished.

A further critical change during this time occurred in 1963, when George Eastham successfully challenged 'Newcastle United's legal right to retain him as a player against his wishes and thus obtained player freedom of movement, which was long a basic right in other occupations'.[15] These changes played a significant role in the way football was to transform from practice to entertainment and Jimmy Hill best represented this change during that time. In arguing that 'professional footballers had effectively subsidized the game for the working class for many years', and that the new affluence of the working class and their affordance of beer, travel and food, meant that football too was to become a commodity, Hill 'envisaged the footballer as an entertainer, and thus football was part of the entertainment business whose market equals were television, cinema and theatre'.[16]

However, it is interesting to note that whilst Hill successfully demonstrated the contradiction of the maximum wage with organic developments in social life and the increasing affluence of Keynesian society, paradoxically, the 'appeal to freedom of contract and the free market in order to set wages was actually antithetical to the Keynesianism which informed British social life at that time'.[17] So then, Hills arguments actually 'contravened the central Keynesian and corporate premises on which the league was based in the late 1950s' and thus according to King 'constituted a moment when new conditions were implemented, necessitating the complete replacement of the League's political economic structure'.[18]

The result of these changes remained the same and with the 'decline of social barriers, footballers grew in confidence and became more independently minded'[19] and thus the top level players began to 'demand the kind of salaries commensurate with the rarity of their skills'.[20]

Over 30 years later, a landmark case won by Jean-Marc Bosman enabled a new almost 'postmodern era of player mobility'[21], where all EU players were now able to secure the freedom of movement once their contract with the club had expired. Whilst this revolutionizing of the European transfer system emerged out of the social, cultural and political conditions of the 1990s, it is important to recognize its relationship with the legacy of the early Europeanization of British football and particularly, the abolition of the maximum wage in 1961. The significant and revolutionary 1960s period then, set the context for the acceleration of modernity during the 1990s, specifically the cultural changes in player as 'postmodern' celebrity star and football as a globally mediated entertainment spectacle.

'From heroes to stars': the early development of consumer culture

Whilst British football has always held an element of 'stardom' and 'commercialism', with names attached to products long before World War I, this commercialism accelerated intensely from the late 1950s onwards. Giulianotti draws on Featherstone's account of how the 'social role and perceived attributes of famous people have changed over the century' and specifically notes how 'traditional heroes embodied the quest for virtue and glory, with the heroic being an intrinsic part of the individuals moral character and graceful talent'[22] for example, players such as Stanley Matthews, Puskas and Bobby Moore, who also represented and signified the values of society at that time.

As the new early 1960s affluent society grew and became more consumer minded, 'the best players were able to reap the transient benefits of that consumerism' (Walvin 1994: 178)[23] by obtaining larger wages and transfer fees which enabled greater mobility 'dislocating them from their local working class contexts'.[24] As a result of these changes, players often became valued for their consumer value and 'price tag', rather than their talent on the pitch or 'intrinsic worth'.

In examining Critcher's developments from 'traditional working class hero' to the 'transitional and "embourgoised" new middle class' gentleman and the 'dislocated superstar' to the 'superstar businessman', Horne, Tomlinson and Whannel discuss a range of cases which perhaps best demonstrate this transition ranging from Matthews to Charlton, Ball to Best and Keegan.[25] This transformation led 'top professionals to become dislocated from their natural environment and often acquired the international celebrity status of a star within the wider entertainment industry'[26] and so football culture would further accelerate from its traditional form to a more modern style. As top players began to become more aware of their consumerism, they started to develop individual styles and identities, which in some cases would 'cut them off from their footballing forebears and working class fans'.[27] This cultural change in the 'socialization and embodiment of self'[28] at this critical turn in football and society was part of a combination of social and cultural processes through the late 50s and 60s which would transform top players from valuable team members and heroes to consuming individual stars.

Accelerating modernity: the rise of television and sponsorship

Walvin has documented how initially, the late 50s rise in affluence and consumerism and the subsequent rise in Television culture, contributed to a decline in football attendances, through alternative choices of leisure consumption and the more comfortable option of staying home to watch football as part of the Saturday evening entertainment.[29] However, by the late 1970s, it had become widely accepted by the authorities and supporters that 'television had helped the game's public appeal'.[30]

What the development of football and television throughout the 1960s and 70s did, was to aid the larger process and development of football on the global stage. Now, the World Cup in particular could be seen by millions, throughout countries all over the world and thus would enable football to become a greater political subject for Western neo-liberal governments particularly, aiding the process of Europeanization through the 'widespread coverage of European competitions'.[31] Through the development of the global televised football spectacle then, the World Cup would become the 'oscars' of the sport, in which its sporting social actors were able to perform in front of millions worldwide.

The rise in football and television culture through intermediate modernity also developed the 'sporting drama' and so through the process of 'centrifugal interplay', the sporting drama projected its 'images, characters and catch phrases into broader aspects of culture'.[32]

However, the political and economic effects of televised football and sporting drama also played a crucial role in the political economic division of the British league, whereby big clubs in the top division received more coverage and sponsorship. In relating this to the wider historical transformation of British Society at that time and its paradoxical view of the 'divisive' free market as a way of resolving the crisis of the post war settlement, King notes, that the 'application of the free market to televised and sponsored football, resulted in the increasing impoverishment of the smaller clubs'.[33]

It is important to note also that during the development from intermediate to late modernity since the 1960s, 'football's political economy has undergone rapid modernization with its star players and clubs being incorporated more deeply within the wider commodification of popular culture',[34] and so the 'football experience has become increasingly synonymous with track side advertising, shirt sponsorship and the merchandising of club paraphernalia'. The development of sponsorship in particular is significant, because it plays a critical role in the larger development of the paradoxical rise of the individual star product and team franchise. As these modernizing process accelerate, the nature of football player and supporter identity change from traditional local, and in most cases proletarian hero, to the modern global star product of Western cultural imperialism and neo-liberalism.

Bishop has provided a semiotic analysis of the changing nature of professional sports logo's drawing on the theories of Baudrillard, Jameson and Debord to explain how the sports team logo, once a sign of allegiance, has been transformed via forces such as television, and changed the relationship between fan and team. The critical rise and impact of sponsorship is demonstrated through the way in which fans have been reduced to buying an endless stream of team-related products, and as Debord would argue, which led their actions being 'channeled into the global construction of the spectacle'.[35]

Football and revolutionary popular culture: 'El Beatle' and the modern superstar

If conservative 'pipe smoking' Duncan Edwards was the 50s, then 'El Beatle' George Best was the 60s[36] and perhaps best captures, the relationship between football and popular culture within society at that time. There is a clear relationship between the accelerated development of football and popular culture throughout the 60s and the development of hero to star within the growing mediated consumer and entertainment culture during late modernity.

Giulianotti notes how in some cases during this transformation, sporting heroes became celebrities extrinsically through the 'practicing and honing of an attractive and colourful self before the evaluative gaze of others'.[37] Through the accelerated development of the media, the promotion of stardom and celebrity took centre stage, whereby football became part of the larger entertainment business with its stars and celebrities becoming key ingredients of the revolutionary 1960s popular culture.

The new football celebrity 'joined the young stars in other culture industries notable television, fashion and popular music',[38] such as the Beatles and thus become advertised and consumed as a 'glamorous' product. It is important to recognize the significance of 1960s society and culture and in particular the 'political, sexual and cultural revolutions'[39] and how this relates to the critical change in football as a pure proletarian and national practice during early modernity to a complex and paradoxical late modern, mediated, entertainment spectacle.

In his discussion of 'creative modernity' and the life of Hanif Kureishi, Redhead notes the significance of the 'love' generation, the new men 'influenced massively by feminism and gay and lesbian politics in a host of contradictory ways, borne on a wave of love, sex, drugs and rock 'n' roll before punk, post-punk and dance culture eclipsed 1960s and 1970s hedonism for ever'.[40] As music culture changed, for example, the rise of the Rolling Stones, Bob Dylan, David Bowie, Led Zeppelin and football culture also changed and the 'boundaries between sport and entertainment were becoming increasingly blurred'.[41]

In considering the relationship between the 'glamorous' modern superstar and 70s popular music culture, Redhead suggests that, 'glam rock had married together previously opposed subcultural styles with Glitters "Come on, come on" from "I'm the leader of the Gang (I am)", ringing out inadvertently via Match of the Day microphones'.[42] Furthermore, he draws attention to the confusing politics of youth styles throughout the 70s suggesting that bands like The Specials and Madness managed to break down barriers between black and white in terms of musical styles, whilst exploring the 'complex challenge that youth culture has made to established (and changing) notions of masculinity and sexuality in specific contexts such as pop and football'.[43]

During this revolutionary period of the 1960's and 1970's, the complex relationship between football, popular music, stardom and celebrity, gender and technology started to accelerate in a more intense fashion.

The politics of post-Fordist Britain and Thatcherism

Walvin has discussed the relationship between the crowd troubles of the 1970s and 1980s and broader social changes for example, older men quitting football for the 'new domesticated pleasures provided by improved homes and car ownership', which left 'sparse terraces in the hands and control of younger fans'.[44] These young fans often 'sought to earn prestige by "taking the end" or "kop" which belonged to their rivals'.[45] As a result, the police and authorities introduced 'perimeter fencing, caging fans into specific ends and segregating home and visiting supporters into different ground sections'.[46]

In his discussion of British post-Fordist society and its relationship to consumer culture and society developing throughout the 1980s and early 1990s, King draws on the work of Lash and Urry to explain how new economics of signs and space allowed entrepreneurs to 'commodify the identity of the football club'[47] which provided the foundation for the new consumption of football in the 1990s. As Thatcherism and post-Fordism developed then, so did a new post-Fordist commodity, 'concerned with the creation of identity, endowing its customer with meaning, rather than acting as a tool with a function'.[48]

The adoption of free market ideology and its promise to defend the affluence created under Keynesianism actually led to industrial production decreasing and which in some of the more industrial proletarian communities, resulted in increased unemployment. The relationship between post-Fordism, the New Right Conservatism of Margaret Thatcher and football culture was significant, in that an 'authoritarian and populist law and order agenda, led by Thatcherites and Reaganites, created a mood of hostility to the perceived lawlessness of the crowd'.[49]

The New Right's response to the rise of hooliganism was to develop 'draconian proposals to control, curtail and criminalize football crowds'[50] at the same time that 'nationalized industries were privatized and neo liberal attitudes displayed contempt for the professions, as most areas of public life became subject to market forces'.[51] What we discover then, in examining the relationship between the politics of the 1970s and 1980s, is a microcosm of the larger changes in modernity, where through 'transitions from old to new, reverential to rebellious, acceptance of tradition to assertiveness of lifestyle, contradictions in cultural forms burst through'.[52]

The formation of the English Premier League in 1992

In setting the context for the 'new' consumption of football in the late modern era and consider how this further facilitated the transition of footballers as local heroes to global celebrity stars, it is appropriate to consider King's discussion of the political and economic effect of Sky television and the Premier League's New Deal. King notes how 'BSkyB communicated notions of the free market which were central to the reformation of post-Keynesian British society' and locates the 'meaningful symbolic conjuncture' of television coverage as a free market idea embodying 'Thatcherite idealism'.[53]

The *mis en scene* of this new broadcasting development was built upon Thatcherite political ideology. This establishment of free-market hegemony through the development of Sky television, opposition to licence fee and concern for consumer choice was part of a larger change in modernity, which saw the rise of greater individualism and blurring of the 'structural boundaries between the old lower middle classes and the affluent upper working classes'.[54]

The development of free market values within the new consumption of football in the early 1990s represents a critical and significant change in late modernity, where through Thatcherism's attainment of a hegemonic position in contemporary British culture, the development of Sky television and particularly through the lens of the Premier League contract with football, 'ideas of consumer choice, individualism and enterprise' are ensured and central to the viewers 'ritual consumption of football'.[55]

The 'breakaway phase' of the Premier League from the Football League may have 'revitalized the economic fortunes of the top clubs, however the very fabric of the smaller clubs and the national game were threatened'.[56] The Premier League and new cultural politics of football have become then a site for multinationalism and 'new breed of entrepreneurship',[57] enabling the expansion of football business and the development of top clubs to become public limited companies.[58]

In considering the cultural and commercial reinvention of English football since the late 1980s and specifically the close relationship between the 'new' football post 1992 and celebrity culture, Williams has suggested that the English Premier League represent's a 'commercial, economic and global entertainment miracle'.[59] Williams' argument is appropriate, in the sense that he links this development of 'new' football with other cultural changes, such as the development of a late modern 24 h news culture and Buckley's suggestion that new media is primarily concerned with stories of 'empty stars, cod personalities and celebrities whose fame is largely self-referential'.[60]

Furthermore, Williams considers Whannel's 'vortextuality' as a way of examining how such celebrity focus in late modern sport is the product of a wider ideological process, whereby 'the growth of media outlets and the vastly increased speed of circulation of information have combined to create the phenomenon of a "vortex" effect'.[61] 'New' football has become then, an accelerating product of late modernity; a 'mediated spectacle and vehicle for insatiable consumerism as a forum for physical pleasures, cultural affiliation and playful creativity'.[62]

Notes

1. Williams, 'Protect Me from What I Want', 101.
2. Walvin, *The People's Game*.
3. King, *The End of the Terraces*, 26.
4. Carter, *The Football Manager*, 81.
5. Walvin, *The People's Game*, 169.
6. Taylor, 'Politics and the People's Game', 7.
7. Ibid.
8. Walvin, *The People's Game*, 172.
9. King, *The End of the Terraces*, 40.
10. Ibid.
11. Ibid.
12. Walvin, *The People's Game*, 74.
13. Ibid.
14. Wagg in King, *The End of the Terraces*, 43.
15. Walvin, *The People's Game*, 176.
16. King, *The End of the Terraces*, 44.
17. Ibid.
18. Ibid.
19. Carter, *The Football Manager*, 90.
20. Critcher in Williams and Wagg, *British Football and Social Change*, 74.
21. Giulianotti, *Football a Sociology of the Global Game*, 121.
22. Giulianotti drawing on discussion of Featherstone, *Football a Sociology of the Global Game*, 58.
23. Walvin, *The People's Game*, 178.
24. Giulianotti, *Football a Sociology of the Global Game*, 116.
25. Horne, Tomlinson, and Whannel, *Understanding Sport*, 50.
26. Giulianotti, *Football a Sociology of the Global Game*, 124.
27. Walvin, *The People's Game*, 33.
28. Giulianotti, *Sport a Critical Sociology*, 117.
29. Walvin, *The People's Game*, 178.
30. Giulianotti, *Football a Sociology of the Global Game*, 91.
31. Walvin, *The People's Game*, 181.
32. Corner in Boyle and Haynes, *Power Play*, 79.

33. King, *The End of the Terraces*, 53.
34. Giulianotti, *Football a Sociology of the Global Game*, 88.
35. Bishop, 'Stealing the Signs'.
36. Burn, *Best and Edwards*.
37. Giulianotti , *Football a Sociology of the Global Game*, 118.
38. Ibid.
39. McDonald and Carrington , 'The Ontological Impossibility of the Black Streaker', 11.
40. Redhead, 'Creative Modernity', 3.
41. Carter, *The Football Manager*, 118.
42. Redhead in Williams and Wagg, *British Football and Social Change*, 146.
43. Ibid.
44. Walvin, *The People's Game*, 192.
45. Giulianotti, *Football a Sociology of the Global Game*, 49.
46. Armstrong and Giulianotti, *Football Cultures and Identities*.
47. King, *The End of the Terraces*, 27.
48. Lash and Urry, *Economies of Signs and Space*, 4.
49. McDonald and Carrington, 'The Ontological Impossibility of the Black Streaker', 17.
50. Ibid.
51. Carter, *The Football Manager*, 101.
52. McDonald and Carrington, 'The Ontological Impossibility of the Black Streaker', 4.
53. King, *The End of the Terraces*, 109.
54. Giulianotti, *Football a Sociology of the Global Game*, 147.
55. King, *The End of the Terraces*, 109.
56. Horne, Tomlinson, and Whannel, *Understanding Sport*, 52.
57. Ibid.
58. Conn in Horne, Tomlinson, and Whannel, *Understanding Sport*, 52.
59. Williams, 'Protect Me from What I Want', 101.
60. Buckley in Williams, 'Protect Me from What I Want', 104.
61. Whannel in Williams, 'Protect Me from What I Want', 104.
62. Horne, Tomlinson, and Whannel, *Understanding Sport*, 52.

References

Armstrong, Gary, and Richard Giulianotti. *Football Cultures and Identities*. Basingstoke: Palgrave Macmillan, 1999.
Bishop, Ron. 'Stealing the Signs: A Semiotic Analysis of the Changing Nature of Professional Sports Logos'. *Social Semiotics* 11, no. 1 (2001): 23–41.
Boyle, Raymond, and Richard Haynes. *Power Play, Sport, the Media and Popular Culture*. Essex: Pearson Education, 2000.
Burn, Gordon. *Best and Edwards: Football, Fame and Oblivion*. London: Faber and Faber, 2007.
Carter, Neil. *The Football Manager: A History*. London: Routledge, 2006.
Featherstone, Mike. *Undoing Culture*. London: Sage, 1995.
Giulianotti, Richard. *Football: A Sociology of the Global Game*. Cambridge: Polity Press, 1999.
Giulianotti, Richard. *Sport: A Critical Sociology*. Cambridge: Polity Press, 2005.
Horne, John, Alan Tomlinson, and Gary Whannel. *Understanding Sport: An Introduction to the Sociological and Cultural Analysis of Sport*. London: Spon Press, 1999.
King, Anthony. *The End of the Terraces. The Transformation of English Football in the 1990s*. London: Leicester University Press, 1998.
Lash, Scott, and John Urry. *Economies of Signs and Space*. London: Sage, 1994.
Mcdonald, Ian, and Ben Carrington. 'The Ontological Impossibility of the Black Streaker: Towards a Sociology of Streaking'. Unpublished paper submitted to the ASA Annual Conference, New York, 2007.
Redhead, Steve. 'An Era of the End, or the End of an Era: Football and Youth Culture in Britain'. In *British Football and Social Change*, ed. John Williams and Stephen Wagg. Leicester: Leicester University Press, 1991.
Redhead, Steve. 'Creative Modernity: The New Cultural State'. *Media International Australia incorporating Culture and Policy* 112 (2004): 9–27.

Taylor, Matthew. 'Politics and the People's Game; Football and Political Culture in Twentieth Century Britain'. Idrottsforum.org. http://www.idrottsforum.org/articles/taylor/taylor070117.html (accessed November 17, 2007).

Walvin, James. *The People's Game: The History of Football Revisited*. London: Mains, 1994.

Williams, John. '"Protect Me from What I Want": Football Fandom, Celebrity Cultures and "New" Football in England'. *Soccer and Society* 7, no. 1 (2006): 96–114.

Williams, John, and Stephen Wagg. *British Football and Social Change: Getting into Europe*. London: Leicester University Press, 1991.

Iconic figures in African football: from Roger Milla to Didier Drogba

Wycliffe W. Simiyu Njororai

Department of Health and Kinesiology, University of Texas at Tyler, Tyler, TX, USA

The rise of celebrity culture is a theme that has attracted a significant amount of attention within the realm of sport and culture related studies in sociology. Indeed sportsmen and women were the pioneers of celebrity status in ancient Greek society. Associating sporting accomplishments with celebrity has now been magnified by the media and the ensuing debate on the celebrity–media nexus and the cultural changes due to globalization have acquired considerable significance in academic studies. In this essay, I endeavour to focus on Roger Milla and Didier Drogba who captured the hearts of soccer-lovers worldwide in the late twentieth and early twenty-first centuries. I will try to capture the essence of the celebrity status of these two soccer icons by evaluating their images in relation to debates surrounding African soccer, sports labour migration and the state of the domestic game. It is my argument that the two rose to iconic status because they ventured outside the continent to compete at the highest level while still maintaining and contributing heavily to the success of their national teams. The career trajectories for Milla and Drogba reveal the dynamics and dilemma that potentially successful African football players have to negotiate.

Introduction

Association football is a national pastime in many African countries. The popularity of the sport is such that one can reasonably argue that it is integrally linked to the cultural identity of the African continent. The game is played and cherished in all regions of Africa even though the iconic players that have made a global impact have come from West and North Africa. Yet for most African countries, football is a western sport that was only introduced in the late nineteenth and early twentieth centuries. The colonization of Africa and the subsequent settler communities introduced the game to African people who were keen to pick up the sport. Since its introduction by western settlers, soccer has been in an ongoing process of growth and development. The period when Africa was under colonial rule witnessed the laying of the foundations for the development of the sport. Some of the aspects that made the game to be embraced with ease by the African people include the following:

(1) Soccer was inexpensive requiring very little special equipment. The ball was also easy to substitute with an improvised one.
(2) The athletic-oriented lifestyle that was already evident in indigenous singing and dancing blended well with the physical attributes required in soccer.

(3) The opportunity was granted to the indigenous people to participate and form teams.

(4) The migrant workers on various plantations and in urban areas, who had an opportunity to engage in leisure time activities found an exciting outlet for expression.

(5) Playing fields served as a vehicle for symbolic freedom and therefore resistance to external domination.

(6) Indigenous people were offered a medium through which to express their ethnic and national pride.

Thus upon gaining independence, many African countries were quick to affiliate with international sports organizations including FIFA being one of the most popular ones. The international affiliations provided an avenue to take part in international competitions, and by 1970 Africa had a direct access to the World Cup football finals tournament. Since then, there has been an increase in Africa's representatives including one between 1970 and 1978, two between 1982 and 1990, three in 1994 and five since 1998 except in 2010 when Africa had six representatives when South Africa hosted the 2010 World Cup.[1] Apart from World Cup participation, individual players were keen to turn professional away from the African continent; and among the trend setters were iconic figures such as Roger Milla of Cameroon. The outstanding performance of Cameroon and Algeria in the 1982 World Cup opened doors for many African players to play professional football in Europe. It is no wonder that countries that repeatedly represent Africa at the World Cup are those that have a high proportion of players playing away from the African continent. The professionalization of sport and the emergence of television and the spectacle of live football transformed the images of outstanding African soccer players. Lee and Lin advances the view that historically sport stars were people who were praised for their talents and also considered ideal types or role models.[2] This is particularly so in the context of African soccer where very few stars were known outside their home countries before the onset of televised soccer and professionalism. In the contemporary context of globalization, professional soccer players have been 'transformed into celebrities located within the ever-expanding web of the entertainment, advertising, fashion, and media tabloid industries'.[3] This contemporary period emerged in the late 70s spear-headed by players such as Roger Milla from Cameroon and accelerated into the twenty-first century as headlined by Didier Drogba of Cote D'Ivoire. Both Milla and Drogba are symbols of achievement as well as potential of African football on and off the field of play.

According to Lee and Lin, the attributes that contemporary sports stars possess include a combination of skill, achievement, personality and media-cultivated image that temporarily elevates them as cultural and promotional icons.[4] In the realm of soccer, each nation has heroes. However, the increasing globalization has created some intriguing global-local manifestations of soccer celebrities. In African football context, the scarcity of international success has created a situation where Africa, though a continent with 53 independent nations, is easily identified as one entity. Thus players such as Roger Milla, George Weah, Apedi Pele, Mustapha Rabah Madjer, Mahmoud El Khatib, Stephen Keshi, Tony Yeboah, Mark Fish, Kalusha Bwalya, 'JJ' Okocha, Didier Drogba and Samuel Etoo, among others, attract attention and a huge following across the continent without regard to nationality. As a continent, Africa has come a long way and star players have played a significant part in putting

Africa on the world map. However, for purposes of brevity, this essay will focus on the accomplishments spanning from Roger Milla to Didier Drogba by situating their journey to iconic status in the larger contest of celebrity status, typology of sport labour migration, evolution of the African game and the place of the media in the popularization of African football stars.

The concept of iconic figures and sports athletes

Professional sport, particularly association football, generates an institutional climate highly conducive to the construction of celebrity status, which is synonymous with iconic figures. According to Bolsmann and Parker, sports performers become famous by way of various means including their physical and cognitive abilities, their 'off-field' exploits and their charismatic demeanor.[5] Sports stars, unlike others, who according to Boorstin's often quoted phrase, are simply '... well-known for their well-known-ness',[6] have to earn their status through hard work and accomplishment on the field of play. A sports 'celebrity' is a term that is controversial and has eluded precise definitions. Nevertheless, the term celebrity is also synonymous with related terms such as – 'stars', 'superstars' 'heroines', 'heroes', 'icons' – all of which appear to elicit different meanings and reactions. However, celebrity is characterized by notions of fame, notoriety, charisma and exception, and therefore celebrity-hood is a commodification of the human form; the epitome of economic fetishism.[7] Celebrity is an enduring characterization of modern civilization and capitalism which seek to translate images into trade-able commodities in the market place. It is, therefore, an integral part of the modern day culture and it is a representation of people who 'are coveted and traded via a complex nexus of media networks'.[8] According to Bolsmann and Parker, celebrity permeates every thread of the social fabric and celebrity sports stars represent the epitome of vicarious achievement and conspicuous consumption.

However, like the case is with some sports getting more media coverage than others, sports stars also receive unequal coverage. Indeed the summation by Bolsmann and Parker captures this inequality in the coverage by stating thus:

> The intensification of the modern-day sport-media relationship has not been entirely uniform in terms of the amount of attention some sports have come to attract in comparison to others. To this end, there is a related tendency to ignore, or at least overlook, a broader range of sporting heroes; individuals that, to all intents and purposes, carry a significant amount of popular cultural kudos and leverage (as national and international celebrities) and yet who, for one reason or another, are not seen in quite the same light as some of their more mediatized contemporaries.[9]

This description aptly describes the sport celebrities that happen to come from the African continent. As a continent, Africa is seen as a back-water region more characterized by wars, deaths, HIV-AIDS, political instability, corruption, hunger among the many malaise that bedevil the continent. Sports figures from Africa, therefore, rarely get as much media attention as their counterparts in the western world. However, even with the constraints of their background and limited exposure, sport heroes have stood out as an epitome of the African spirit. This African spirit is demonstrated by the free running and graceful style exhibited by the Ethiopian and Kenyan runners from the Eastern African region; the explosive movements of the Western African runners; the skilful and highly artistic soccer exhibited by the players from Cameroon, Ghana, Nigeria, Senegal, Egypt, Morocco, Tunisia and Cote D'Ivoire. Thus, the sporting achievements of the individual sports stars on the African continent are highly celebrated and embraced given the amount of sacrifice, persistence and the sheer strength of will that one has to navigate to become a world champion or a player of international repute. In this context, the individual accomplishments of the sports person mirror the hopes and aspirations of millions of ordinary people from local to the global stage.

The globalization of sport can, therefore, be viewed as a centripetal force that menaces indigenous sport cultures and dissolves identities built and maintained around shared sport experiences at a local level.[10] These shared experiences have been enhanced with the developments in media as well as technology that have contracted the globe into a village. Indeed as the globalization of sport has been frequently explicated and theorized within the context of global and local tensions,[11] one wonders, yet marvels at the extent to which the globalization of sport has influenced and transformed today's sports identities – identities of athletes, identities of sports communities and identities of sports fans – and how tensions between the globalization of sport and local adjustments have been displayed across various types of identification.[12] Indeed, global diffusion of sports cultures, constant flow of athletes across national borders, and uniformly broadcast and consumed sports events worldwide have significantly challenged uniquely distinguished and preserved national/local identities and, as a result, have created a mixture of identities with regard to nations, athletes and sport fans.[13]

In particular, the increasing migration of African players from one country to another and their transnational media appeal deserves special scholarly attention to more systematically theorize the ways in which their identities are defined, metamorphosed and played out in the torrential stream of the globalization of sport. The growing tendency of soccer labour migration and the global consumption have unquestionably demonstrated the global flow of capital and de-territorialization of sports economy.[14] It is also noteworthy that, cross-national athletes are also representative vehicles of citizenship, national identity and nationalism associated with their respective countries of birth and origin, and by extension, continent.[15] For that reason, they have been regarded as cultural symbols of the global-local nexus as well as global marketing resources possessing resonant identities with local sports fans.[16] It is these notions of cross-national athletes and their transnational identities and appeal that the iconic figures of Roger Milla and Didier Drogba epitomize as African footballers in a global arena.

Typology of sports/soccer migrants

Maguire[17] and Magee and Sugden[18] developed typologies to categorize the migrant athletes. Maguire's typology of international sports labour included mercenaries, settlers, nomads, cosmopolitan, pioneer and returnees. This categorization was based on interviews with athletes drawn from soccer, basketball, cricket and rugby. This typology was very close to that developed by Magee and Sugden after interviewing soccer players in England. Their typology of migrant athletes included mercenary, settler and nomadic cosmopolitan, ambitionist, exile and expelled. One can argue that the categories applicable to African footballers over the years include mercenary, nomadic cosmopolitan, settler, returnee and ambitionist. These categories are not mutually exclusive, however, as they overlap in some instances. To clarify, a brief description of each of the applicable categories follows:

(1) *Mercenary*: A mercenary athlete is one who is motivated by earning capacity and who migrates for reasons of economic reward. This motivation for financial gain could be on a short-term basis.[19] The careers for athletes are short. It is therefore prudent to maximize the opportunity to earn as much as possible so as to invest in their future. Soccer players from Africa move to other countries to play the game because of better monetary compensation. Similar movements have characterized the transfer of allegiance by some Kenyan runners moving to Bahrain and Qatar on financial grounds.[20]

(2) *Nomadic Cosmopolitan*: According to Magee and Sugden,[21] athletes who fall in this category include individuals who are motivated by a desire to experience different nations and cultures. Maguire explains that this group of athletes is motivated by cosmopolitan engagement with migration where the desire is to seek new experiences.[22] For soccer, this category could include some who move to new leagues such as MLS in USA, New Zealand and China, not so much for money but to wind down their careers in new places. For African players, these could be a minority. However, the nature of some sports such as athletics circuit involves athletes moving and competing in different countries around the world.[23] Athletics agents have therefore strategically set up camps for their athletes to train and stay while on the competition circuit, which qualifies them as nomadic in lifestyle. In the soccer contest, players who change clubs regularly exhibit nomadic tendencies. Indeed Roger Milla played for several clubs in France before returning to Cameroon while Didier Drogba also changed clubs within France before moving to Chelsea in England and later on moved to China and then Turkey in 2013 to wind down his career. The nomadic streak in the human is always that of seeking a new opportunity.

(3) *Settler*: This category of players is composed of those who move to another country to compete and continue to stay beyond the end of their active careers. Indeed, Maguire describes this group as sports migrants who subsequently stay and settle in the society where they perform their labour.[24] There have been many African born players who turn out for other countries such as Eusebio from Mozambique turning out for Portugal. This category also includes players who change their nationality in favour of countries where they ply their trade.

(4) *Returnee*: This group of players may move to compete in another country, but are obligated to return to their homeland to participate in international competitions. Such players give-in to the lure of home soil which overcomes any of the advantages of staying in the host country.[25] The case of many African players fits into this category as the players move abroad to improve their game but still return to represent their nations in international competitions. One of the characteristics of Roger Milla and Didier Drogba is the commitment to their respective national teams of Cameroon and Cote D'Ivoire. They both sacrificed a lot to commute from Europe to represent their countries in international contests whenever they were invited. They therefore contributed immensely to lifting the profile and achievements of their national teams at continental and global levels.

(5) *Ambitionist*: This category transcends a number of categories. However, athletes in this category are characterized by three dimensions: (i) the desire to achieve a sport career anywhere, (ii) the preference for playing in a certain location as compared to elsewhere and (iii) the desire to improve one's career by moving to a higher-quality league.[26] This category of players ventures into new countries with a desire to elevate themselves and, more importantly, to continue to excel in the game. This is particularly true for young African players who aspire to move to Europe at any cost even if it means starting off in the 3rd Division in little known leagues with the hope of moving to more prominent ones.

Academic interest in African football

There has been a plethora of academic materials concerning association football in Africa since Versi[27] called for more research and studies on the state of the game. Indeed a lot of recent academic literature focuses on the historical, political complexities and labour migration of African players,[28] and some studies that have focused on specific regions of Africa including Southern Africa[29], Eastern Africa[30] and West Africa.[31] Whereas these studies are highly informative and meticulously detailed, there have been few that focus on how high profile sports participants have been received at a popular cultural level[32] across the continent and specifically on how the individual soccer stars fit in with the current globalization of the sport nationally and globally. In turn, those accounts which have concentrated more readily on soccer have had a tendency to focus on the de-skilling of the African game and the struggle for the continent to gain acceptance in the FIFA family. These studies and the resultant literature have therefore failed to focus on the wider influence of individual players who have been the successful products of the whole migration experience from Africa to Europe and their loyalty to their home nations, which elevated those nations to global significance. According to Bolsmann and Parker,[33] the popular cultural impact of celebrity/star players is a necessary consequence of the more recent globalization of soccer in which labour migration and media advancement have played such a vital part. For African players, understanding their struggles and the circumstances leading to their migratory tendencies help explain why and how individuals such as Roger Milla and Didier Drogba have emerged as celebrities.

Background of African football

Football was introduced into Africa in the late nineteenth century by missionaries, sailors, soldiers and traders who were of French, English, Belgian and Portuguese origins. Throughout the period of colonization, football quickly gained popularity amongst the black African population while white colonials preferred to play cricket and rugby. The game was characterized by racial divisions from the onset, with whites first playing and popularizing football. Some of the earliest documented football matches were played in South Africa as early as 1862[34] and football-related associations were formed in 1879 and 1891 in Pietermaritzburg and Cape Town, respectively,[35] leading to the founding of the South African Football Association (SAFA) in 1892. Football then spread around the African continent by missionaries, settlers and soldiers.

By the 1960s when most African countries gained their independence, football was already entrenched and many nations were quick to affiliate with CAF and FIFA. Although the initial stages of the game were characterized by discrimination against the indigenous people, gradually they embraced the sport and made it their own. The popularity of football was so immense that as early as in 1899, blacks in South Africa played the game and had a team, Orange Free State Bantu Football Club, play in England. To date, the game of football is highly celebrated as a cultural institution. For example, Karl Alexander, who lived for a time in Africa to study the game, stated thus:

> And then I came to Africa, Morocco to be precise, and its football-crazy streets, beaches, pitches and people. In coming to Africa, the part of me that disappeared when I left the 'beautiful game' back in August immediately came rushing back into my life, but in a different way. No more would I be playing the game constantly, attending practices every day in the heat or cold, hanging out with my teammates or representing the 'Bobcats' of Bates College. Instead, I found myself submerged in a football culture, a place where the people literally ate, breathed and lived football. I was immediately intrigued and inspired. In my 16 years of playing the game I had never seen football so important, so interplayed into a society that it literally became a life-changing game.[36]

Although his thoughts were on football in Morocco, that description is befitting to how the game is celebrated across the continent. For in Africa, more so than in Europe, South America or any other place on this planet, football encompasses the essence of the continent. The sheer passion for and the management of the game mirrors in many ways the politics, the culture and the economy on the African continent. Alexander captures this deep-rootedness of football by stating that the 'people are so interwoven into football that it is steadily becoming, quite literally, a matter of life and death for people'. He also adds that football has been a key player in its political and cultural makeup throughout its history. Indeed, football plays a big part in politics too including many politicians starting their careers in soccer before moving into competitive politics, politicians using its popularity to gain votes and to cultivate nationalism. In fact, success on the field of play can also enhance national unity as witnessed in 2006 in Cote D'Ivoire when there was a ceasefire between warring factions after the Elephants qualified for the World Cup. The game of football, therefore, stands as a symbol for political and social action in Africa.

Media and football nomads from Africa

A key factor in what has come to define football in Africa over the past quarter century has been the drastic increase in the commoditization and glorification of the game through the international media.[37] The growth as well as the liberalization of the media worldwide had a major impact on the international broadcasting of soccer games and sports news through satellite television. This impetus started in the 1980s, what once could only be seen in football stadiums and local matches could now be seen from the comfort of a home television set via a satellite dish.[38] From the late 1980s onwards, the proliferation of African radio and satellite television stations emerged largely through the liberalization of African media content which began to gain the rights to football broadcast and analysis.[39]

New media structures in Africa, as with the rest of the world, have provided a way to interact, communicate and experience other cultures and societies. For football in Africa, media availability has made it possible to support any team at any point in time, diffusing local alliances and allowing different nations and populaces around the continent to support the same club team at the click of a remote button.[40] New media technologies have fostered the creation of new cultural landscapes in Africa which no longer are limited to the continent. New cultural micro territories and allegiances have been created as major European clubs have stamped their presence on African football media. As a consequence of their loyalty, a lot of merchandize for various international soccer brands are now widely accessible across the African continent. Indeed media coverage of international soccer sparked off a sense of international curiosity throughout the continent. This curiosity as well as familiarity of the game along with the players has also created a new cadre of international celebrities in the game of soccer. The new media spaces have given African footballers as well as their followers, including aspiring talents, an international vision of the game.[41] The media, being a powerful socialization medium, provides African footballers with an 'illusion of facility', the notion that making it as a professional footballer is an easily obtainable and incredibly rewarding vocational option that can be achieved by anyone including them.[42] This has created a hunger and thirst to pursue the dream of playing the game professionally and preferably in Europe.

For African football migrants in particular, the proliferation of internationally mediated sporting events and television consumption has indeed led to the popularity of emigrating for vocational purposes.[43] According to Raffaele Poli, the impact of football media on African football migration is enormous.[44] He states that it is undeniable that football and its promulgation through the mass media have contributed to the increase in African youth of the desire to succeed through emigration and that an increase in football publicity contributes to perpetuating the naivety of millions of young African adolescent to aspire towards elite football status. Apart from the few players who succeed, thousands of others attempt without success. Despite many such failures, the glitter of the successful footballers such as Samuel Etoo and Yaya Toure, who were among the 10 highest paid footballers in the world in 2012,[45] creates a desire for many young players to try it out by moving abroad using both legal and illegal means to get a shot at professional football status in Europe. It is this same media that promoted and enhanced the images of iconic players such as Roger Milla and Didier Drogba.

One of the consequences of the media coverage of football stars is the representation of African football superstars as iconic legends and national heroes to look up to by young talents. For decades, the footballing world has utilized football celebrities (i.e. Pele, Diego Maradona, Ruud Gullit, David Beckham or Ronaldinho) to commercialize the game of football through merchandizing and taking advantage of the player's idol status.[46] For African football celebrities, the meaning of player commoditization takes on a new and much more powerful form. Seen as locally grown superstars, international football celebrities in Africa such as Cote D'Ivoire's Didier Drogba, Ghana and Real Madrid's Michael Essien or Togo and Tottenham Spurs' Emmanuel Adebayor are prime examples of the success, fame and fortune which can spur from professional football.[47] The downside is that only showing the success stories of the few professional players, who have made it as footballers in Europe, the African media is portraying a distorted image of true professional football in Africa.[48]

Through his studies in Cote D'Ivoire on the migration of African footballers, Raffaele Poli accurately depicts the extremity of how African football superstars are used to urge the idea of football as a profession among Ivoirian youth. According to him:

> The media ignores almost systematically, that, in comparison to the African players who attain glory and prosperity through football, the vast majority of footballers from the continent who attempt their chances in Europe fail and [subsequently] find themselves often in precarious situations. By only concentrating on the success stories, the media feed the illusion of an easy way, which is a notion shared by many young Africans.[49]

However, the media presence of successful athletes, who mostly ply their trade overseas, creates a desire among the youth to also elevate their standards as well as whetting of their hopes and hunger for success. The only unfortunate aspect is the portrayal of the athletic success as being an easy profession. For example, Poli conducted a survey with the Ivorian Under-17 national team, where 18 of the 23 players he asked said that, once in Europe, finding a professional club to play for would be easy.[50] Such optimism was not shared by their team's trainer who felt that only three or four of them had necessary talent to break through in Europe. But for African youth, any career path way that offers hope for a break through poverty is worth the attempt. The failure by the media sources to balance the proclamation that a life in professional football is easy to achieve with the reality of struggle, corruption, exploitation and neo-colonial undertones along the way would help open the eyes of the aspirants. For example, Roger Milla's journey to iconic status was not without challenges. In an interview with FIFA.com, he stated that starting out as a professional footballer is like a journey into the unknown.[51] He stated that he didn't know what kind of obstacles he would face in his career. However, due to his ambition, he was able to develop his game by learning from some great players thereby making progress quickly and winning titles too.

Although he was talented and could have moved to France at a tender age of 18 to join Saint Etienne, a major force at the time, the soccer administration in Cameroon blocked the deal and Milla had to wait another seven more years before making the journey to France, where Valenciennes was his first port of call. This resilience and persistence to overcome administrative pitfalls in the African game characterize a lot of the players who have gone on to accomplish much at the international level. Such challenges have to do with the administrative weaknesses of the African game and the sheer corruption and ill will that pervade the sport. However, successful athletes tend to have an inner drive and passion that drive them to success no matter what challenges they encounter. Thus even at an early age, Milla was introduced to the world of migration as his father, who worked with railways, was forever on the move. Despite the nomadic life, Milla kept his eyes on football. Milla emerged from the barefoot games of his boyhood with a nickname, Pele. His excellent technique and scoring touch were already evident, and by the time he was 18, he was playing first-team football at one of Cameroon's leading clubs, Leopard de Douala. After winning the league championship there in 1972, Milla moved on to Tonnerre Club de Yaounde the next year and further success followed.[52]

In 1976, Milla's career on the international stage got off to an auspicious start as he helped Tonnerre capture the CAF African Cup Winners' Cup and collected the African Golden Ball for the continent's best player. Twelve months later, the French club, Valenciennes lured him across the Mediterranean to Europe. Milla struggled to make his mark at Valenciennes, however, and he fared little better after heading south to AS Monaco, spending half his time on the bench and the other half injured. A spell at Bastia did little to enhance his reputation either, his impromptu trips to Cameroon antagonizing the coaching staff. Unfortunately for African Footballers based abroad, the frequent call ups to the national teams create bad blood between the players and their clubs. Saint-Etienne, newly relegated to the second division, proved his salvation when they signed the now 32-year-old in 1984. There he rediscovered the path to goal, scoring 22 times in 31 appearances over two fruitful seasons. He flourished even further after moving to Montpellier, a club where he felt at home, and where his dribbling and scoring ability came to the fore. By the time he called time on his professional career in France, in May 1989, he had 152 goals to his name.

On the other end, Didier Drogba's journey to professionalism followed a unique trajectory that involved victory over isolation, family sacrifice and apprenticeship away from Africa. Didier Drogba was born in Abidjan on 11 March 1978. He spent his childhood in his native Cote D'Ivoire and his adopted country, France. According to the information from his website, he first left the country of his birth at the age of five to stay with his uncle, Michel Goba, who was by then a professional footballer. Although it was a difficult decision to make for Drogba's parents, they let him to go because it gave him a real chance to succeed in life. For three seasons, therefore, Didier travelled with his uncle from one club to another akin to a nomadic lifestyle of some African ethnic groupings. This early exposure to club football and migratory lifestyle laid a foundation that would later project Drogba to stardom. After returning home at the age of eight, he linked up with his old friends to organize football matches as often as possible utilizing whatever empty spaces were available. His homecoming was however short-lived as after only three years, the country was hit by a serious economic crisis prompting his now job-less parents to send him back to France.

In the meantime, his uncle, after a spell at Besançon, had returned to Dunkerque, taking Didier back to northern France once again. It was here that he was to join his first football club. Initially he played right back, a position that was not approved of by his uncle as in football, people only look at the strikers. This forced the young Didier to change and try out at the centre-forward position. This change in position later defined his career. But of significance in the early age of Drogba was the experiencing of the migrant tendencies that characterize a soccer player as he moved from club to club with his uncle. Additionally, the sacrifice of living away from his biological parents characterizes the long winded journey to success that is not unique to him. Many African families let go their children to stay with relatives if they deem it necessary for the children's future success either academically or in the realm of sport. It was in 1991 when Drogba was 13 that his parents chose to move to France. Meanwhile, the teenage tendencies of losing focus and getting distracted led to a significant drop in academic performance. He dropped from the top of the class to the bottom where he had to repeat a year of school. His parents reacted, like any other parent who puts significant value to education, by immediately banning him from football for a year and sending him to live with his cousin. At the age 15, he signed up with Levallois, and it was here, in the suburbs of Paris, that the young Didier Drogba slowly began to make a name. At Levallois, Didier demonstrated his commitment from a very early stage. He showed discipline by staying away from the partying lifestyle and late nights. He went on to become the star of the Under-17 team.

Didier continued his apprenticeship as a footballer which entailed overcoming the frustration of being on the bench. He had to learn patience, and to respect his manager's decisions. Even though he was the 'best in the team', he did not get much playing time. Despite this lack of time on the pitch, the young attacker attracted interest, with Guingamp, Le Mans, Lens and Paris Saint-Germain following his performances very closely. Unfortunately, he fractured his foot, during a match against Caen, tripping on a sprinkler head and ending up in plaster. Around this phase of life, Didier faced a huge challenge in injuries which hampered his progression into the professional ranks. By the age of 19 years, he finally became a professional footballer. However, injuries continued to plague his career including breaking two metatarsals, a fibula and an ankle. He seemed to be dogged by bad luck. And yet this was also the time at which Isaac, the first of his two children, was born. The birth of his son woke him up as it was a turning point in his life. However, Didier continued to look for an opportunity to improve himself. But it was not until the age of 21 that he signed a professional contract at Le Mans. He later moved to Guigamp as he was being played out of his position as a winger and not a striker at Le Mans. It took Didier Drogba close to twenty years in France to eventually taste division one league football at the age of 24.

Drogba did not emerge from any known youth club or competition. The curly-haired striker broke forth to limelight in the 2002-03 French Ligue 1 season at Guingamp, where he scored 17 goals in 34 appearances. Landing a £3.3 million deal at Olympic Marseille in 2003 – his second Ligue 1 club – Drogba's career would accelerate at lightning speed. His two amazing seasons at Marseille which culminated in a UEFA Cup final, would achieve for him three major things that shaped his career very positively. Firstly, Drogba honed his skills of precise heading, running aptly with the ball and netting goals from any angle without wasting a second to think. Secondly, it gave him an easy access to Ivory Coast's national team – the Elephants. In an era when the whole nation was being seduced by the youngsters from Asec Mimosas, Ivory Coast's elite football club with a youth academy, Drogba bust in and immediately made an impact. Third and most important, Drogba won the public's love and trust, and this opened doors for him to Chelsea after signing a record breaking deal of £24 million, which made him the most expensive Ivorian footballer in history. At Chelsea, Drogba achieved the peak of his bliss as he led them to a European Champions League title in May 2012. Didier Drogba's is therefore justifiably an iconic figure adored by millions of fans across the globe. Indeed no other player in Ivory Coast's football history has shot himself to the height where Didier Drogba currently stands. He is no longer just a football star in the West African nation, but a cardinal reference with which strangers identify Ivory Coast.[53]

The accomplishments and images of Milla and Drogba

Appendices 1 and 2 show the accomplishments of both Roger Milla and Didier Drogba, respectively. The superlative achievements of these two African footballers attest to the sheer strength of will and dedication on their part. The striving for victories, awards and titles is at the heart of competitive sport and a passionate desire for players. According to Roger Milla, cited by FIFA.com, his lifelong desire was to win awards as they give him great pleasure.[54] This sentiment is echoed by Didier Drogba, who was voted Chelsea's greatest player of all time in a poll of 20,000 fans in October 2012[55] because of his accomplishments at the club. According to Didier, the accomplishment made him feel honoured and proud because so many big players have been at the club before and during his time. And when you consider that he was voted ahead of other legends at the club such as Frank Lampard and John Terry speaks volumes about the impact that Didier made on the field and fans. One thing that drove both Milla and Drogba was the love of the fans and their desire to please them. According to Drogba, his ambition of joining Chelsea was to win all the major trophies in England. And according to Milla, it is the great reception from the African community in the north of France, where he was based that inspired him. Throughout their careers, both Milla and Drogba had a great love affair with their fans. According to Milla, without the fans a player is nothing as they are a source of happiness, memories and inspiration.

Both Milla and Drogba left lasting images in the eyes of the fans. For Milla, in particular, his accomplishments and displays at the 1990 World Cup are forever engraved on the minds of those who watched the game. Roger Milla, the Cameroon striker and African football icon, exploded back on to the international scene at the ripe old age of 38 after a brief retirement from the game. As a veteran of the game, he was blessed with an enduring burst of pace and an unerring eye for goal that left defenders mesmerized. Milla's legacy and iconic status were defined by his contribution in taking Cameroon into the quarter-finals of the 1990 FIFA World Cup in Italy, a feat that was hitherto, uncharted territory for an African team. Incredibly, he also played four years later in the United States where he scored a goal too, raising his goal tally at the World Cup to five. Roger Milla's presence at the 1990 World Cup is even more memorable when one considers that he was summoned out of retirement on the eve of the tournament.

Although he had already achieved plenty with Cameroon, making history as part of the team that qualified for the 1982 FIFA World Cup in Spain, when the 'Indomitable Lions' made their first appearance on the world stage, Milla captured the hearts and minds of spectators worldwide. In the 1982 campaign, despite a first-round exit Cameroon returned home unbeaten.[56] And after winning the CAF African Cup of Nations for a second time in 1988, Milla announced his retirement from the international stage and after memorable testimonials in Douala and Yaounde, attended by almost 100,000 spectators, he moved to Reunion Island in the Indian Ocean to live out what he thought would be a peaceful semi-retirement. Playing in the FIFA World Cup was not under consideration until there was a crisis in the national squad that was wrought by conflict. This crisis prompted the Cameroonian press to begin bidding for Milla's return. The clamour received widespread public support and the country's President, Paul Biya, made a telephone call pleading with Milla to come out of retirement and answer his country's call. This was a clarion call to national duty that he could not turn down.

Therefore it was at the age of 38 that Roger Milla moved out of retirement into the international limelight and put on a show that lit the soccer world and one that he thoroughly enjoyed as a footballer. According to FIFA.com, Milla

> lit up Italia 90 with his bursts of pace, his jinking runs, his clever passes and, of course, that hip-wiggling Makossa dance around the corner flag with which he celebrated each of his four goals. A late substitute in Cameroon's stunning 1–0 victory over holders Argentina in the tournament's opening game, it was in their second group fixture against Romania that he wrote his name into the FIFA World Cup record books. Coming off the bench after 58 min, he became the oldest goalscorer in the

tournament's history when breaking clear of the Romanian defence to fire Cameroon in front with 13 min remaining. Ten minutes later he struck again.[57]

That victory assured Cameroon a place in the second round where Milla proved the hero again, his two goals in extra time against Colombia sending the Indomitable Lions to the quarter-finals, the furthest an African nation had reached. The first was sublime, the old man carrying the ball past Perea and Escobar before driving it beyond Higuita with his left foot. The second a gift from the goalkeeper, whose attempt to dribble round Milla ended up with the Cameroonian finishing into an empty net. 'He wanted to dribble past me. You don't dribble past Milla', said the hero of the hour. Even in the subsequent 3–2 quarter-final loss to England, Milla shone, winning the penalty from which Emmanuel Kunde struck their first goal, then putting Eugene Ekeke through for their second. Milla, who had always craved recognition as a footballer, could be proud: not only would he be crowned African Footballer of the Year but the performances of his team, along with Egypt at Italia 90, led to the announcement that there would be a third African team at future FIFA World Cups.

Similarly, but on a different stage and generation, Didier Drogba, the Ivory Coast striker spear headed Chelsea's 2012 European Champions League title with amazing heroism. He not only helped eliminate the title defending Champion and anointed favourites, Barcelona, but went ahead and grabbed the equalizer against Bayern in May's European Cup Final, before slotting home the decisive spot-kick in the penalty shoot-out against the German giants. This was the moment that Didier Drogba cemented his legendary status in the memory of soccer lovers around the world and in particular, the Chelsea fans. No wonder that the Chelsea fans voted him the greatest player in the history of the club ahead of other stalwarts including second-placed England midfielder Frank Lampard and skipper John 'Captain, leader, legend' Terry who came in fourth place.[58] According to Drogba, to make history, a player has to win big prizes for the fans and the club if the fans are to make you a big figure in the club's history. Thus Drogba's heroics in the Allianz Arena proved to be transformative, from a hero to an iconic figure with a legacy not only to Chelsea, but to African football and the entire beautiful game worldwide. It was while riding the peak of his achievement that he announced his decision to leave Chelsea for Shanghai Shenhua in China at the age of 34 before moving on to Galatasaray in Spring 2013.

Conclusion: legacies of Mill and Drogba

Maguire's typology of migrant athletes identifies those who are motivated by earning capacity and who migrate for reasons of economic reward as mercenary. Thus Didier's move to China could easily be situated within that paradigm of a mercenary who needed to squeeze as much money as possible from the club before age catching up with him. On the other hand, Didier could also be categorized as a cosmopolitan migrant who needed to find new opportunities but with less stress via public expectation for success. This latter paradigm is in-line with Didier's background when he kept moving with his uncle and later on in his own career even venturing beyond France where he first started. This advantage of moving from one country to another incidentally is what remains as a regret in Roger Milla's resume. This is because during the course of his stints with Valenciennes, Monaco, Bastia, Saint Etienne and Montpellier, in which time he scored 111 goals in 312 matches, Milla became one of the finest centre-forwards on the planet, but was never able to showcase his finishing skills elsewhere. According to Milla, cited by FIFA.com, there were no such thing as agents back then, and it wasn't easy to get a move abroad. It is something of regret for him as he would have loved to play in Germany, Spain or Italy.

Apart from their footballing achievements, both Milla and Drogba have distinctive and expressive personalities that are very entertaining to the spectator. For Roger Milla, the iconic corner flag celebration at Italy 1990 is one of the classic images of the entire World Cup. The expressive dance personified the African dance tradition as an expression of joy and vivacious spirit. Yet, according to Roger, he hadn't planned on doing that makossa dance at all. It was an impromptu innovation that was meant to blend player celebration with the fan base that always supported him on the field of play. The dance was a fitting celebration as a reward to the fans who had demanded for his inclusion on the national team roster. Roger asserted that one of the things he was proudest about was the fact that the people of Cameroon urged him to make a comeback to help their national team at Italia 90.

Humanitarian causes and service to others is a legacy that sets Roger Milla and Didier Drogba apart from the regular footballer. Since his retirement from soccer, Milla derives pleasure from helping others. As a travelling ambassador for Cameroon and UNAIDS (the United Nations Joint Programme on HIV/AIDS), the ex-footballer has been helping to raise awareness among African youngsters about the risks the virus poses. He is passionate that:

> All our teams and resources need to understand that this pandemic exists, that lots of people have died and more will do so in the future. We need to get as many people as possible to protect themselves because the continent really needs its children.

Apart from the HIV/AIDS awareness cause, Milla also played a prominent role in promoting South Africa 2010, an event that revealed the love and passion of the African people. Prior to the event, Milla and other soccer leaders went out of their way to show that Africa could stage a World Cup that was just as good as the previous ones. Indeed Roger Milla spent time rallying the people on the African continent to come together and support the 2010 World Cup in South Africa.

Roger Milla also devotes whatever spare time he has to helping others less fortunate than himself through his 'Heart of Africa Foundation'. This foundation provides aid to pygmies in the east of Cameroon and the orphans and children of the streets of Yaounde. In addition, Milla envisages helping former Cameroonian sports stars reintegrate into society especially those that have now been reduced to living rough. One of his future dreams is to set up an academy for up-and-coming centre-forwards in Cameroon to unearth and nurture the Samuel Eto'os of tomorrow. According to FIFA.com, no matter how successful the Cameroonian legend's new academy is, it is sure to be a long, long time before another Roger Milla emerges to grace the world stage.

Notes

1. http://www.fifa.com/worldcup/archive/southafrica2010/index.html (accessed February 27, 2013).
2. Lee and Lin, 'The Global Flows of International Professional Baseball System'.
3. Ibid., 286.
4. Ibid.
5. Bolsmann and Parker, 'Soccer, South Africa and Celebrity Status'.

6. Boorstin, *The Image*.
7. Bolsmann and Parker, 'Soccer, South Africa and Celebrity Status'.
8. Ibid., 111.
9. Ibid., 110.
10. Washington and Karen, 'Sport and Society'.
11. Andrews and Ritzer, 'The Grobal in the Sporting Glocal'. Also see Lines, 'Media Sport Audiences – Young People and the Summer of Sport '96'.
12. Jun and Lee, 'The Globalization of Sport and the Mass-mediated Identity of Hines Ward in South Korea'; Giulianotti and Robertson, 'Recovering the Social'.
13. Maguire, '"Real Politic" or "Ethically Based"'; Lines, 'Media Sport Audiences – Young People and the Summer of Sport '96'.
14. Thibault, 'Globalization of Sport'.
15. Rojek, 'Sports Celebrity and the Civilizing Process'.
16. Gladden, Irwin, and Sutton, 'Managing North American Major Professional Sport Teams in the New Millennium'; Silk and Andrews, 'Beyond a Boundary?'
17. Maguire, '"Real Politic" or "Ethically Based"'.
18. Magee and Sugden, 'The World at Their Feet'.
19. Ibid.; Maguire, '"Real Politic" or "Ethically Based"'.
20. Njororai, 'Global Inequality and Athlete Labour Migration from Kenya'.
21. Magee and Sugden, 'The World at Their Feet'.
22. Maguire, *Global Sport*.
23. Njororai, 'Global Inequality and Athlete Labour Migration from Kenya'.
24. Maguire, *Global Sport*.
25. Ibid.
26. Ibid.
27. Versi, *Football in Africa*.
28. See Cornelissen and Solberg, 'Sport Mobility and Circuits of Power'; Darby, 'Out of Africa'; Darby, Akindes, and Kirwin, 'African Football Labour Migration to Portugal'.
29. Alegi, *Laduma!*; Bolsmann and Parker, 'Soccer, South Africa and Celebrity Status'.
30. See Njororai, 'Global Inequality and Athlete Labour Migration from Kenya'. Also see Waiswa, 'Analysis of Factors Influencing Football Development in Selected Districts in Uganda'.
31. Ugor, 'Small Media, Popular Culture, and New Youth Spaces in Nigeria'.
32. Bolsmann and Parker, 'Soccer, South Africa and Celebrity Status'.
33. Ibid.
34. P. Alegi, *Laduma!*
35. Ibid.
36. Alexander, 'Chasing the Dream: Globalization and its Role on Sub-Saharan Football Migration' (2010), http://karlkicksitinsa.blogspot.com/2012/07/globalization-and-its-role-on-sub.html (accessed November 27, 2012).
37. Ibid.
38. Tiesler and Coelho, 'Globalized Football at a Lusocentric Glance'.
39. Alexander, 'Chasing the Dream'.
40. Andrews and Ritzer, 'The Grobal in the Sporting Glocal'.
41. Ugor, 'Small Media, Popular Culture, and New Youth Spaces in Nigeria'.
42. Poli, 'Migration and Trade of African Football Players'.
43. Tiesler and Coelho, 'Globalized Football at a Lusocentric Glance'; Alexander, 'Chasing the Dream'.
44. Poli, 'Migration and Trade of African Football Players'.
45. http://www.therichest.org/sports/highest-paid-football-players/ (accessed December 10, 2012).
46. Cornelissen and Solberg, 'Sport Mobility and Circuits of Power'.
47. Ibid.
48. Poli, 'Migration and Trade of African Football Players'.
49. Ibid.
50. Ibid.
51. FIFA.com 2010.
52. Ibid.

53. http://www.goal.com/en/people/c%C3%B4te-divoire/497/didier-drogba/profile (accessed December 11, 2012).
54. FIFA.com 2012.
55. Walters, 'Top Drog: Chelsea Fans Pick Euro Hero Didier as Club's Greatest Ever Player. Mirror Football', http://www.mirror.co.uk/sport/football/news/didier-drogba-voted-chelseas-greatest-1,410,537 (accessed December 11, 2012).
56. Cameroon had three draws against Peru, Poland and Italy, with the Poles going on to finish third and Italy becoming world champions.
57. FIFA.com.
58. Walters, 'Top Drog'.

References

Alegi, P. *Laduma! Soccer, Politics and Society in South Africa*. Scottsville: University of KwaZulu-Natal Press, 2004.
Andrews, D., and G. Ritzer. 'The Grobal in the Sporting Glocal'. *Global Networks* 7 (2007): 113–53.
Bolsmann, C., and A. Parker. 'Soccer, South Africa and Celebrity Status: Mark Fish, Popular Culture and the Post-apartheid State'. *Soccer & Society* 8, no. 1 (2007): 109–24.
Boorstin, D.J. *The Image: A Guide to Pseudo-events in America*. New York: Atheneum, 1961.
Cornelissen, Scarlett, and Eirik Solberg. 'Sport Mobility and Circuits of Power: The Dynamics of Football Migration in Africa and the 2010 World Cup'. *Politikon* 34, no. 3 (December 2007): 295–314.
Darby, P. 'African Football Labour Migration to Portugal: Colonial and Neo-colonial Resource'. *Soccer & Society* 8, no. 4 (2007): 495–509.
Darby, P. 'Out of Africa: The Exodus of Elite African Football Talent to Europe'. *Working USA: The Journal of Labor and Society* 10 (December 2007): 443–56.
Darby, P., G. Akindes, and M. Kirwin. 'Football Academies and the Migration of African Football Labor to Europe'. *Journal of Sport & Social Issues* 31, no. 2 (2007): 143–61.
Eriksen, T.H. 'Steps to An Ecology of Transnational Sports'. *Global Networks* 7, no. 2 (2007): 154–65.
Falcous, M., and M. Silk. 'Global Regimes, Local Agendas: Sport, Resistance and the Mediation of Dissent'. *International Review for the Sociology of Sport* 41 (2006): 317–38.
Giulianotti, R., and R. Robertson. 'Recovering the Social: Globalization, football and Transnationalism'. *Global Networks* 7, no. 2 (2007): 144–86.
Gladden, J.M., R.L. Irwin, and W.A. Sutton. 'Managing North American Major Professional Sport Teams in the New Millennium: A Focus on Building Brand Equity'. *Journal of Sport Management* 15 (2001): 297–317.
Grainger, A. 'From Immigrant to Overstayer: Samoan Identity, Rugby, and Cultural Politics of Race and Nation in Aotearoa/New Zealand'. *Journal of Sport and Social Issues* 30, no. 1 (2006): 45–61.
Jun, J.W., and H.M. Lee. 'The Globalization of Sport and the Mass-mediated Identity of Hines Ward in South Korea'. *Journal of Sport Management* 26 (2012): 103–12.
Lee, P.-C., and C.-Y. Lin. 'The Global Flows of International Professional Baseball System'. *The Sport Journal* 10, no. 4 (2007), http://www.thesportjournal.org/article/global-flowsinternational-professional-baseball-system
Lines, G. 'Media Sport Audiences – Young People and the Summer of Sport '96: Revisiting Frameworks for Analysis'. *Media Culture & Society* 22 (2000): 669–80.
Magee, J., and J. Sugden. '"The World at Their Feet": Professional Football and International Labor Migration'. *Journal of Sport & Social Issues* 26, no. 4 (2002): 421–37.
Maguire, J. *Global Sport: Individuals, Societies, Civilizations*. Cambridge, MA: Polity Press, 1999.
Maguire, J. '"Real Politic" or "Ethically Based": Sport, Globalization, Migration and Nation-state Policies'. *Sport in Society* 11, no. 4 (2008): 443–58.
Njororai, W.W.S. 'Distance Running in Kenya: Athletics Labour Migration and Its Consequences'. *Leisure/Loisir* 36, no. 2 (May 2012): 187–209.

Poli, Raffaele, 'Migration and Trade of African Football Players: Historic, Geographic and Cultural Aspects'. *Africa Spectrum* 41, no. 3 (2006): 393–414.

Rojek, C. 'Sports Celebrity and the Civilizing Process'. *Sport in Society* 9, no. 4 (2006): 674–90.

Rowe, D. 'Sport and the Repudiation of the Global'. *International Review for the Sociology of Sport* 38, no. 3 (2003): 281–94.

Silk, M.L., and D.L. Andrews. 'Beyond a Boundary? Sport, Transnational Advertising, and the Reimagining of National Culture'. *Journal of Sport & Social Issues* 25, no. 2 (2001): 180–201.

Njororai, W.W.S. 'Global Inequality and Athlete Labour Migration from Kenya'. *Leisure/ Loisir* 34, no. 4 (2010): 443–61.

Thibault, L. 'Globalization of Sport: An Inconvenient Truth'. *Journal of Sport Management* 23 (2009): 1–20.

Tiesler, N.C., and J.N. Coelho. 'Globalized Football at a Lusocentric Glance: Struggles with Markets and Migration, Traditions and Modernities, the Loss and the Beauty: An Introduction'. *Soccer & Society* 8, no. 4 (2007): 419–39.

Ugor, Paul, 'Small Media, Popular Culture, and New Youth Spaces in Nigeria'. *Review of Education, Pedagogy, and Cultural Studies* 31 (2009): 387–408.

Versi, A. *Football in Africa*. London: Collins, 1986.

Waiswa, K.A. 'Analysis of Factors Influencing Football Development in Selected Districts in Uganda'. Unpublished MSc thesis, Kyambogo University Kampala, Uganda, 2005.

Washington, R.E., and D. Karen. 'Sport and Society'. *Annual Review of Sociology* 27 (2001): 187–212.

Appendix 1. Roger Milla's affiliations, appearances, goals and achievements

Clubs, appearances and goals	Achievements	Details
(1) Valenciennes, Monaco, Bastia, Saint Etienne and Montpellier. Scored 152 goals in 312 matches (2) Appeared in World Cup Football final tournament in 1982, 1990 and 1994; played 10 matches and scored 5 goals. He was the 3rd top scorer in 1990 World Cup and oldest to score in World Cup match in 1994 at age 42 (3) Took part in 1984 Olympic Football Tournament, played 3 matches and scored 1 goal	(1) A two-time winner of the CAF Africa Cup of Nations, the African Golden Ball, the French Cup and the CAF Cup Winners Cup, and Cameroonian league title (2) A member of the FIFA 100 (the select band of greatest living footballers), African and Cameroonian player of the century and Knight of the Legion of Honour (3) CAF Africa Cup of Nations winner: 1984, 1988 *Individual* CAF Africa Cup of Nations joint-top scorer: 1984 (four goals), 1986 (four goals) CAF Africa Cup of Nations best player: 1986 (4) **Club honours** 1972 and 1973 Cameroon League and Cup Champion 1975 African Cup Winners Cup 1980 and 1981 French Cup winner 1987 French second-division champion (5) *Individual* FIFA 100 CAF Best African Player of the last 50 years: 2007 African Footballer of the Year: 1976, 1990	• Date of birth: 20 May 1952 • Birthplace: Yaounde, Cameroon • Roger Milla now passes on his experience as a player while working as a member of FIFA's Football Committee and Technical Study Group • Milla had been semi-retired for seven months, playing on the island of Reunion, when he returned to the Cameroon squad for Italia 90 • Ambassador for Cameroon and UNAIDS
International career Cameroon: 1978–1994 **Clubs** 1970–1973 Leopards de Duala (CMR) 1974–1977 Tonnerre de Yaunde (CMR) 1977–1979 Valenciennes (FRA) 1979–1980 Mónaco (FRA) 1980–1984 Bastia (FRA) 1984–1986 Saint-Étienne (FRA) 1986–1989 Montpellier (FRA) Saint-Pierre de la Reunion (Reunión) Pelita Jaya (Indonesia)		

Sources: FIFA.com (2012). Roger Milla, the pride of the Indomitable Lions at http://www.fifa.com/classicfootball/players/player=79318/bio.html.

Appendix 2. Didier Drogba's Club affiliations, appearances, goals and achievements

Clubs, appearances and goals	Achievements	Details
Current club: Galatasaray	Winner of the Champions League with Chelsea in 2012	• Date of birth: March 11, 1978
Previous clubs: Shanghai Shenhua, Vannes, Levallois, Le Mans, Guingamp, Marseille, Chelsea	Winner of the Premier League with Chelsea in 2005, 2006, 2010	• Height: 189 cm
	Winner of the Carling Cup with Chelsea in 2005, 2007	• Weight: 84 kg
Ivory Coast International 85 appearances, 56 goals	Winner of the FA Cup with Chelsea in 2007, 2009, 2010 and 2012	• Position: Striker
Number of Ligue 1 matches: 80	Winner of the Community Shield with Chelsea in 2005, 2009 Golden Boot winner with Chelsea in 2006	
Number of Ligue 1 goals: 39 Number of Premier League matches: 223	Vice champion of the Premier League with Chelsea in 2007, 2008 Finalist of the Champions League with Chelsea in 2008	
Number of Premier League goals: 100	Finalist of the Carling Cup with Chelsea in 2008	
Number of European Cup matches: 83	Finalist of the Community Shield with Chelsea in 2006, 2007 Finalist in the UEFA Cup with Marseille in 2004	
Number of European Cup goals: 45	African Footballer of the Year 2006 and 2009	
World Cup Final Tournament appearance in 2006 and 2010, 5 matches played and scored 2 goals	Finalist of the African Cup of Nations with Ivory Coast in 2006 and 2012 Semi-finalist of the African Cup of Nations with Ivory Coast in 2008	

Flawed heroes and great talents: the challenges associated with framing soccer legends in the NASL

Fernando Delgado

Department of Communication Studies and Theatre Arts, UW–River Falls, River Falls, WI, USA

The essay explores the ways that the North American Soccer Leagues (NASL) attempted to frame footballing stars in terms that North American fans would understand and embrace. The impetus for this approach was economic and influenced by the success of Pelé. However, the essay argues that the approach was deeply flawed and missed the obvious challenge of replacing Pelé – that he was irreplaceable. Nevertheless, the NASL and its boosters sought to position several stars as the natural successors to Pelé, including Franz Beckenbauer, George Best and Johan Curyff. The essay thus explores how these NASL stars were framed and how these frames would ultimately become limited.

Suppose you are a journalist assigned to write a story about a sport that is unfamiliar to most of your readers. The readers who know something about this sport knit it by its reputation for being low-scoring, unmanly and working class. Moreover, they think that this sport goes against their national identity and really belongs on foreign soil, where it began in the first place. Under such conditions, you probably would not expect your story to be aided by the announcement that a new player – a foreigner who grew up in rural poverty and is best known for his finesse rather than his strength has been recruited. And yet 25 years after soccer promoter, Clive Toye brought the Brazilian soccer star Pelé to play in the North American Soccer Leagues (NASL), no event has had a more significant effect in bring attention to the sport of soccer in the United States.[1]

In the afterglow of David Beckham's triumphant departure from Major League Soccer (MLS) in the fall of 2012, it would be easy to proclaim professional football in North America a finished product and highlight the professional game's new history from the league's inception in 1996. Concomitant with this move would be an observation of the incredible distance the professional game has travelled since Pelé signed with the New York Cosmos in 1975. But these tendencies would miss the continuities and similarities between the two leagues (despite MLS's ambivalence toward connections with the NASL) and the impact of the NASL on MLS. They would also elide the considerable and continuing economic, cultural and sporting challenges that confront the development of football as a spectator sport in North America. Indeed, while most trace MLS' lineage and foundation to the US hosting the 1994 World Cup, Hopkins observes that despite the demise of the NASL it would be unfair not to praise the incredible part it played in shaping the future of many great US [and we should add Canadian] soccer players and the role it played in enticing kids around the country to start kicking a ball.[2]

While the MLS is known for both buying and developing young players and selling them on to larger and more prestigious leagues (e.g. Clint Dempsey, Tim Howard and Josy Altidore), works such as Tossell's have typically focused on the NASL's strategy of purchasing predominantly lower tier British players or others well past their sell date.[3] But a review of both leagues demonstrates the common thread of acquiring experienced international players who also have developed some brand identity. The development of that individual brand identity has been seen as an important adjunct to any qualities on the pitch because it could resonate with potential ticket buyers and sponsors in North America. MLS has invested in any number of players well into their thirties (with varying degrees of on and off-field success) such as Carlos Valderrama, Lothar Mattheus, Youri Djorkaeff and, most famously, David Beckham in the hopes that on-field success and all forms of revenue would simultaneously increase.

This strategy is also visible in any number of developing leagues, such as those in Australia, Qatar and China, but the judicious acquisition of known international players who are capable of delivering the goods on the pitch is a risky proposition. The memories of the NASL suffer because of the perception that the NASL only contracted with players who no longer had ability or never had that ability. While some of that is true, the work of Colin Jose provides evidence that the NASL was also investing in players at various stages of their careers, including those far nearer to their peaks than the league was given credit for.[4] To be sure the likes of Gordon Banks, Colin Bell and Eusebio (to name but three) were nearer retirement and attempting returns from catastrophic injuries. But others such as Johan Neeskens, Hugo Sanchez and Trevor Francis were surely at or nearing the apex of their careers.

This essay, however, is not meant to be an abbreviated history of football in North America or the NASL, for there are several efforts that are excellent.[5] Rather, the focus here is on how investors, marketers and journalists attempted to legitimize football by following the model of Pelé and constructing the NASL around and through global icons and stars. In this fashion, they hoped to develop and enhance the league's standing by educating increasingly large and sophisticated audiences to meet short-term goals (financially sustain individual clubs and the league) and longer-term goals (acquire the right to host a World Cup and be seen as a peer on the international football scene). Of course these goals and strategies confronted a complex landscape where ethnic communities had long and very involved histories with the game, domestically and internationally, while other communities of sports fans were apathetic or openly hostile to the sport, and a yet a third group of spectators and fans was curious and engaged – the legacy of Pelé was to energize grassroots participation in football – but naïve in terms of the scale and scope of the global game and its stars.

Nevertheless, the league and its various clubs with sufficient financial resources acquired many well-known international players in an effort to meet these goals. Among them are the football icons that are the centerpiece of this analysis – Franz Beckenbauer, George Best and Johann Cruyff. Each of these players graced the plastic and natural turf pitches of the NASL and, in turn, each was seen as the logical corollary or inheritor of the Pelé model and legacy. Yet, through their individual playing styles and personal attributes they also created challenging and confounding frames for NASL's supporters to translate for erstwhile fans, soccer moms and the youth supporters they brought to the stadia from the mid-1970s to the ultimate demise of the NASL by the mid-1980s. The attempt to frame these icons in terms that would appeal to North American soccer audiences demonstrates just how challenging it is to construct stable and meaningful media frames for consumers and audiences. By focusing on the efforts to frame Pelé's inheritors, the essay will highlight the manner in which US football and NASL boosters sought to explain football's royalty to a largely unsuspecting and unknowing audience of North American football newcomers.

Apprentices, journeymen, stars and a few North Americans

In the efforts to establish professional football as a force in the US and Canadian cultural and sporting landscape, the NASL (1968–1984) stands out as the largest and arguably most successful attempt at securing a toehold for football as a spectator sport prior to MLS. At its heyday, the NASL drew healthy crowds and was home to foreigners past their prime, others who had never made their mark back home, youngsters (both foreign and North American) striving to make their reputation, and stars at various points along their career. Above all, the NASL was the first North American attempt at creating a viable professional soccer league that had, at least for a short period of time, a major infusion of financial investment (in the forms of billionaire Lamar Hunt and corporate investors such as Time-Warner and Gulf + Western) and mainstream media coverage. For all its flaws, NASL fans had ready access to a constellation of the world's footballing stars and celebrities (perhaps some North American spectators were not truly sure of their value and worth in these pre-ESPN, FoxSports and internet days). While the ultimate impact of the NASL can be debated, its legacy was felt and can be measured by the number of managers, owners and players who became integral to the MLS.

Of course, any conversation about the NASL starts and seemingly ends with Pelé's arrival in 1975 and while he certainly stands out in world footballing terms as *the* icon of post-War soccer, the NASL was home to many other stars and icons. While works such as Colin Jose's encyclopedic coverage of the league provide detail into the clubs and players of the NASL, a broader view of the league suggests that its fans were appreciating the talents of a wide range of global football stars.[6] As Tossell observes, 'Pelé would be followed to the NASL by a veritable who's who of world football'[7] – an observation reinforced by a review of the World Cup Rosters between 1970 and 1978. However, across the decade and a half of the NASL's history three athletes, beyond Pelé, stand out as sporting icons hosted by the league: Franz Beckenbauer, George Best and Johan Cruyff. These three talents, because of their relevance to the league and sport but also because of the complexities they created for those covering and promoting the league at the time serve demand our attention as subjects of inquiry into the heroes of US professional football.

Clearly, the arrival of Pelé in 1975 immediately engendered a highly competitive and inflationary model within the NASL, a model built around the acquisition of name players that was economically unsustainable in the absence of robust television contracts and other forms of revenue to support the teams and growth of the

NASL. But the impact that Pelé had, especially off the field by virtue of his star power and celebrity, encouraged the Cosmos and other teams to pursue players with international reputations. As Lanfranchi and Taylor have pointed out, 'The post-Pelé era arguably introduced a further type [of import] – the high-profile star international such as Beckenbauer, Cruyff, Best, Eusebio, and Carlos Alberto'.[8] Thus, NASL clubs moved forward, particularly from 1977 through 1980, acquiring these international stars and first-division talents, either to replace or supplement Pelé, and they were seen as vital to the eventual success of the league and certainly to the individual clubs that contracted them. In a North American sporting landscape that was star-driven, these footballing heroes were perceived as crucial to the league's attempts to improve the quality of play, draw media and fan attention, and garner the respect of the rest of the footballing world.

The strategy became an arms race that was economic folly. As Elliott and Harris write, 'Part of NASL's strategy to develop the sport occurred through the signing of some of the most well-known players in the world'.[9] But to attract such talent the clubs, in particular the Cosmos, were going well beyond market value and fiscal prudence. For example, Johan Neeskens was offered $2 million annually over five years a sum that would be unmatched because 'no European club could offer him anything like the same financial package'[10] and NASL coach Hubert Vogelsinger noted how 'since Beckenbauer got his million from the Cosmos, every player wants to be paid twice as much as he is really worth'.[11] Though neither Beckenbauer's nor Neeskens' contracts were representative of most players in the NASL it took just a few inflated contracts, in a era where good attendances were in the 18,000 range and the local and national television contracts were yielding scant revenue for the league to bankrupt most clubs. As Wangerin observes, the attention paid to the Cosmos' constellation of stars and their periodically gaudy attendances masked another reality in the league such as in Southern California where 'a rather more humbling 5295 were scattered inside the Los Angeles Coliseum for a playoff game between the Aztecs and Dallas [Tornado]'.[12]

The economic model and its flaws were known and even commented on as the NASL was reaching its apex. Wangerin recalls the various strategies identified by an NASL strategic planning group formed in 1977, among the plans developed was more modest expansion and the need to address the economic disparities in the league.[13] As Paul Kennedy wrote, at the near high point of the NASL, 'if the North American Soccer League's recent history is any indication, for every successful franchise, there will be another that will float along in a pool of red ink and a third that will sink'.[14] And driving up the costs was the escalating price of player acquisition and salaries since very few clubs were developing their own (North American) talent. The perception was that in order to grow the game, NASL clubs needed to find the next Pelé, as Nick Matavulli wrote in *Soccer America*, 'the "we need Pelé clubs", instead of concentrating on marketing soccer, will be looking for another instant success'.[15] Whatever marketing strategy would be deployed, the collaboration of the mass media was central to the economics of the NASL:

> New cities seem to be drawing well, but none of the standard soccer centers are drawing flies and there is great question that the Cosmos would be soaring so high without the magic draw of Pelé. Even the greatness of a George Best or a Franz Beckenbauer is not sufficient to pull people who have heard hardly a word about their greatness in the US press.[16]

But the allure of star power was too great. The league had tasted some success, there was growing media attention, and the Pelé/Cosmos model had been shown to work in both the trophy cabinet and in the turnstiles. In the end, the dependency on international players, often on severely inflated wages, would not only be economic suicide it would also stunt the development of American and Canadian players, something not addressed until 1983's Team America entry into the NASL – too little, far too late. Wangerin provides insight into this conundrum of using establishing players from abroad vs. trying largely untested North Americans, "while the NASL continued to be dominated by foreign imports, it had always been assumed that 'in a few years' the league would become predominantly American",[17] yet the structure of how teams were run mitigated this strategy as

> the league's managers, almost all of them British, were much more comfortable rummaging through the Football League for durable tradesmen looking for summer work rather than traipsing across North America in pursuit of unproven or unfamiliar names, be they young collegiate or capable semi-professionals.[18]

Ignoring the domestic market suggested that many NASL clubs (one notable exception being the Chicago Sting under the direction of Willy Roy) were focused on short-term returns. Newsham recalls how 1979 heralded a next stage of expansion with 'the rest of the NASL squads bolstering their squads, confident that national television exposure would lead to healthier crowds and increased revenue'.[19] But these newly contracted stars were not the likes of Pelé. They had neither the celebrity that crossed cultural boundaries nor the magnetic personality that attracted neutrals to the game. Moreover, few of the arrivals saw themselves in a missionary role with a charge to grow the global game in North America; a role Pelé surely embraced wherever he went. Coupled with the stagnant development of true US and Canadian stars who could draw North American fans who 'identified' with the home-grown talent, the NASL struggled to truly sustain the impact of Pelé, a challenge exacerbated by over-aggressive and not well thought-out expansion into cities that could not adequately support a club. The loss of Pelé was significant because the league now had no beacon that could successfully carry the game's appeal beyond the stadia and playing fields. But rather than fold up shop with the departure of Pelé, NASL's leadership took energy from his time in the league and sought to create energy around the established and arriving international stars. The league's job, abetted by those in the media with personal or professional interests in seeing the game grow, was to frame these stars so that audiences, consumers and fans would embrace them just as Pelé was embraced. It would prove to be an interesting but difficult strategy.

Constructing media frames

Thus, we turn to the mechanics of how such international stars as Beckenbauer, Best and Cruyff were sold or framed for the North American football audience. Given the centrality of the mass media, in this particular instance print media, in articulating information about international footballers to casual and avid fans in North America in the 1970s and early 1980s, the considerable scholarly inquiry into and application of media frames is entirely relevant. Indeed, at its core, the study of media frames is about the relationship between audiences, their interpretations and engagement with media representations of people, issues, values and themes.

At its core, framing is a function of how the mass media operate for, as Scheufele observes, the 'mass media have a strong impact by constructing social reality'[20] for audiences and readers. According to Gitlin, media producers (seen as elite and controlling) use frames as a manner to select, emphasize and exclude certain topics, issues and meanings.[21] Von Sikorski and Schierl note how 'journalists regularly use media frames to turn complex issues and occurrences into newsworthy events by selecting and transferring specific aspects of reality into comprehensible news stories'.[22] Rhee argues that because media frames impact how readers/viewers interact with news texts 'it is important to ask how news frames influence the individual's interpretation'.[23] And, staying focused in the news, Scheufele concludes, 'the framing and presentation of events and news in the mass media can thus systematically affect how recipients of the news come to understand these events'.[24]

The marketers and journalists who strove to build a growing and dynamic fan base for football and the NASL sought frames that could elicit positive reactions from actual and potential fans; legitimate the game and league; and continue to be seen as credible for those fans and cognoscenti who were knowledgeable about the global game. While it may be true that many US sports writers and editors were openly hostile to football, there were others – Jules Furth, Paul Gardner, Frank Dell'Appa, George Vescey – who were clearly supporters of the game and the NASL. They often functioned like public relations experts insofar as they had to translate meaning, history, context and tactics to North American readers. As Satterlee has observed, 'to educate and at the same time to interest their audience became a common rhetorical predicament for authors who wrote about Pelé [and presumably the NASL] in the mid-1970s', a readership that was often presumed to be a 'soccer illiterate audience'.[25]

The writers' efforts were thus more consonant with the view that media frames, Semetko and Valkenburg have shown, shape or select reality for media consumers by narrowing and organizing news content[26] as they strove to educate and convert. The writer who sought to attract readers and fans to the game would follow the suggestion of Entman who observes that media frames 'highlight some bits of information about an item that is the subject of a communication'.[27] As a result, frames are part of a mass-mediated social construction of reality or, as Gamson and Modigliani observe, 'the frame suggests what the controversy is about, the essence of the issue'.[28] Following Gamson and Modgliani's language here, the desire for the NASL was to communicate the essence of the stardom of Pelé's followers, the next round of footballing stars who would fill his gap and nudge the popularity of the game forward and legitimize the league.

Insofar as the print media texts chosen here are partisan in the sense that they are focused on celebrating and reinforcing football to relatively naïve and comparatively uninformed US fans of the professional sport, the framing of football icons playing in the NASL from the post-Pelé arrival in 1975 through the demise of the league in 1984 follows along both conventional journalist ethics and a desire to recruit a larger fan base for the league and sport. Thus, it can be reasonably argued that the writers and editors in regional newspapers and periodicals such *Soccer America* participated in intentionally constructing frames for these heroes that highlighted the players' truly global stature while also grappling with any personal or character issues that might prove negative. The goals of media outlets could coincide with the commercial and economic interests of the NASL and its teams. Thus, the observation made by Tucker that the purpose of such media framing activities is 'to define particular aspects of reality in ways that support specific interests'[29] aptly captures the purposefulness of framing NASL football heroes.

In fact, the media framers who supported and sought to expand football's popularity in the US were not simply battling (potential) fan ignorance of or apathy toward the sport but also other powerful, and primarily print, media framers who were overtly hostile to the sport and the NASL. As Clive Toye, a seminal figure in the development of the NASL, recalls:

> Prescott Sullivan of the *San Francisco Examiner* wrote: 'In Europe as in South America they go raving mad over the game. Pray that it doesn't happen here. The way to beat it is constant vigilance and rigid control. If soccer shows signs of getting too big, swat it down …' Dick Young, *New York Daily News* sports editor and columnist and all-around man of influence in those days, once said to one of his young reporters: 'Don't waste your time on soccer, young man; it's a game for commie pansies'.[30]

Aligned with the hostility for old guard sports writers was the basic insularity of many (particularly non-ethnic) sports fans for whom football was either alien or exotic. As Wangerin observed of the NASL's efforts to import footballing talent, principally from the United Kingdom:

> The acquisition of such ageing international talent may have improved the quality of play, but it had little impact at the gate, as the [San Antonio] Thunder quickly discovered. Few Texans had heard of [England World Cup hero] Bobby Moore, and if they had it was bound to be the one who played wide receiver for the Minnesota Vikings and had changed his name to Ahmad Rashad.[31]

In this environment, then, it was critical for NASL's media framers and like-minded marketers to construct an appealing image of the game that was connected to the global context of the game to assure legitimacy both home and abroad. But the effort also had to make the presence of the given star locally meaningful to fans that might fill the home stadium. In simpler terms, the goal was to build through and beyond the singular icon and persona of Pelé who, with his arrival in New York, became the symbol and lighthouse for the league. As Hopkins observes in his analysis marketing football in the USA, 'Soccer to most American corporations, and indeed Americans, meant just one thing: PELE'.[32] Thus, the introduction of other true global icons was necessary to any hope at expansion and legitimation. But the introduction of such players needed to be supported by PR, marketing and media coverage that educated and reinforced positive messages about the sport, league and the presumed stars that would legitimize the NASL in and beyond North America.

As a consequence, the frames that emerge needed to (1) construct the player as a star, reminding fans and readers that this player is outstanding and has successfully competed at the highest level; (2) humanize the star and suggest why each was in North America playing for their respective teams. In this way, the goal was to pursue the fan by elevating them through identification or association with the star. The third and final component arises from the first two. Superstars in any sport are often arrogant and impolitic. Moreover, they can – in the way that in recent times English footballer Paul Gascoigne has shown in the tabloid press – be extraordinarily flawed as humans, and this can further complicate positive associations among fans, the media, the athlete and the sport or league. In the following section, I explore how these three themes are shot through the frames provided by the NASL and principally through their media allies.

They really are superstars

The case for Beckenbauer, Best and Cruyff to be footballing superstars would seem to be self-evident to experienced followers of the global game but the audience that was sought for North American football was not largely composed of such fans and writers. The case had to be bluntly made and the framing for such stars had to be clear, obvious and redundant. Thus, the official NASL media guide for 1978 suc-cinctly states that Beckenbauer is 'considered to be one the finest players in the his-tory of the game'.[33] Of course, while one must accept that all sports journalism can be prone to hyperbole, Pelé's putative successors had to be framed as near his equal (and in many cases they were, if for no other reason that they were nearer to their peak as athletes). And this connection to Pelé but also the extension of world-class talent beyond the strict parameters of Pelé's time in the league is well articulated by NASL Commissioner Phil Woosnam:

> Prior to Pelé's arrival, no one could have imagined that our fans would have the oppor-tunity to see such world-renowned players as Beckenbauer, Carlos Alberto, Best, Moore, Hunt, Ball, Banks, Bogicevic, Chinaglia, Marinho, briefly Cruyff, playing for NASL clubs.[34]

Thus, from this foundation, the superlatives that frame the footballing talents of Beckenbauer, Best and Cruyff present each player as a legitimate star of global stat-ure who, like Pelé, is in North America to take football to the next level and be accessible to fans. For example, Cruyff's ability as a playmaker is presented in sym-phonic terms: 'Just as the conductor of a symphony is able to direct and orchestrate a team of musicians to a coordinated effort, so does Johan exude a dynamic leader-ship in molding his ensemble to a high winning percentage'.[35] This construct of leadership and sublime skill also extends to others. One account concludes that 'everything that can be said about Beckenbauer has already been spoken ... the Kaiser can do it all'.[36] As one writer, extolling Beckenbauer's midfield play and influence, observes, 'the perfect example [of midfield play] is Franz Beckenbauer, the fabulous Kaiser Franz, one of the world's premier performers who left his native West Germany to join the Cosmos'.[37] With Cruyff there was no doubt about his status when he was introduced, 'Cruyff, a three-time European player of the year has been called the best in the world since Pelé retired',[38] and fortuitously here he is swapping Barcelona's *blaugrana* for LA Aztec orange and white.

In California, where first Best and then Cruyff tried to help the Los Angeles Aztecs recreate the Cosmos vibe in the other media centre in the US, the need for a superstar is clear. Aztecs co-owner Larry Friend breathlessly described Cruyff as

> absolutely incredible. The last time I saw one athlete turning on a crowd like this was in 1960 when Elgin Baylor was a rookie the [NBA's Los Angeles] Lakers ... every time he makes a run people expect him to do something special.[39]

No doubt Friend and his fellow investors were first among those who with such lofty expectations. Unfortunately, football is a more complex game with fewer opportunities for even one sublime player to dominate the ball and the game. Worse, many of the fans could not appreciate the small and quiet things that players like Cruyff could do off the ball to create space and opportunity for his teammates. No, what they expected was Cruyff to do it all, all of the time. And, to make matters worse, neither Cruyff nor Best was surrounded by the quality talent that was evident in the Cosmos starting 11 as well as on its bench.

Before Cruyff arrived, Best was to provide the magic that sparked professional football in Southern California. Indeed, Best is often framed as the pinnacle of midfield play: 'If he [a midfielder] can score, defend, and be a playmaker he's a superstar. Like George Best of the Los Angeles Aztecs'.[40] His fame and notoriety preceded his actual arrival and he was certainly was 'the world-class superstar from Northern Ireland',[41] supremely talented and mercurial (both on and off the field). His turn of play and showmanship actually approached that of Pelé in terms of thrilling fans. Best's undoing, as it would be throughout his career were his own personal demons and addictions. But fans and writers alike were prepared to embrace and elevate Best to the peak of world football – even comparing him with Cruyff (who had not yet arrived in the NASL) and repeating a common refrain, ascribed to English footballer Derek Dougan: 'Cruyff was manufactured on earth; Best was made in heaven'.[42] Best's arrival provided the opportunity to bookend American football with King Pelé and the Irish pretender. Even a match between the Cosmos and Aztecs could tax the footballing superlatives and metaphors. Though the LA fans would boo the absence, by injury, of the immortal Kaiser of West Germany, the game itself was a 'right royal gathering with King Pelé, King George the Best of Ireland, "Il Duce" Giorgio Chinaglia, Bonnie Prince Charlie Cooke, and a regal entourage'.[43] Of course, because he was the equal of Pelé, 'Best dazzled the Cosmos defense'.[44]

In this frame these and other stars that arrived on North American soil had to serve the role of growing and energizing the base. But, as we shall see in the next section thrilling play on the field did not always translate into popularity and ticket sales in the way Pelé's arrival in 1975 had instantly changed the league.

But heroes have flaws

If players have come close to achieving Pelé's greatness during the rise of the media age and interdependency with football, few of these players have matched his charisma or ability to elicit the affection of fans. A solid and stolid professional like Beckenbauer certainly could not. As Newsham writes in his history of the New York Cosmos, 'Beckenbauer lacked the natural charisma and gregarious nature that Pelé possessed … his quiet demeanor hadn't really endeared him to the crowd in the same way they had taken to the Brazilian'.[45] Cruyff was similarly quiet though he appeared to recognize the missionary purpose of his presence in the NASL, 'maybe I can help the sport grow here in America. It seems a shame that such a world wide sport is not yet accepted in this great country'.[46] Whatever Cruyff's intention to develop the popularity and stature of the sport, he (like Beckenbauer) could not translate this into the kind of energy and fervour that Pelé was able to create.

There are indications of perhaps why. Newsham observes how Beckenbauer's Cosmos teammate Giorgio Chinaglia, who would quickly displace Pelé as the face of the club, noted that while Beckenbauer was excellent as a player there was no indication this his presence would lead to greater ticket sales or increased advertising revenue in the US. These two stars possessed none of the cross-platform celebrity that Pelé brought with him nor did they exude or embrace the showmanship necessary to pull fans in. For example, Cruyff, escaping the scrutiny and pressures of Spanish and European football, is relatively anonymous in Los Angeles where 'he is able to walk around without being hounded by autograph seekers and the usual groupies . . . his low profile affords him a cocoon of privacy', perhaps welcome by

Cruyff and his family but exactly opposite of what the club and league owners desired from their high-priced star.

Beckenbauer, often described in match reports as smooth, composed, professional and sublime, did not bring the same effervescence to the stadia that Pelé or even lesser lights such as Rodney Marsh to the stadia of North America. Moreover, at the end of the season Beckenbauer (when not on world tour with the Cosmos) retreated back to his home in Switzerland. While his was the face of the adidas sporting goods company and German football, Beckenbauer's position, style and personality did not themselves to be the heir to Pelé's legacy. He was merely exceptional as player when the NASL needed another star of unquestioned status and appeal among North American spectators trying to find a reason to stay with the league. Beckenbauer was the true professional at a time when the NASL was almost best known for outlandish promotions, fan participation and elements like the cheerleader Krazy George, he of the ripped shorts, drum and ridiculous antics as he led fan chants, most notably with the San Jose Earthquakes.

Perhaps that is why George Best was so important to that early post-Pelé period. Here was a true footballing star that also brought other elements to the media circus. The cerebral Cruyff and the quietly strong Beckenbauer were no match for Best coming out of self-imposed exile. The LA Aztecs knew this non-footballing dimension could bring other media attention beyond the sports pages. Thus,

> on the day he arrived in the USA, the media was handed a list that was supposed to contain the highlights of Best's career … instead it looked more like the rap sheet of a juvenile delinquent.[47]

As one account of his initial presentation to the Southern California press attests:

> Celebrity arrivals in Los Angeles tend to be media events, and George Best was no exception. Lights, camera and 'let's see some action, George', was the attitude of the LA press, which had prepared for the arrival of soccer's most famous bad boy by reading through his lurid collection of British notices. George Best, in classic British tradition, was not amused.[48]

Football has long been full of wayward geniuses. The likes of Garrincha, Paul Gascoigne, Diego Maradona each provide common enough examples of creative footballers who battled demons off and on the pitch. Combined with footballing subcultures, particularly prevalent among the British, that embraced or encouraged alcohol consumption we should not be surprised that a George Best emerges in the 1960s as a sublime footballer who was combustible on and off the pitch. It is perhaps perfect then that Best arrives as the West Coast's version of Pelé but also as the temperamentally opposite persona to Pelé. Whereas Pelé brought lightness and fame, Best brought a brooding darkness that assured notoriety and, by the time he left Los Angeles for Fort Lauderdale and then San Jose, headlines associated with his alcoholism, indiscipline and disappearances from his clubs. Still, he brought the NASL headlines, though it is unclear as to how such headlines would encourage soccer moms and dads to see his antics.

Indeed, even as Best promised to do better there was anticipation that the proverbial wagon would have him off and he would disappear for a few days. As the media described him upon his sale from Los Angeles to Fort Lauderdale, 'the former English Footballer of the Year comes to the Strikers with the reputation, deserved or underserved, of a free spirit, and individualist, a difficult player to coach'.[49] He was thus, apart from the footballing brilliance, everything that Pelé was not. No one would have expected Pelé to disappear from the Cosmos for days on end but Best, attracting all manner of attention, would go 'AWOL four times this [1979] season',[50] frustrating his teammates and mystifying management. The irony of many of his disappearances was that 'chances are they [management] could have found him at Bestie's Bar in Hermosa Beach', the drinking establishment owned by Best.[51] And, though he often did the business on the field, it was Best's sins that provided the greatest amount of media coverage for his clubs and the league. Periodically, the on and off field would intersect as when he would show up to games drunk or when his temperament would get the best of him, as when Strikers coach Ron Newman substituted Best and his temper flared on his way to the locker room. Still, in the best spirit of friendship and co-dependency, coach Newman was able to get past this unprofessional outburst, 'He's an Irishman, and we forgive all Irishmen. He has a hot blood temper. But we're good friends. We had a couple of beers and made up'.[52] It is unlikely these breaches of discipline and public displays of unprofessionalism and alcoholism would be readily tolerated today but for the NASL a spectacle meant coverage and interest and that is why someone like Best was signed in the first place.

Conclusion

Perhaps the downfall of the NASL was the failure of stars such as Beckenbauer, Best and Cruyff who could not sustain the energy Pelé brought to the league from 1975 through 1977. But their failure was not on the pitch or the result of their fading skills as footballers. In the end their failure was simply that they were not Pelé. In a developing market, the NASL was reaching out to new fans – middle-class suburbanites in most cases who would morph into the next generation's 'soccer moms' – and, as Willy Keo observed a month before Pelé's testimonial match in 1977, 'they know little beyond the name of Pelé. He is surely as rare as Haley's comet if not a one-and-only'.[53] The NASL was a grand and often highly entertaining experiment – clubs with an international flavour unmatched until the advent of the Champions League, Bosman ruling and global television altered the composition of clubs in Europe during the 1990s – with a few embarrassing moments of amateurism and American hubris thrown in for good measure. True football fans attending NASL matches could take with them tremendous memories of having seen some of the greatest players of the 1960s and 1970s on display (even if some of them were bit beyond their prime). Indeed, even a tired and well-pastit George Best could produce a brilliant goal for the San Jose Earthquakes that lives on, via YouTube, in our internet age and gives some indication of what such heroic footballers brought in to the NASL pitches.

However, in trying to market the sport around world footballing heroes, they too soon found Pelé rather than building to his arrival; thus what followed was forever informed and distorted by what Pelé represented and could bring; and the error was to presume that every other footballing star had his personality and charisma and that every erstwhile footballing fan would see these heroes through the same rose-coloured lenses as they saw the King himself. The danger in building a model around heroes is that in sport heroes will inevitably fail us and if we have not built a well of affection for the game itself or a willingness, perhaps a maturity, to transfer our identification and fanaticism to the next hero we lose interest in the game. This process in an already saturated sporting landscape that is North America was death to the NASL. Yet, for a relatively short period of time, the NASL attracted a constellation of stars that, if you were paying attention, would take your breath away. It remains a shame that the league's promoters, boosters and marketers could not see their way through the glitz and the glam to frame the game and its stars in a way that encouraged the organic identification of fan to star, of spectator to hero. I suspect the league would have lasted longer and the game, at least in the US, would better off. Still, how does one learn to do this when the original template was arguably the game's greatest and most popular player? When you begin with the greatest idol all that follow have the patina of falseness.

Notes

1. Satterlee, 'Making Soccer a "Kick in the Grass"', 305.
2. Hopkins, *Star-spangled Soccer*, 29.
3. Tossell, *Playing for Uncle Sam*.
4. Jose, *North American Soccer League Encyclopedia*.
5. See the works of Allaway. Allaway, *Rangers, Rovers, and Spindles*; Allaway, *Corner Offices and Corner Kicks*; Allaway, Jose, and Litterer, *The Encyclopedia of American Soccer*.
6. Jose, *North American Soccer League Encyclopedia*.
7. Tossell, *Playing for Uncle Sam*, 77.
8. Lanfranchi and Taylor, *Moving the Ball*, 160.
9. Elliott and Harris, 'Crossing the Atlantic from Football to Soccer', 563.
10. Lanfranchi and Taylor, *Moving the Ball*, 161.
11. Matavulli, 'Hubert Vogelsinger', 5.
12. Wangerin, *Distant Corners*, 211.
13. Ibid.
14. Kennedy, 'The Economics of Soccer', 6.
15. Matavulli, 'When Pelé is Gone', 8.
16. Keo, 'A Little NASL Chit Chat', 22.
17. Wangerin, *Soccer in a Football World*, 155.
18. Ibid.
19. Newsham, *Once in a Lifetime*, 168.
20. Scheufele, 'Framing as a Theory of Media Effects', 105.
21. Gitlin, *The Whole World is Watching*.
22. Von Sikorski and Schierl, 'Effects of News Frames on Recipients' Information Processing in Disability Sports Communications', 114.
23. Rhee, 'Strategy and Issue Frames in Election Campaign Coverage', 27.
24. Scheufele, 'Framing as a Theory of Media Effects', 107.
25. Satterlee, 'Making Soccer a "Kick in the Grass"', 310.
26. Semetko and Valkenburg, 'Framing European Politics'.
27. Entman, 'Framing: Toward a Clarification of a Fractured Paradigm', 53.
28. Gamson and Modigliani, 'The Changing Culture of Affirmative Action', 143.
29. Tucker, 'The Framing of Calvin Klein', 143.
30. Toye, *A Kick in the Grass*, 113.
31. Wangerin, *Soccer in a Football World*, 175.
32. Hopkins, 28.
33. *1978 North American Soccer League Guide*, 59.
34. Woosnam, 'From the Commissioner,' 3N.
35. Furth, 'Cruyff', 17.
36. Kuzbyt, 'The Cosmos', 9.
37. Kapelian, 'Mini-clinic: Midfielders', 54N.
38. Robledo, 'Fatigued Cruyff Dazzles in LA', 8.
39. Robledo, 'Cruyff Draws Fans to Rose Bowl', 14.
40. Kapelian, 'Mini-clinic: Midfielders', 53N.
41. Stephens, 'Los Angeles Relied on their Best Man', 15.

42. Robledo, 'George Best: Playboy or Playmaker', 3N.
43. Pugh, 'David and the Aztec Gang Lasso the Cosmos', 14.
44. Ibid., 14.
45. Newsham, *Once in a Lifetime*, 195.
46. Robledo, 'Fatigued Cruyff Dazzles in LA', 8.
47. Robledo, 'George Best: Playboy or Playmaker', 5N.
48. 'George Best: Winner', 62.
49. Serni, 'Best Plans to Become a New Man', 7.
50. Sheldon, 'Best AWOL Again', 7.
51. Ibid.
52. Sheldon, 'Strikers Find Magic in Win', 8.
53. Keo, 'A Look at Logic and Fairness', 21.

References

Allaway, Roger. *Rangers, Rovers, and Spindles: Soccer, Immigration and Textiles in New England and New Jersey*. Haworth, NJ: St. Johann Press, 2005.

Allaway, Roger. *Corner Offices and Corner Kicks: How Big Business Created America's Two Greatest Soccer Dynasties, Bethlehem Steel and the New York Cosmos*. Haworth, NJ: St. Johann Press, 2009.

Allaway, Roger, Colin Jose, and David Litterer. *The Encyclopedia of American Soccer History*. Lanham, MD: The Scarecrow Press, 2001.

Elliott, Richard, and John Harris. 'Crossing the Atlantic from Football To Soccer: Preliminary Observations on the Migrations of English Players and the Internationalization of Major League Soccer'. *Working USA: The Journal of Labor and Society* 14 (2011): 557–70.

Entman, Robert. 'Framing: Toward Clarification of a Fractured Paradigm'. *Journal of Communication* 43 (1993): 51–8.

Furth, Jules. 'Cruyff'. *Soccer America*, December 20, 1979, 16–8.

Gamson, William, and Andre Modigliani. 'The Changing Culture of Affirmative Action'. In *Research in Political Sociology*, ed. Richard Braungart and Margaret Braungart, 137–77. Greenwich, CT: JAI Press, 1987.

'George Best: Winner'. *Soccer Corner*, June, 1977, 62–3.

Gitlin, Todd. *The Whole World is Watching: Mass Media in the Making and Unmaking of the New Left*. Berkeley: University of California Press, 1980.

Hopkins, Gary. *Star-spangled Soccer: The Selling, Marketing and Management of Soccer in the USA*. New York: Palgrave Macmillan, 2010.

Jose, Colin. *North American Soccer League Encyclopedia*. Haworth, NJ: St. Johann Press, 2003.

Kapelian, Varten. 'Mini-clinic: Midfielders'. *Kick Magazine*, June 10, 1978, 53N

Kennedy, Paul. 'The Economics of Soccer'. *Soccer America* 14, May 11, 1978, 6–7. 18.

Keo, Willy. 'A Look at Logic and Fairness'. *Soccer America* 23, September 6, 1977, 20–1.

Keo, Willy. 'A Little NASL Chit Chat'. *Soccer America*, August 23, 1977, 22.

Kuzbyt, Bob. 'The Cosmos'. *Soccer America*, March 30, 1978, 9.

Lanfranchi, Pierre, and Matthew Taylor. *Moving the Ball: The Migration of Professional Footballers*. New York: Berg, 2001.

Matavulli, Nick. 'When Pelé is Gone'. *Soccer America* 13, no. 5 (August 2, 1977): 8–9.

Matavulli, Nick. 'Hubert Vogelsinger. In Tune in San Diego'. *Soccer America* 14, no. 18 (May 4, 1978): 9–10.

Newsham, Gavin. *Once in a Lifetime: The Incredible Story of the New York Cosmos*. New York: Grove Press, 2006.

1978 North American Soccer League Guide. New York: NASL, 1978.

Pugh, Brian. 'David and the Aztec Gang Lasso the Cosmos'. *Soccer America*, July 5, 1977, 14–5.

Rhee, June Woong. 'Strategy and Issue Frames in Election Campaign Coverage: A Social Cognitive Account of Framing Effects'. *Journal of Communication* 47 (1997): 26–48.

Robledo, Fred. 'George Best: Playboy or Playmaker'. *Kick Magazine*, June 7, 1978, 3N–5N, 57N–58N.

Robledo, Fred. 'Cruyff Draws Fans to Rose Bowl'. *Soccer America*, June 7, 1979, 13–4.

Robledo, Fred. 'Fatigued Cruyff Dazzles in LA'. *Soccer America*, May 31, 1979, 8.

Satterlee, Thom. 'Making Soccer a "Kick in the Grass:" The Media's Role in Promoting a Marginal Sport, 1975–1977'. *International Review for the Sociology of Sport* 36 (2001): 305–17.

Scheufele, Dietram. 'Framing as a Theory of Media Effects'. *Journal of Communication* 49 (1999): 103–22.

Semetko, Holli, and Patti Valkenburg. 'Framing European Politics: A Content Analysis of Press and Television News'. *Journal of Communication* 50 (2000): 93–109.

Serni, Jim. 'Best Plans to Became a New Man'. *Soccer America*, July 6, 1978, 7.

Sheldon, Bill. 'Best AWOL Again'. *Soccer America*, August 2, 1979, 7, 16.

Sheldon, Bill. 'Strikers Find Magic in Win'. *Soccer America*, April 5, 1979, 8.

Stephens, Phil. 'Los Angeles Relied on their Best Man'. *Soccer America*, August 23, 1977, 15.

Tossell, David. *Playing for Uncle Sam: The Brits' Story of the North American Soccer League.* Edinburgh: Mainstream Publishing, 2003.

Toye, Clive. *A Kick in the Grass.* Haworth, NJ: St. Johann Press, 2006.

Tucker, Lauren R. 'The Framing of Calvin Klein: A Frame Analysis of Media Discourse about the August 1995 Calvin Klein Jeans Advertising Campaign'. *Critical Studies in Mass Communication* 15 (1998): 141–57.

Von Sikorski, Christian, and Thomas Schierl. 'Effects of News Frames on Recipients' Information Processing in Disability Sports Communications'. *Journal of Media Psychology* 24 (2012): 113–23.

Wangerin, David. *Soccer in a Football World: The Story of America's Forgotten Game.* Philadelphia, PA: Temple University Press, 2008.

Wangerin, David. *Distant Corners: American Soccer's History of Missed Opportunities and Lost Causes.* Philadelphia, PA: Temple University Press, 2011.

Woosnam, Phil. 'From the Commissioner'. *Kick Magazine*, May 19, 1979, 3N.

Why Zico is called the 'God of Soccer' in Japan: the legacy of Zico to Japanese soccer

Yoshio Takahashi

Graduate School of Comprehensive Human Sciences, University of Tsukuba, Tsukuba, Japan

This essay will shed light on the reasons why Brazilian football player Zico has become the 'God of Soccer' in Japan by discussing Zico's unique character and actions and the social condition surrounding him, as well as the role played by the image of a hero held by the Japanese. The study uses the existing literature on Zico's tenure in Japan along with Zico's own writings and anecdotes to reflect upon his legacies from various angles. While it emphasizes the ability of an interpreter in constructing Zico's image, it also encapsulates the key moments and images Zico elicited in Japan, including his brilliant style of play, his memorable hat-trick in his opening J-League match and his figure as a father of Japanese football. The essay will try to show that Zico's emphasis on the importance of family, as in building a 'Zico Family', as well as his strong sense of obligation, professionalism and integrity contributed to creating his image as a legendary human being in Japan.

Introduction

It was September 2012. Zico, the head coach of the national team of Iraq, arrived at the stadium in Japan for the Japan vs. Iraq match in the final round of the Asian qualifying competition of the FIFA World Cup 2014. Prior to kick-off when Zico was introduced, Japanese supporters let out a huge cheer and Zico reciprocated by waving his hands. Earlier, despite being the coach of the opponent team, Zico was surrounded by fans who begged for his autograph at the Japanese airport. The following day Zico visited the training grounds of Kashima Antlers, the J. League club he helped build, interacting with the players and the head coach, Jorge de Amorim Campos (Jorginho), renewing their friendship. There is a bronze statue of Zico at the home stadium of the Antlers for which he played. In the Cheerio Shopping Centre, always crowded with local shoppers, there is a square named after Zico where a huge bronze statue stands. To this day, the Japanese considers Zico the great 'God of Soccer'.

When Zico was 14 he joined Brazil's famed Clube de Regatas do Flamengo soccer club, and he went on to lead his team to the Copa Libertadores and the Toyota Cup victories in 1981 and the Brazilian champion title four times (in 1980, 1982, 1983 and 1987). Zico was transferred to Italy's Udinese Calcio in 1983 where he scored 19 goals in the 1983–1984 season and finished second among top goal scorers. He represented Brazil on the national team for the FIFA World Cup in 1978, 1982 and 1986. According to his official website, during his four years in the minor league and 23 years as a professional player, Zico appeared in 1180 matches and scored 826 goals. As a national team member, Zico scored 66 goals in 88 matches, including the unofficial ones. Zico, along with Socrates, came to represent brand Brazilian soccer in the 1980s. Zico retired as a player in 1989, and the following year the newly elected Brazilian President Fernando Collor de Mello appointed him as his Minister of Sports. Zico stayed at this political assignment for about a year.

On 21 May 1991, Zico, then 38 years old, accepted an offer to join the Sumitomo Metal Industries Soccer Club in Kashima, Japan. The media at first could not understand why Zico chose to sign with an amateur club from Japan, an under-developed soccer nation, and they wrote many speculative articles about the surprising move. Yoshiyuki Ohsumi, a Japanese soccer journalist, said in 1994 that Zico's move to Japan give the impression of 'a panda hired to attract attention' rather than a soccer superstar transfer. Zico later explained in 2002 that if the offer was to return to the pitch just as a player, he would never have accepted the transfer to Japan, no matter how much money he was offered. He argued that what gave him the motivation to return to the pitch in Japan was the grand project that required his experience and skills. He was asked to help the club secure a place in Japan's first fully professional soccer league that was officially set to be launched in 1993. The launch of a professional soccer league was part of Japan's strategy to win the bid for hosting the 2002 FIFA World Cup. The inception of a home club was also to help revitalize the town of Kashima through soccer.

Zico played for Sumitomo in 1992, the last season before the old Japan Soccer League was disbanded, and finished as the league's top scorer. When the J. League was launched in 1993, the small town club, renamed Kashima Antlers, was not expected to compete with richer, more glamorous clubs. But Zico helped the Antlers to win the J. League Suntory Series and a runner-up finish in its inaugural season. After he retired as a player in 1994, Zico stayed on as the Antler's technical director, leading the team to become an elite club in the league. In July 2002, Zico was appointed head coach of the Japanese national team and was entrusted with the responsibility to manage the 2006 FIFA World Cup squad. It is a fact, however, that even Zico, whom the Japanese considered a great figure, was not immune to criticism by the media once he became head coach of Japan.

According to Fujita, there have been a total of 1384 players of foreign nationalities that played in the J. League between 1993 and 2011, of which over 60%, or 862, were from Brazil.[1] The second largest group was from South Korea, followed by the former Yugoslavia, Argentina, the Netherlands, Australia and Germany. When the J. League was launched in 1993, there were a number of renowned players with national caps including Gary Lineker (England), Pierre Littbarski (former West Germany) and Ramon Diaz (Argentina), who joined Japanese club teams. They were later followed by star players, such as Salvatore Schillaci (Italy), Guido Ulrich Buchwald (former West Germany) and Dragan Stojkovic (former Yugoslavia). But despite such inflow of big names in Japanese soccer, Zico's position as a legend remains supreme. In the Kashima Antlers locker room, there is a board with the words expressing Zico's spirit: 'The Antlers Family is built upon dedication, loyalty and respect'. Zico's influence goes beyond the boundaries of soccer. Not only has he been named an honorary citizen of Kashima, but he has also been commended by the Prime Minister of Japan for his services rendered to the entire nation.

Despite Zico's great contributions to soccer in Japan, it has never been analysed why Zico stood out to earn the status of the 'God of Soccer' in Japan. The term 'God of Soccer' is of course not the one that the monotheistic Brazilian media would use. According to Sawada, Japanese people honour myriads of gods and deities, and therefore the respect for Zico as a presence greater than man is recognized in the expression, 'Zico the God'.[2] This essay will try to analyse the reasons why Zico has become the 'God of Soccer' in Japan by discussing Zico's unique character and actions and the social condition surrounding him, as well as the role played by the image of a hero held by the Japanese. The study uses the existing literature on Zico's tenure in Japan along with Zico's own writings and anecdotes to reflect upon his legacies from various angles. While it emphasizes the ability of an interpreter in constructing Zico's image, it also encapsulates the key moments and images Zico elicited in Japan, including his brilliant style of play, his memorable hat-trick in his opening J-League match and his figure as a father of Japanese football. The essay will try to show that Zico's emphasis on the importance of family, as in building a 'Zico Family', as well as his strong sense of obligation, professionalism and integrity contributed to creating his image as a legendary human being in Japan.

Methodology

The study has used available literature on Zico, ranging from his own writings to writings on him by several authors and journalists. Writings in Japanese have been translated to get the Japanese perspective on Zico. Similarly, anecdotes written by Zico have been used to gain an understanding of Zico's personality and actions. The Japanese works mainly used for this essay include the ones written by the Kashima Antlers trainer, Zico's interpreter, and a Japanese writer residing in Brazil. The selection of these sources was corroborated by Japanese materials compiled by the Kashima Antlers. Zico's trainer provided a glimpse of Zico when he was not at a match, focusing on his achievements as seen from someone who worked very closely with him. Zico's interpreter communicated what Zico said and his writings represented the spirit of Zico. The writer in Brazil, a soccer reporter, helps us understand what the Brazilian media thought about Zico in Japan. Compilations by the Kashima Antlers like 'Arigato Zico' and 'Obrigado! Zico' include words of gratitude for Zico, which throw light on the deification of Zico by Japanese people in general and Kashima Antlers fans in particular.

Sporting hero and foreign players: Zico and Lineker

Before the J. League gained status in Japan, in popular sports like professional baseball and sumo wrestling, foreign athletes were collectively referred to as *gaijin*,[3] *suketto*[4] (one who helps) or *gaikokujin*. In these sports, the heroes were always the Japanese athletes[5] and foreigners were the villains out to oust the heroes, or they were considered outsiders who did not understand the Japanese spirit of *wa* or harmony. Foreigners usually signed a hefty contract so when their performance was poor, they were dubbed as *ponkotsu gaijin*, meaning they were decrepit and useless. There were some foreign athletes who became popular in Japan, one of whom is sumo's Takamiyama Daigoro. His great fighting spirit and his determination to never miss a bout no matter what injuries he might be carrying – a Japanese character trait known as *gaman* – were much admired.[6]

In such context, Moffett attributed the new concept of a hometown club, clever marketing, and the star players as the reason why soccer and the totally different professional league made headlines.[7] In an underdeveloped soccer market such as Japan where there were no world-class star players, it was imperative to hire players from abroad. According to Moffett, Zico was in a class of his own among all the international players who were transferred to Japan.[8] More importantly, Zico, being a striker, could score goals, thus constituting one of the factors that make a player popular. This is because strikers are higher profile, and their main ability, setting up and scoring goals are more readily appreciated by football novices than the stopping and subtle positioning of defensive players. In fact, Zico accomplished a hat-trick in the opening match at the home stadium of the Antlers, and made a striking J. League debut.

Moffett[9] also examines the case of Gary Lineker who was not able to make any remarkable contributions while in Japan. Nagoya Grampus Eight signed Lineker because he was a world-class striker, was known for fair play and never once received a yellow or red card and was also known for his tea-and-cake gentility from England. The Japanese also found Lineker attractive because he had a sunny personality, was an intelligent sportsman and a logical soft-spoken person. Lineker was a pure striker and was not used to the short passes his team frequently used. Grampus could not produce many chances for Lineker, and he scored very few goals. The team struggled in defence and finished in a disappointing ninth place out of ten in their first season. Lineker offered his advice to the team but later said he wondered about the translation. Unable to become a hero, Lineker left Japan. Moffett also claims that Diego Maradona was unable to become a hero despite his popularity in Japan because the strict Japanese law against drug use prohibited him to enter the country.[10]

Social condition and personal relationships surrounding Zico

It is important to understand the social condition of the time Zico agreed to play in Japan. Zico arrived in Japan in 1991, a time when the Japanese economy began to slump. When the Japan Football Association's intent to bid for the FIFA World Cup and plans to establish a professional football league were announced in 1989, the Japanese economy was at its peak with a rush of resort development projects underway and many corporations achieving record profits. In 1985, the Japanese government started promoting financial deregulation, measures to boost domestic demand and policies to open up the market in an effort to resolve pressures from the US government resulting from Japan–US economic frictions. Amendments to the Immigration Control Act in 1990 allowed Japanese Brazilians to seek work in Japan. The population of Brazilian citizens who signed up for an Alien Registration totalled 2250 in 1987; but the number surged to 56,429 in 1990 and to 119,333 in 1991. The rapidly increasing Japanese Brazilian workers painted the image of Brazil.

The institution of a new professional soccer league (the J. League) and the bid for a global sports event (the FIFA World Cup) brought on the construction of new stadiums nationwide and boosted domestic demand, while also promising to revitalize local communities with the use of the facilities after the World Cup. Sumitomo Metal Industries, the parent company behind Zico's Kashima Antlers, was committed to improving the living standards of its employees by bringing about a change to the township of Kashima through soccer. Moffett depicted Japanese society back in those days as follows:

> Japan's boardrooms – always sensitive to image and alert to the spirit of the times – would pay attention. They were also under pressure to be better corporate citizens, and give back to society rather than just generate bigger profits. Kiichi Miyazawa, Prime Minister from 1991 to 1993, declared that Japan's mission after achieving economic greatness was to become a 'lifestyle superpower'. Football was the perfect vehicle for corporations to demonstrate both their largesse and their embrace of the creative workplace.[11]

At the same time, NHK launched a satellite broadcast service in 1989, making world sports more accessible. Before Zico's arrival in Japan, world soccer was not available on Japanese television and baseball was the most popular sport in the country. The only programme offering world soccer content was 'Diamond Soccer', which basically covered European soccer.

Though Pele came to Japan as a member of Santos FC from Brazil to play against the Japanese national team, the Japanese only knew of Brazilian soccer through Japanese Brazilian players such as Nelson Yoshimura and Sergio Echigo, who were playing in Japan's football league. The brilliant technique of Brazilian soccer captivated Japanese fans. However, the level of Japanese soccer was not very high because it was not so popular at that time. When Zico first arrived in Japan, he was said to have commented that the level of the game in Japan 'is like sandlot soccer played on Sundays'.[12]

Zico's success in Japan can also be attributed to his relationships with the managements of the Kashima Antlers club and the Japan Football Association. The Antlers head coach, Masakatsu Miyamoto, had full confidence in Zico, handing over the command of the team to him.[13] Lineker pointed out that Ryuzo Hiraki, the Grampus head coach, had no experience as a manager, and if Zico had also played under such an inexperienced coach, he would not have been able to instil his expertise to the team. If we look closely at Zico's personal contacts and the people who supported him, we find that Saburo Kawabuchi, the first chairman of the J. League who headed the project team that worked on the launch of the new professional league, played a major role. Kawabuchi wanted to see the Kashima Antlers become a success story that embodied the philosophy and objective of the J. League because it would symbolize the ideal model of a club with strong ties to its hometown, thereby revitalizing the community. Kawabuchi learned of Zico's interest from a Japanese Brazilian named Luis Antonio Takasaki and strongly recommended Zico to Sumitomo Metal. It was also Kawabuchi who, as president of the Japan Football Association, appointed Zico as head coach of the Japanese national team in 2002.[14] Also, at the government level, the Ministry of International Trade and Industry (presently called the Ministry of Economy, Trade and Industry) was discussing the revitalization of the sports industry which included the support towards the establishment of a professional soccer league. The key figure at the Ministry was Takeo Hirata, who later would join the Japan Football Association as General Secretary in 2002 and support Zico in his role as head coach of the national team. Hirata was also involved with the Sumitomo Metal club, and he met Zico for dinner at a hotel the day Zico set his foot in Japan back in 1991. Soon after, Hirata would assume a position at the Japanese Embassy in Brazil, all the time staying in touch with Zico, and he developed a relationship of trust with the Brazilian soccer superstar.[15]

The fact that the second J. League Chairman came from the Kashima Antlers demonstrates how much the J. League authorities supported the Japanese club in which Zico was involved.

Zico in the eyes of his interpreter

In 1994, Paulo Roberto Falcão was appointed the head coach of the Japanese national team. Together with Zico, Falcão was a key member of the Brazilian national team during the 1982 and 1986 FIFA World Cups. Falcão claimed that language as well as the nature of the Japanese played a critical role making Zico so much revered and deified in Japan. When a foreigner speaks through an interpreter, there is an inevitable time lag that often spoils the mood. For a foreigner who does not speak the local language, the interpreter plays a crucial role as a filter that communicates what he or she wants to express.[16]

Moffett argues that before Zico instructed the players, he had to first train the interpreter.[17] Zico's interpreter, Suzuki, used exactly the same body language from the bench as Zico, sometimes shouting in the same tone. Suzuki was almost like Zico's double. Suzuki states, 'When doing simultaneous interpretation, people tend to pay more attention to the interpreter, but I try very hard to avoid that. The presence of the speaker is very important'.[18] When Suzuki translated Zico's words, he reflexively considered how the Japanese would interpret the translation. As a result, he would sometimes use a roundabout expression or other times would use totally different words. Zico would demand Suzuki to 'fully understand what I am trying to say before interpreting into Japanese'.[19]

Suzuki's ability as an interpreter had a significant impact in constructing Zico's image. Suzuki gave a good summary of Zico's personality and actions in his writings. According to him, Zico hated to lose and when the match kicked off he would do everything he could to win.[20] Zico would speak sharply, but he was always sound and fair.[21] He cared for the fans and would always say, 'Because of the fans, we are professionals and we are who we are'.[22] Zico placed great importance on communication, and he was flexible if the reason was clear and just.[23] Zico always said that professionals must perform their task to the fullest. To quote Suzuki, Zico used to say, 'Always keep your word, be responsible till the end, and never betray someone's trust'.[24] Such images of Zico were continually communicated to the Japanese through his interpreter.

Zico as seen by his trainer

Before he even met Zico, Kishida, the trainer, always understood that Zico was an incredibly talented soccer player and a respectable human being who would be a world leader in soccer as well as in sports. He describes his first meeting with Zico: 'When our eyes met, I felt a thrill run down my spine. As I said my first greetings, I was full of excitement and awe like a little boy'.[25] He also mentions: 'You'd expect someone who is praised as god to have a sharp gaze, but Zico had a look so profound that it almost took you in. His eyes were truly charismatic'.[26] Speaking of the buzz at the clubhouse when word reached there that Zico would be coming: 'Everybody was moving about this way and that, and we couldn't concentrate on anything'.[27] Zico's charisma was instantly felt by everyone who played with him, but as a charismatic figure Zico never isolated himself. He made everyone around him – players and staff – aware that they were part of the Zico family. Kishida recalls that Zico glared fiercely at him when he once was listening with his eyes closed in a staff meeting.[28]

Zico in Japan: image construction in Brazilian media

Through Sawada, a Japanese Brazilian journalist based in Brazil, the Japanese were able to obtain information about Zico that were not available in Japan and to learn how Zico was evaluated in Brazil. For example, Sawada revealed that the real reason why Zico decided to come to Japan was because he wanted to secure funds to open and manage his own football school and club in Brazil. He also wrote that the facilities of the Sumitomo Metals club Zico joined were poor compared to Brazil, but Zico never gave up and played as hard as he could. Sawada also introduced comments from Zico's friends and acquaintances in Brazil, offering a glimpse into Zico's character. According to these comments, Zico was serious-minded, hard-working, modest, simple and unpretentious, loyal, and punctual. He had a strong sense of obligation and a strict personal and work ethic; he kept his promises; he didn't hold a grudge; and he was a passionate and patient leader.[29]

The appeal of Zico in Japan

'Arigato, Zico', compiled by the Kashima Antlers FC, includes 86 words of gratitude for Zico. The club president, Suzuki, expressed his feelings about a father-like Zico who was strict yet kind-hearted:

> Zico patiently educated our young players, displayed artistic soccer in front of thousands of fans, taught us what a true professional is with the kind compassion of a father. His every action left a lasting impression that still comes alive today.[30]

Words of gratitude also mentioned Zico's outstanding soccer skills, spectacular plays, overhead kicks, hat-tricks, heel kicks, free kicks and the magic he displayed with his foot. There is no doubt that Zico mesmerized Japanese fans with his techniques, even if he had reached 40 and was probably feeling his limits physically in terms of age. The hat-trick he scored at the J. League opening match was especially a memorable and great achievement. Everything about him when he played – his earnestness, mental strength, righteousness, innocence, the way he insisted or got angry on the pitch – was part of Zico's charm.

According to his trainer Kishida, in real life Zico fulfilled the role of a father more than anyone in his family, and was both strict and compassionate at the same time. Apparently, work does not come first over family. A photo and an article subtitled, 'A father wears a smile of joy at his young son's play', introducing Zico attending his second son's match immediately upon returning to Brazil, demonstrates Zico's strong love for his family.[31] In his interviews, Zico emphasized the importance of learning about friendship, passion and cooperation through soccer and of building an honest and fair relationship with everyone.[32] In fact, the superintendent of the players' dormitory where Zico used to drop by from time to time described him as a friendly person who always bound them into a family, often telling jokes.[33] As a member of the Sumitomo Metals team before the J. League was launched, Zico requested that he be treated the same as every other player in terms of the seating arrangement on the bus and accommodation.[34] Such actions made him extremely popular as well as accessible in Japanese eyes.

Zico's legacies

Zico had an enormous influence on Japanese soccer. Ohsumi argues, first and foremost Zico was able to leave a strong impression upon young Japanese players as to how to play soccer with one's imagination.[35] Zico's playing style represented the very essence of Brazilian soccer. Moreover, Ohsumi claims, Zico showed the Japanese the ways to give everything for the victory of the team with determination and commitment. When instructing others, Zico always placed importance on basic skills. He adopted the style of first listening to what the other person has to say before offering his own opinion, and if there were disagreement he would discuss matters thoroughly to make the person understand and reflect on his teachings. At training, Zico would use trial and error to find the most logical way. He was also very punctual. Although Zico strongly believed in fair play, there was an incident that aroused criticism at the second leg of a J. League championship match in January 1994 when he spat on the ball before Kazuyoshi Miura took a penalty kick and received a red card. However, it was later revealed that the stadium and the refereeing were far from neutral, which caused Zico to become a bit emotional. There was a lesson to be learnt about soccer from Zico relating to this incident.

Zico's role in Japan did not stop at passing on soccer techniques. From the day Zico arrived in Japan, as Kishida points out, Zico was not only a player on the team but he also tried to bring change to the Japanese sports culture.[36] In other words, Zico's training methods, conditioning and metal preparation had the potential to bring to light the problems of Japan's old-fashioned attitude towards sports. For example, when Zico first came to Japan, he stayed at the club dormitory for single players and educated them about their diet. Zico demanded everyone to be conscious about being a professional player. He tried to discipline the amateurish Japanese players to live like professionals.

Why Zico was considered 'God'

Many would situate the hypothesis of Zico's deification in Japan in the context of religious customs of the Japanese. While this is largely true, as this essay has tried to show, the social condition on the eve of Zico's arrival in Japan and his personal relationships in the Japanese soccer community played a crucial role in the process. It was Zico's commitment that went beyond soccer to help change Japanese society, creating his image as more than a soccer star among the Japanese outside of the soccer arena. Japan's economic growth and its bid for hosting the 2002 World Cup in the context of globalization helped develop soccer from being a minor sport to a successful professional sport, creating the need for world-class players. In football the Japanese had to learn everything unilaterally, and that was what established the difference from the way professional baseball or sumo treated foreigners. More importantly, Zico not only contributed as a player but also virtually coached the team he played for. Zico helped bring in other talents from Brazil and was instrumental in developing the team to its status as one of the strongest in the league. Needless to say, Zico's exceptional soccer technique captivated the hearts of many Japanese fans. Thus, Zico truly became the father of today's Japanese soccer.

How Zico became 'God' in the eyes of the Japanese depended a great deal on the interpreter who communicated Zico's words to the players, the media and the Japanese fans. Those who could not speak or understand Portuguese had to depend totally on the interpreter Suzuki's translation. Suzuki was always conscious of how the Japanese would respond or react to Zico's words he interpreted, and his interpreting skills helped minimize any negative reactions toward Zico. In addition, the unique qualities of Zico's character both as a player and as a human being, revealed in the writings of people close to him, such as the team trainer or the Japanese journalists in Brazil also made Japanese people embrace Zico as a cult figure. For instance, Zico was depicted as a strict but warm-hearted father, which is an image that the Japanese like. Similarly, Zico's emphasis on the importance of family, as in building a 'Zico Family', was also a concept greatly valued in Japan. His strong sense of obligation, professionalism and integrity contributed to creating a respectable image of Zico as a human being.

Though Zico was in charge of the national squad of Japan for the 2006 FIFA World Cup, the team failed to qualify for the knockout stage. While there were some adverse criticisms of Zico as a manager for the failure, but many also claimed that the Japanese national team was not good enough to fully understand and act on the soccer philosophy of Zico the God. Even if the result was disappointing, Zico would always be loved and admired as the 'God of Soccer' in Japan.

Notes

1. Fujita, 'Football Migrants in the J. League'.
2. Sawada, *Zico Aratanaru Chosen*.
3. According to Robert Whiting, gradually, gaijin became the word used for white people and kokujin or gaijin for blacks, but was not applied to other Asians or Arabs. In the late 1980s, the use of the word 'gaijin' fell out of favour in newspapers, on TV and in official government documents, replaced instead by the more formal 'gaikokujin' (person from another country).
4. Suketto literally means 'ones who helps'. For Whiting, the implication is that one is there not as a member of the group but as an outsider with special skills or expertise to impart. A suketto is hired – indeed often overpaid – to raise the skill or technology level in his field, to refrain from any wa-damaging activities, and then to depart quietly so that his pupils can practise what they have learnt from him. The term has been applied not only to foreign ballplayers but to engineers, technicians, bonds traders and others in the long string of experts Japan has employed to raise its level of competition.
5. *The Yomiuri Shimbun, Osaka* (1996) picked up sporting heroes of post-War Japan, but there was no foreign player in the list.
6. Wikipedia, http://en.wikipedia.org/wiki/Takamiyama_Daigor%C5%8D (accessed April 27, 2013).
7. Moffett, *Japanese Rules*.
8. Moffett talked about one significant exception – the great Zico. Here was a player that combined star quality with a determination to improve the Japanese game. Zico was everything Japanese football wanted from a foreign player.
9. Moffett, *Japanese Rules*.
10. Ibid.
11. Ibid.
12. Kishida, *Kamisama ga Sakka wo Kaeta*.
13. According to Suzuki, Miyamoto yielded authority to Zico after the game with the representative of Croatia of the Italy training camp ahead of the first season. Suzuki, *Zico Spirit no Dentatsusha*.
14. Sawada, *Zico Aratanaru Chosen*, 117.
15. Hirata, 2007, 110–2.

16. Kashima Antlers FC, *Obrigado! Zico*, 71.
17. Moffett, *Japanese Rules*.
18. Suzuki, *Zico Spirit no Dentatsusha*, 100.
19. Suzuki, *Kami no Kuno Zico to ita 15 nen*, 210–2.
20. Ibid., 24.
21. Ibid., 30.
22. Ibid., 74.
23. Ibid., 90.
24. Ibid., 98.
25. Kishida, *Kamisama ga Sakka wo Kaeta*.
26. Ibid.
27. Ibid.
28. In order to centralize consciousness, Japanese people may close eyes and may hear a speech. Kishida was not sleeping and was concentrating consciousness. But Zico assumed that Kishida was dozing, and therefore got enraged.
29. Sawada, *Zico Aratanaru Chosen*.
30. Kashima Antlers FC, *Arigato Zico Nihon jin ni Yume to Kandoh wo Ataetekureta Kamisama eno Kanshajo*.
31. Kashima Antlers FC, *Obrigado! Zico*, 60.
32. Ibid., 64.
33. Ibid., 25.
34. Ibid., 22.
35. Ohsumi, *Zico ga Nihon ni Nokosshitamono*.
36. Kishida, *Kamisama ga Sakka wo Kaeta*.

References

Fujita, Tomohiro. 'Football Migrants in the J. League: Feature and Trends'. *Japan Journal of Sport Sociology* 21, no. 1 (2013): 101–10.

Hirata, Takeo. *Sakka to iunano Senso Nihon Daihyo Gaikoukoushou no Urubutai* [War Named Soccer – National Team and Back Stage of Diplomatic Negotiations]. Tokyo: Shinchosha, 2007.

Kashima Antlers FC, ed. *Arigato Zico Nihon jin ni Yume to Kandoh wo Ataetekureta Kamisama eno Kanshajo* [The Letter of Thanks to God Which gave Japanese People a Dream and Impression]. Tokyo: Goma Syobo, 1994.

Kashima Antlers FC, ed. *Obrigado! Zico* [Thank you! Zico]. Tokyo: Fusosha, 1994.

Kishida, Kodo. *Kamisama ga Sakka wo Kaeta* [God Changed a Soccer]. Tokyo: Rippu Shobo, 1994.

Moffett, Sebastian. *Japanese Rules: Why the Japanese Needed Football and How They Got It.* London: Yellow Jersey Press, 2002.

Ohsumi, Yoshiyuki. *Zico ga Nihon ni Nokosshitamono* [What Zico Left to Japan]. Tokyo: Fusosha, 1994.

Sawada, Hiroaki. *Zico Aratanaru Chosen* [Zico – New Challenges]. Tokyo: Linebooks, 2002.

Suzuki, Kunihiro. *Zico Spirit no Dentatsusha* [Messenger of the Zico Spirit]. Tokyo: NEC Media Products, 2002.

Suzuki, Kunihiro. *Kami no Kuno Zico to ita 15 nen* [Suffering of God for 15 Years which were with Him]. Tokyo: Kodansha, 2007.

The Yomiuri Shimbun, Osaka. 'The Hero Sengo Sports no 40 Nin' [The Hero – 40 Players after World War Two], 1996.

Of magic and mania: reflections on the fan following of Brazilian football and Pelé in Calcutta

Souvik Naha

Swiss Federal Institute of Technology Zurich, Zurich, Switzerland

Why do Indians celebrate Brazilian football? Is it because Indians do not have local stars to root for? Why does it have to be Brazil? Why was a generation of football fans in Calcutta in awe of an exotic South American footballer called Pelé? This essay responds to these conundrums by analysing transnational football fandom from perspectives of cultural diffusion and image-making. It situates circulation of culture in a historical study of the impact of Brazilian football, with particular emphasis on Pelé, as borne out by fan culture in India. It examines if the similarities between India and Brazil in the global meridian of development had any bearing on football fandom. Next, it studies particularly how Pelé's visit to Calcutta in 1977 was registered by the overlapping categories of fans, politicians and journalists. By doing so, it offers a model of understanding moral/cultural networks of transnational fandom in terms of hero/icon/legend worship.

Introduction

The football fans of Calcutta are as fervent as their counterparts elsewhere when it comes to celebrating world football.[1] On the day of an important match, work schedules are openly defied. During FIFA World Cups, flags of the participating nations, particularly Brazil and Argentina, flap throughout the city and its outskirts. Neighbourhood walls are painted with graffiti featuring global football stars, and haircuts of icons emulated at every saloon. Jerseys bearing names of footballers and accessories like wristbands are in great demand. Football books and newspaper supplements are published and consumed widely. The matches are telecast live at restaurants, hotels, nightclubs and shopping malls. During the World Cup in 2010, a newly opened mall in Calcutta organized food carnival, quiz shows, tattoo and face-painting boutiques and chat shows with celebrities and sports personalities to attract customers. A giant wrought iron football along with a 5-ft Jacumi, the World Cup 2010 mascot, was installed at the entrance of the hotel Hindustan International.[2] The hotel also laid out an experimental menu which included, among others, vodka-based 'Bosque Smoke', gin-based 'Capello Lamborghini' and Rooney's 'Nomicks Cooler', fish-based dishes like 'Mesmerised Like Messi' and 'Between The Posts', a potato platter called 'Kaka's Chip' and a Mexican dessert imaginatively called 'Ronaldo's Banana Kick'. New Kenilworth Hotel served cocktails from or popular in each of the 32 participating countries.[3] Over 300,000 users subscribed to Waka

Waka, the Cup theme song, as their mobile ringtone, and millions downloaded the song from internet.[4] And the weirdest of them all, kite-makers came out with a World Cup special series of kites inscribed with different images of every team.[5] The fervour foregrounds the public's enchantment with world football. However, the enthusiasm was reserved mostly for the Latin American teams Brazil and Argentina, which is evident from a press report, one among many, following their ouster from the 2010 World Cup:

> 'After Brazil crashed out of the quarterfinals, the only attraction was Argentina. But everything seems to have gone haywire. Now I am least interested in this World Cup,' Tamal Das, an MBA student, told IANS ... The streets of Kolkata are still adorned with huge posters of Kaka, Robinho, Messi and Maradona. Flags of Brazil and Argentina are still fluttering atop houses, but the interest has died down... The soccer crazy city is now gunning for revenge against Germany and the Netherlands, who knocked out Argentina and Brazil.[6]

In the words of another correspondent, 'a pall of gloom descended over the entire city. It was almost as if Kolkata had gone into mourning'.[7] Paul Beckett, South Asia bureau chief for *The Wall Street Journal*, wrote about the overwhelming support for Brazil in India, so much that Brazil's defeat proved to be equivalent to India being eliminated, chiefly in Calcutta where 'supporting Brazil or Argentina seems almost as important a birth rite as supporting Rangers or Celtic if you are in Glasgow'.[8] Calcutta's Brazil fixation started arguably after the latter's World Cup victory in 1958. In the decade that followed, the surge in radio commentary and press coverage reinvented the public sphere around sports – enlisting more followers across social divides.[9] Brazil's run of three World Cup wins between 1958 and 1970 coincided with media expansion and the reinvention of fan culture by the stream of mediated information. An 'imagined world' around Brazilian football was arguably created as part of public ideality.[10] Prior to Argentina's twin Cup victories in 1978 and 1986, and the predominance of Diego Maradona in world football, Brazil was the nation and Pelé the individual that football fans in Bengal raved about. The attachment was cemented by Pelé's visit to Calcutta to play an exhibition match. It was hardly the first time that Pelé was received so enthusiastically in a country not in the big league of global football. In 1969, Pelé travelled to Lagos, Nigeria, then in the midst of a brutal civil war, to play an exhibition match. Both the warring parties, the western Nigerians and the Biafrans agreed to a 48-h ceasefire so that people could enjoy watching Pelé on the football field.[11] While it is not uncommon for fringe nations to worship global icons, the making of such fan culture is a matter of historical significance, basic to the understanding of formation of charisma and flow of culture.

Writings on the cultural diffusion of sport have followed two major directions. Firstly, there are critiques of Eurocentric sporting ideologies like Olympism, and explorations into the transnational character in modern sports such as cricket and football.[12] Cricket has been important to discussions of globalization of sport as a critical framework of studying international relations, colonial and imperial history, and the rise of the non-West.[13] A somewhat different model of analysis has been used to study the production and consumption of global football leagues such as the English Premier League in transnational contexts.[14] The second approach, mostly sociological in method, addresses issues of immigration, assimilation and multiculturalism.[15] This essay situates diffusion in a historical study of the impact of Brazilian football, with particular emphasis on Pelé, as borne out by fan culture in India, a disparate geopolitical entity. It does so by analysing how Pelé's visit to Calcutta as part of the Cosmos club which played Mohun Bagan was registered by the overlapping categories of fans, politicians and journalists. This is a study of transnational football fandom at two levels – circulation of culture and hero worship.

Dreaming of Brazil: social history of football in India and Brazil

Football fans from all around the world have been awed by Brazilian football, and Indians are no different. Boria Majumdar gives a number of reasons as to why football fans in Calcutta loved Brazil. Firstly, admiration for the Brazilian style of play, aggressive yet elegant, was commonplace in Calcutta as elsewhere in the world.[16] The craze reached such levels in post-independence India that Brazil was nearly assigned copyrights for curved passes, free kicks that curled in elliptical orbits, bicycle kicks, mesmerizing set pieces and dribbles within the smallest conceivable space. The ideal Brazilian player – 'crafty, agile and impossible to catch' – is compared to Curipira, the guardian of animals and trees in indigenous myths, a legend said to be personified by the aboriginal player Garrincha.[17] Alex Bellos sums up the world's fascination with Brazilian football players by saying: 'the phrase 'Brazilian soccer player' is like the phrases 'French chef' or 'Tibetan monk'. The nationality expresses an authority, an innate vocation for the job – whatever the natural ability'.[18] As European football was increasingly swallowed up by techniques and formations in the 1960s, individual ability and emotive quality set Brazilian football apart from the rest of the world.

Additionally, Majumdar argues that the colonial histories of Calcutta and Brazil had fostered a sense of solidarity which was manifested in football fandom.[19] Like Calcutta, a major entrepot and administrative bastion of the British Empire, Brazil was a Portuguese colony and subject to exploitation for three centuries. However, this connection drawn by Majumdar is misplaced since the colonial contexts of India and Brazil were utterly different. In India, football was introduced as a colonial sport and later framed by Indians as an instrument of resisting colonialism. On the contrary, football was first played in Brazil long after it became independent of Portuguese rule. Brazil was acknowledged as a kingdom under the sovereign state of the United Kingdom of Portugal, Brazil and Algarves in 1815, and formed an independent state, the Empire of Brazil, in 1822. It is said that British sailors played football in the Brazilian shores in 1864.[20] Rumours of a priest starting the game in a Sao Paulo school in the 1870s and of games played by British and Brazilians working for the Sao Paulo Railway in 1882 are not supported by evidence. Charles Miller, son of English coffee planters in Sao Paulo, has been recognized as the organizer of the first widely reported game of football in Brazil – in Varzea do Carmo near the junction of the Avenue Gasometro and Santa Rosa Street – in 1895.[21] However, Richard McBrearty, curator of the Scottish Football Museum at Hampden, gives Thomas Donohue, a Scottish dye expert who travelled to Brazil in 1893 to work in a factory in Bangu, credit for importing football in the country.[22] Donahue's team involved people across races, but the same cannot be said about any other representative squad of the time.

The organization of football in Brazil till the mid-twentieth century bore no structural resemblance to any sport in India. Majumdar contends elsewhere that major sports such as cricket were very much democratized and considerably more representative of the society in colonial India compared to the form sports have taken after the country's independence in 1947.[23] In the same period, football in

Brazil developed differently. Brazilian society to this day remains markedly segregated along class divides and income inequality, which is reflected in the formation of clubs and regulation of football. Robert Levine has schematized the development of football in Brazil in four periods: 1894–1904, when football was largely confined to the private urban clubs of the immigrants; 1905–1933, when the sport became very popular with substantial improvement in playing standard; 1933–1950, the phase when professionalism replaced the amateur playing structure; and the post-1950 phase when, aided by talented players, Brazil became widely recognized as the leader in world football, and the game itself elaborately commercialised and 'an unchallenged national asset'.[24] An overview of the four phases establishes that the organization of football in India and Brazil at any given temporal context were far from coextensive.

Records of non-white ethnic groups participating in football in the first phase are hard to find. Although it has been written that by playing football immigrants could assert better Brazilianness and create ethnic cohesion, available sources indicate otherwise.[25] The more widely accepted opinion, in the words of Muniz Sodré, is that in the first three decades of the twentieth century football was looked upon as a 'discriminatory class ritual'. Sodré describes early Brazilian football as a privilege of the propertied whites – merchants, great landholders and foreigners – in exclusion of the native poor.[26] Nevertheless, a number of European companies encouraged workers to play football so that a sense of belonging to the workplace community could be fostered culturally. It seemed that the factory directors had adopted the public school pedagogy of promoting football to systematise and control institutional environment.[27] By the end of the 1920s, the status quo was displaced by professional recruits. At this stage, it has been noted, local intellectuals condemned football as a game tarnished first by its European origin and then by its popularity among working-class immigrants, blacks, *mestizos* and *mulatos*.[28] Similar to the experience in the UK, intensification of urban-industrial society and growth of populism in national politics reinvented football as a mass spectacle. The high level of competition in local leagues and the necessity to build a large fan base required that players were now recruited on merit, from among every ethnic constituency of the society. The players, most of who came from underprivileged, semi-literate backgrounds, treated club contracts as vehicles of social mobility.[29] This was especially true for black footballers, for whom football became a means of social emancipation.[30] Although there was no restriction on blacks and mulattos to play professional football, they remained in public esteem for only so long as their careers lasted. This covert racist inclination affected not only rebellious blacks like Leonidas da Silva but also unobtrusive blacks like Domingos da Guia, who apparently 'played like an Englishman'.[31] Racist stereotypes of emotional instability and indiscipline of non-Caucasians were emphasised to explain Brazil's defeat to Uruguay in the final of the 1950 World Cup and then to Hungary in the 1954 World Cup.[32] To avoid such 'national tragedies' in the future, the managerial structure of the game were overhauled and made highly professionalized. Aided by a bunch of supremely talented footballers, especially Pelé, Garrincha and Didi, Brazil won the next two World Cups in 1958 and 1962, nullifying the racist critiques and elevating Brazilian football to the realm of magic.[33] The victory of 1970 fortified Brazil's claim as the number one football nation.

In comparison to Brazilian football, Indian football was relatively more centralized and less professional. Unlike Brazil which was independent at the time when football was introduced to the country, India encountered football as a colonial sport.

Indians started playing football in the 1870s. Initially the game was restricted among the urban gentry and middle classes. Afterwards, it became an emblem of anti-colonial nationalism, manifested undeniably in Mohun Bagan's victory over East Yorkshire regiment in the Indian Football Association Shield final in 1911. The triumph challenged fundamental views on the racial superiority of white Europeans over Indians, and assumed political significance as an inspirational symbolic victory for the oppressed over their oppressors at a juncture when revolutionary terrorism was at its peak and Calcutta was the hotbed of a nationalist movement against British colonialism.[34] In the colonial period itself, football participation conformed and reinforced communal, ethnic and regional identities, premised upon which football thrived as a mass spectator sport.[35] The Indian Football Association (IFA) was established as the administrative body for Bengal/Indian football in 1892 and the supreme all-India governing institution, the All India Football Federation (AIFF), was set up in 1937. After independence from British rule in 1947, India was invited to participate in the 1950 World Cup in Brazil. However, the AIFF's inability to organise funds for foreign travel and their failure to understand the tournament's importance as a global event forced India to withdraw. Nevertheless, till the mid-1960s India was considered to be one of the top three in Asian football. In both the 1951 Asian Games in Delhi and the 1962 Asian Games in Jakarta India won the gold medal in football, and finished fourth in the 1956 Olympics in Melbourne. Evidently, the development of football in India and Brazil followed separate arcs.

Majumdar makes a more pertinent point that the compulsion of asserting postcolonial identity persuaded Indians to support Brazil in football matches against European countries. According to him, 'in the Brazilians, the Bengalis find their poor, non-white clones, who can meet their dream of meeting the imperialists and neo-colonialists head on'.[36] Football is the ethos that consolidates Brazil as a nation, similar to India, where cricket and Hindi films are perhaps the only symbols of national unity. Furthermore, the image of Brazilian football as an informal everyday activity practised by the working class, the unemployed and the vagabonds dovetailed particularly well with the sport's tradition in 1960s' Calcutta where unemployment and civil unrest was widespread. Brazilians footballers came mostly from underprivileged families. They were not produced by scientific training in academies or reared through educational curriculums; they were brought up in the streets, parks and beaches and depended on exceptional skill and passion. As Majumdar sums up, football fans in Calcutta exalted the Brazilian stars who came from lower-middle-class households and became world icons, and attempted to emulate them. In addition to class, the hegemonic culture of sportsmanship was particularly significant in constructing this football solidarity. This issue is taken up in the next section.

The dream begins: Pelé and cultural ethos in Bengali sport writings

Pelé's international career was over before television network was set up in India, video cassettes were easily available to the public and correspondents travelled abroad to cover football World Cup matches. His status as a hero was derived from images upheld by the sport press or biographers, which were in turn based on writings published outside the country. John Lowerson had accorded much importance to printed word and the author–reader complex in the creation of the aura and moral values of heroism.[37] According to Lowerson, these values were consumed by 'a constituency whose creation has been well charted, at least in terms of its core, the burgeoning schools and colleges of the late Victorian middle classes'.[38] The ethics of morality and fair play were diffused through educational institutions and clubs situated in the metropolis and the colony.[39] Missionary schools and colleges took up the responsibility of circulating sports as means to facilitate moral emancipation and physical vigour. Their efforts were complimented by indigenous patrons who imbibed the 'games ethic' and set about implementing the ideals as they befitted the indigenous society. Sport heroes in colonial India were figures who at least textually defied the codes of Caucasian superiority, such as Ranjitsinhji or C.K. Nayudu, whose cricketing performances were celebrated as anti-colonial manifestations regardless of the cricketers' intentions.[40]

Representation of Pelé's charisma was augmented by the authenticity of his sporting performance. Max Weber's contemplations on 'charismatic authority' – virtue which emphasizes heroism by endowing the person with 'supernatural, superhuman' qualities – can be invoked to analyse Pelé's literary representation.[41] As Weber contends, perpetuation of charisma is contingent on aesthetic, ethical judgments made by followers, because of which charisma is unstable and indelibly linked with merit of sporting performance. Aside from being a sporting hero, Pelé was looked upon as a cultural leader of black solidarity. In one biography, Pelé was quoted as having described his first visit to Africa as an uplifting experience. In his words:

> Everywhere I went I was looked upon and treated a god, almost certainly because I represented to the blacks in those countries what a black man could accomplish in a country where there was little racial prejudice, as well as providing physical evidence that a black man could become rich, even in a white man's country ... To these people, who had little possibility of ever escaping the crushing poverty in which they found themselves, I somehow represented a ray of hope, however faint.[42]

Asked by a reporter which people he cherished to have met during his travels, Pelé named Martin Luther King and Nelson Mandela, and regretted to not have met Gandhi.[43] Records declassified in 2012 reveal that in 1970, Pelé was investigated for suspected leftist sympathies. Veronica Cristo, a spokeswoman for the Sao Paulo State Public Archives, told the press that a reader discovered a thin file containing notes on the demand for release of political prisoners, with Pelé's name on the cover. The file contained a description of an interrogation of Pelé due to his alleged involvement with the political struggle in the country, and some news clippings on matches he played in.[44]

It is accepted that sporting heroes have 'common qualities like courage and willpower but they also have specific national and social characteristics'.[45] Yet, the nature of what the reader is able to see, hear and read about is determined and amplified by texts and photographic images, which ensure that the sport star image develops through selected constructions of reality. Pelé's charisma was circulated in Calcutta through articles published in newspapers, sports magazines, occasional biographies, and comments on the radio and at times by videos of his performance. In addition to football skill, the commentators admired his sportsmanship and philosophical observations. Celebration of his personal life was very important to vernacular literature, as are evident from writings on him.

Sports literature in Bengali literature is rife with references to Pelé. The word 'play' often became 'Pelé' in the local speech modulation. Pelé was also a moniker given to any upcoming footballer. The person himself was associated with the pinnacle of excellence on the football field. A novel by the journalist Moti Nandi, published as Pelé was on verge of retiring from Santos, begins with a dream. Prasun, the protagonist who is an aspiring footballer too, dreams of a middle-aged Brazilian driving to his house in a limousine and offering him a contract to play in Santos, which had taken a mythic status as the club Pelé plays for.[46] Similarly, in a fictional account of the Cosmos match, the Mohun Bagan forward Bidesh Bose played magnificently and was offered a chance to play for the Santos second XI by none other than Pelé.[47]

The first literary pieces on Brazilian footballers started to come out in the 1970s when Pelé had been recognized as the king of football and Brazil the undisputed leader in the world game. The introductory sentence of a book, authored by the radio commentator Ajay Basu, claimed that no contender in the football world has achieved, not even the 'scheming Fascist warlords' or 'British thieves', what Brazilian footballers have accomplished.[48] The warlords in question were the Nazi soldiers who wanted to galvanize the World Cup trophy won by Italy in 1938 and extract the gold for war efforts. The thief referred to was Edward Betchley, convicted as one of the conspirators who stole the trophy won by England in 1966, though no conclusive proof was found against him. In comparison, the Brazilians were portrayed as moral souls who did not resort to trickery.[49] Their capital was pure talent. Their football reflected the working of a sound brain and healthy mentality. Basu suggested earnestly that it was not possible for Brasilia or Rio de Janeiro to contain the greatness of Brazilian football; the visible trappings of divinity elevated the footballers to the status of world citizens.[50] Before any Brazilian footballer came to India, Shakti Prasad Poddar from Seorafuli, near Calcutta, spent his life's savings to travel to Brazil and meet Pelé. The craze was accentuated by literary mediations.

Pelé's first biography in Bengali is possibly Jayanta Dutta's *Ami Pelé Bolchi* (This is Pelé Speaking), published in 1972. A revised and expanded edition was published in 1976. The book illustrated Pelé as the paradigm of football-playing. Dutta claimed that football should be played the way Pelé played it – without ever committing fouls.[51] Pelé did not believe that penalties should be looked upon as scoring opportunities as the odds were against the goalkeeper. He was reluctant to score his thousandth goal from a penalty awarded to Santos. But he agreed as the referee pleaded with him not to disappoint the spectators, especially because the referee is the law and should be adhered to respected at all circumstances.[52] Pelé was estimated to be a model human being even outside the football field. The author was moved by his gesture of gifting the farewell-match jersey to a hawker kid, an act construed as giving opportunity to the underdog. On another occasion, he was said to have signed 1500 autographs for fans in two hours at a friend's house. His generosity was well-documented, particularly an incident in which he distributed everything to his fans, including his clothes and car – the scraps of which were taken home as mementoes – and went home wearing underpants.[53] As Pelé became a living legend, his name started to be used for promotion of merchandise, but he did not allow cigarettes and liquor to be associated with his identity.[54] Although Dutta admitted that as a child Pelé often stole nuts from rails wagons, he exonerated him promptly saying that the money received from selling nuts went into purchasing a football, otherwise fans would have been deprived of watching god on the football field.[55]

Within this adulation was embedded a critique of the state of football and physical culture in India. From its status as the Asian football giant in the mid-1960s, India was relegated to the periphery in Asian football at the time the book was published. Dutta acknowledged that Pelé was fortunate to have been born in Brazil.

Had he been born in India, he would have been beaten by his father for playing football instead of studying. Good sporting performances would have earned him a clerical job in a bank. He would have travelled in tram cars and buy his own daily grocery. He would have got an *Arjuna* or a *Padmashri* – governmental awards in recognition of one's sporting accomplishments. Had he been an Indian, playing in the Merdeca tournament in Indonesia would have been his destiny; he would not have ruled the game.[56] The crisis of Indian football was threefold. Firstly, the organizational structure in India was badly managed, with no system of scouting talent and modern scientific training in place. Secondly, football was too poorly remunerated for a large section of aspiring young footballers to take up the game seriously as a career option. Thirdly, unlike in Europe and the Americas, sport had been more of a spectacle than a vocation in India – a compulsory but trivial part of educational curriculum – which had contributed to the lack of professionalism and ability. The evocative tale of Pelé's sporting mobility put the Indian imbroglio in perspective, supposedly to elicit attention and measures to improve sports in the country.

Dutta's observations were replicated and elaborated by Santipriyo Bandopadhyay, another noted sport journalist and author of several books, in *Baller Raja Pelé* (Pelé, the King of Football), published on the eve of the Mohun Bagan-Cosmos match in 1977. In this book, The Pelé mythos was reinforced by narratives of his exclusivity and qualities that distinguished him from others. His goals were imbued with magic. It was said that the Duke of Edinburgh, then on a diplomatic mission to Brazil, identified Pelé, who he had not seen before, by just watching him move on the field during the Santos-Botafogo match in Rio. He left the stadium, and the country, stating that he had no business left unfinished.[57] Pelé's stature as a person was amplified by the story of his hurting himself to protect the Czech goalkeeper Viliam Schrojf from serious damage as the latter had swooped on his feet to snatch the ball during a league game in the 1962 World Cup.[58] The injury ruled Pelé out of World Cup. Other accounts suggest that it was not an effort to save the opposition goalkeeper but a tackle while he attempted a long-distance shot led to the injury, but this version obviously would not fit into Banopadhyay's narrative. His goal by head against Italy in the 1970 World Cup final was said to be scored from a distance of 35 yards, though video evidence shows Pelé to have been well inside the penalty box when striking the cross from Rivelino with his head. Pelé's initial refusal to score his thousandth goal from penalty was stressed to highlight his standing above footballers who would have taken advantage of any opportunity to achieve a landmark. His retirement from football in 1971 was postulated as a desire to give young footballers chance to play. His return to the Santos team on a three-year contract was a move to pull Santos out of financial crisis. Although people stood up in respect whenever Pelé entered a hotel or restaurant, the man personified humility.[59] An ideal family person, not given to addictions, a footballer loyal to the club where he was nurtured, a hero not enticed by money or enamoured of fame – Pelé sat next to god. Pelé's high-profile move to New York Cosmos in 1975, a decision widely criticised even in Brazil, was justified as his responsibility to popularise football in all parts of the world. Lastly, the thrilling possibility of Pelé coming to Calcutta to play in probably his last match was 'good to hope, but scary to believe, lest [the fans] drown in the sorrow of broken hope'.[60]

In both these works and essays in magazines such as *Sportsweek*, *Khelar Asar* (Sportfield) and *Khelar Kagoj* (the Sport Magazine), emphasis on Pelé's initial hardship, development in spite of infrastructure, moral character, love for nation and sports, value system and disregard for statistics enhanced his charismatic authority. The moral masculinity embodied by Pelé was consumed far and wide. Facts such as the government of Brazil having legally prevented Pele's acceptance of a million dollar offer from the Italian club AC Milan by declaring him a 'non-exportable national treasure' were conveniently overlooked. Instead, Pelé was looked upon as a supreme leader of Third World solidarity, who conquered discrimination by cultural performance. As one footballer later wrote, the most well-known person ever is Pelé, ahead of Jesus Christ, Hazrat Mohammad, Gautam Buddha, Alexander, Napoleon, Hitler, Maradona and Gorbachev.[61] Interviews with football followers indicate two overlapping directions in which the devotion to Brazil and Pelé developed. Firstly, Brazilian football championed spontaneity and style over the disciplined regimes upheld by European tradition. Secondly, and more importantly, it operated as a critique of the Eurocentric worldview and crystallized non-conformist public opinion. Bengali sport writers overlooked the fact that the military dictatorship had used Pelé as a spokesperson for the status quo. Pele advocated acceptance of the will of god as responsible for poverty and misery and forbade material aspirations against god's decree.[62] Yet, representations of Pelé's image as the face of Third World solidarity expressed the opposite. When asked why he went to watch Cosmos playing Mohun Bagan, one of my respondents, then a young Marxist historian, said that he wanted to observe keenly the 'one' who had undermined the football manuals produced by Western imperial states and liberal democracies.[63] Another fan, then a clerk with hardly any political inclination, confided that he wanted Mohun Bagan to beat the American and therefore upper-class club but wished Pelé would score so that Indians may learn.[64] Pelé was given a rousing reception when he landed in Calcutta. The match created a stir in the media like nothing else, which the next section analyses to problematise the responses to global football in the periphery.

Living the dream: responses to Pelé's visit to Calcutta

> Like Royalty, they were greeted,
> Cosmos football club, fervently awaited;
> To the Eden Gardens, Calcutta rushed,
> Fantasies ran crazy, both loud and hushed
> The Bengali and his God; his Adonis and Cupid
> Here's a lifetime chance to see Pelé, stupid![65]

Nagendra Prasad Sarbadhikary had kicked a football in 1877. It was the first time that a Bengali had touched a football. To celebrate the centenary of the pioneering kick, Mohun Bagan Athletic Club decided to invite Pelé and his team Cosmos to play an exhibition match in 1977. Cosmos agreed to play them on 25 September as the concluding match of their Asia tour. A scamper for tickets ensued as soon as the news was confirmed. 59,390 tickets were printed, out of which only 19,000 were put on sale, and the rest were distributed among different organizations and institutions. Members of the parliament and the legislative assembly were granted two tickets each.[66] The monarch of Bhutan wrote to Jyoti Basu, the Chief Minister of West Bengal, asking for a ticket.[67] Ticket prices exceeded all previous records for any match played in the country. People did fascinating things for and with the ticket, the account of which is material enough for a separate article. Sudhir Kumar

Ghosh, nearly 70 years of age, gifted a ticket to his son-in-law to earn his gratitude. The generous promise of a television set, at a time when the television broadcast had barely started in the county and the contraption was still a wonder of science, did not sufficiently entice Ranu Roy, a young college student, to surrender the ticket to her elder brother. Subir De, a school student, spent all he had saved for buying new clothes for the Durga Puja, the biggest local festival, to buy a ticket because Pelé would not come every year unlike the festival.[68] Laxmikant Das, former Olympic weight lifter, failed to procure a single ticket out of the 68 allotted to his railway office despite being a sport person.[69] Dolgobindo Maiti purchased 199 coupons to optimize chance to win tickets, and was rewarded with four of them.[70] 48 people were arrested for selling duplicate coupons.[71] The eagerness was epitomized in the following cartoon, published in *Dainik Basumati*, which showed fans flocking to fortune-tellers to know if they would be able to acquire tickets (Figure 1).

An 18-member panel headed by the public works minister Jatin Chakrabarti was formed to supervise the itinerary.[72] A staggering 25,000 strong police battalion were deployed for peacekeeping.[73] It was taken for granted that Pelé would attract more frenzied attention compared to any dignitary to have visited Calcutta, including the Chinese premier Zhou Enlai and Queen Elizabeth II, thereby increasing chances of

Figure 1. *Dainik Basumati*, 14 September 1977, 1.

stampede and riot. So the government decided that no formal cavalcade should be organized for the travelling team. The route to the hotel was kept secret to avoid rush of fans and traffic jam. Instructions were given to the Calcutta Electric Supply Corporation that no power cuts should occur in the Dharamtola region so long as Pelé stayed there.[74] The team was to be put up in Grand Hotel, then the most luxurious hotel in the city. The premises were renovated, intensively cleaned and freshly painted. The best suite was reserved for Pelé.[75]

Hell broke loose as the aeroplane carrying Pelé touched down, late at night. Literally every airport staff frantically ran to the tarmac. The absence of Franz Beckenbauer in the Cosmos team did not bother anyone. The thousands gathered to greet Pelé scaled barricades and raced to watch him from vantage points. In the commotion that came to pass, hundreds, including journalists and camerapersons, were hurt. As the situation went beyond police control, the team were smuggled out on a bus waiting secretly (Figure 2). A number of fans tried to climb the bus, holding on to window panes and doorknob, but were scattered as soon as the bus picked up speed.[76] The Grand Hotel looked like a fortress as police cordoned off every entrance and exit, corridor and swimming pool. Even before daybreak, thousands of young people braved the rain and jostled to catch a glimpse of Pelé. No less than 30 people occupied the tree in front of the hotel. In many a locality, fans resorted to superstitions like bowl planting and stealing containers of slaked lime to ward off rain on match day. A rumour spread that a number of tantrists were performing rain-stopping rituals at the stadium.[77] People from neighbouring districts and even states started to mill in as the day progressed.[78] Special flights and trains were arranged for spectators from Tripura to arrive.[79]

Quite a few souvenirs were published to mark the occasion. One of these *Mohun Bagan Meets Cosmos*, edited by Arijit Sen, which was sold at Rs. 5. Pelé's charisma was used in marketing campaigns by companies as diverse as M.P. Jewellers, Eastern Railway, Televista, Fertilizer Corporation of India, Borolin antiseptic cream, Horlicks health drink and Hewlett's tonic.[80] In the Horlicks advertisement, a local boy aspiring to emulate Pelé was advised to drink Horlicks. Pelé was conceived as a special individual capable of adding marketable value, sanctity and glamour to products.

Figure 2.   Pele on arrival at the Calcutta Airport © Mona Chaudhury.

Pelé's visit was not received with universal enthusiasm. Cosmos club was paid $5000 in advance and another Rs. 3,35,000 in addition to travel and living expenses for a contingent of 27.[81] In a letter to the *Anandabazar Patrika*, Jugal Kanti Roy regretted the massive expenditure undertaken by Mohun Bagan to bring the legend for a single match in a country where sports were deprived of sponsorship and proper planning. He mentioned that the sports journalist and commentator Shyamsundar Ghosh had asked this question to Dhiren De, secretary of Mohun Bagan, in a radio talk show. De speculated that the coming of Pelé would elevate the standard of football and spectatorship in the country. From his experience of watching great international cricketers and good footballers, Roy asserted that the euphoria of spectatorship or lessons learnt from these visits do not last long. Moreover, how would football fans benefit from a match that was barely accessible to most of them?[82] The issue was addressed by the newspaper's editor, Santosh Kumar Ghosh, the next day. Ghosh criticized the cult of the individual underlying the rush for tickets and uproarious reception of Cosmos. He cautioned readers against elevating an individual above the game – an act which contravened the philosophy of team sports as a coordinated exercise of rationality and physical vigour. He disapproved the obsession with deifying and deriving entertainment out of sporting events and sportspersons without critical appreciation of either.[83] However, his newspaper too succumbed to the public craving for news of Pelé. The detailed reports on Pelé's movements and statements, his eating habits and physical features would have embarrassed even the best gossip tabloids.

The fans did not pay attention to any disapproval of their hero's visit. The spectacle of the emperor of football coming to this impoverished country was indeed bewildering. As Dipali Kumar Ghosh wrote:

> Pelé's presence has glossed over all civic problems. Crisis of unemployment, debasement of food ration, paucity of refined rapeseed oil, escalating market prices, distress over children's future – everything has been wiped out. Nobody cares about what Indira Gandhi is saying or if the country is on track of progress.[84]

A report in *Dainik Basumati* conveyed that the spectators longed to witness Pelé' wizardry with the ball, to see the 11 Mohun Bagan players roving around, confused, culminating in goals scored against the home team.[85] The contours of this collective fantasy of an affective community display an eclectic appreciation of the global icon within a palpable localism.[86] According to a report in *The Times of India*:

> [The crowd] wanted Pelé to display his prowess at juggling the ball, taking on and beating a host of rivals, bend the free kicks past a wall of defence into goal beyond the groping hands of the goalkeeper, leap and head down into goal with the power of kicks and also fire shots of binding speed into goal.[87]

However, Pelé could not fulfil local aspirations. He was 38, tired at the end of a tour, and probably unwilling to risk an injury ahead of his farewell match on 1 October. Fans were disappointed, but Pelé's statement at the press conference obviated it all:

> Mohun Bagan should have taken a 4-1 lead in the first half itself for their fine understanding and combination, but they were subdued in the second half... They played in the Brazilian way. They played an up and down game... The local crowd is very nice. I saw so many people who did not get a ticket and waited outside.[88]

Playing in the Brazilian way was the highest compliment any Indian footballer could dream to receive. The phrase certainly reproduced Brazilian football in a deterritorialised context by recognising Calcutta as a site of its practice. Pelé was subtly criticized in match reports for failing to meet expectations, but in the long run his mere presence on the field was inked in awe. As Santipriyo Bandopadhyay later wrote, the Calcutta fans did not have the arrogance to judge or criticize Pelé's play on that day. Watching him and speaking to him was a momentous incident in their lives.[89] The king of football, who was previously accessible only through magazines, was now a phenomenal reality. The footballer Prasun Bandopadhyay admitted to not have deserved to watch such divine play. An out of this world pass to Chinaglia was for him a glance at god.[90] Football lovers thanked Mohun Bagan for organising the match. The goalless display from Pelé in the muddy and slushy field disappointed fans. But flashes of brilliant footwork, magical receiving and passing, and occasional amazing shooting remained etched in public memory.

Conclusion

Despite the rise of Argentina, the fascination with Brazil did not abate. Diego Maradona commanded a huge fan following from 1986 onwards, but Brazil held a special place which has been encapsulated in literature. In a short story by Dibyendu Palit, a clerk harassed by his boss refuses to support any team over Brazil even at the risk of termination of his tenure. When the officer asks around the possible winner in the 1986 World Cup at Mexico, himself favouring France and Argentina, a colleague counsels the clerk to shift allegiance to either of the two. But he refuses to do so.

> 'No, that's not possible'. Kinkar sat up straight, 'Brazil can't lose'.
>
> 'You don't realise. Why do we care if Brazil wins or loses?'
>
> Kinkar stared at him for a short while. Watching Dilip with intent, he said, 'Excuse me. I can be his servant, but can't betray Brazil. Brazil will win. I'll go to him after we lift the Cup'.
>
> Dilip sat down. He looked Kinkar straight in the eyes, 'You're strange. Why do you support Brazil so fanatically?'
>
> 'Because – ,' Kinkar fumbled for words, looking confused and desperate to respond. Taking a brief pause, he said, 'You know why? I feel they are my team, they are like us – '.[91]

The excerpt aptly summarizes what this article has tried to analyse. Despite an apparent lack of familiarity with Brazil at most levels, the people of Calcutta have been so taken by its football that they are willing to sacrifice many privileges and still act as if supporting Brazil is a moral obligation, a necessary choice. This article explored the formative role of mediated information and mobility of a star player in this fandom. By placing the textual perspectives in broader social and sporting contexts, it also unpacked some of the motivations to popularize Brazilian football. The Cosmos-Mohun Bagan match was certainly proof of the extent to which the popularization had succeeded. Having done a combined analysis of both circulation and consumption of country and player image, the article claims to have addressed how cultural legacies are manufactured and sustained globally. There are, however, recent developments to consider.

In recent years, the decline of country-based tournaments and global access to European football leagues though satellite television, internet and merchandising have transformed the demography of fandom. Brazil and Argentina are still the emotional favourites. Brazil's two FIFA World Cup victories in 1994 and 2002 and the emergence of Lionel Messi, Kaka, Diego Forlan and others have kept interest in Latin American football alive. Yet, local preference has undergone a shift in which Latin America has lost its irreplaceability. It was evident in the unusual surge in absenteeism from schools and offices during the semi-final stages of the 2006 World Cup which featured an All-European line up.[92] However, the frenzied reception given to Maradona in 2008, Forlan in 2010, Messi in 2011 and a Brazil all-star team comprising Dunga, Cafu, Roberto Carlos in 2012 showed that Calcutta still persists with *football-arte*.

Notes

1. Calcutta was renamed Kolkata in 2001. The new spelling is mentioned as part of quotations; elsewhere the old name has been retained.
2. 'Kolkata Decks up for Grand World Cup', *The Times of India*, June 9, 2010, http://articles.timesofindia.indiatimes.com/2010-06-09/kolkata/28278727_1_soccer-mania-plasma-soccer-fever.
3. 'FIFA cuisine Lures Kolkata;', *Hindustan Times*, July 8, 2010, http://articles.timesofindia.indiatimes.com/2010-07-08/food-festivals/28285087_1_fish-and-chips-cocktails-waka-waka.
4. Manoj Gairola, 'And the Mobiles went Waka Waka', *Hindustan Times*, July 13, 2010, http://www.hindustantimes.com/India-news/NewDelhi/And-the-mobiles-went-WakaWaka/Article1-571462.aspx.
5. Keval Sharma, 'Kites Flying off Kolkata Shopping Shelves as WC Fever takes a Grip', June 17, 2010. http://topnews.in/sports/kites-flying-kolkata-shopping-shelves-wc-fever-takes-grip-211669.
6. 'Kolkata Fans Losing Interest in World Cup', *Hindustan Times*, July 4, 2010, http://www.hindustantimes.com/sports-news/Football/Kolkata-fans-losing-interest-in-World-Cup/Article1-567368.aspx.
7. Shiv Sahay Singh, 'After Weeks of Fun-filled Rivalry, Bangali Brazilians & Argentines United in Grief', *Indian Express*, July 4, 2010, http://www.indianexpress.com/news/after-weeks-of-funfilled-rivalry-bangali-brazilians—argentines-united-in-grief/642032.
8. Paul Beckett, 'World Cup: Who Do We Support Now?', *India Realtime*, July 2, 2010, http://blogs.wsj.com/indiarealtime/2010/07/02/world-cup-2010-who-do-we-support-now/.
9. The gender dimension of sports consumerism in the 1960s has been discussed in Naha, 'Adams and Eves at the Eden Gardens'.
10. According to Arjun Appadurai, a 'community of sentiment' is a transnational space in which the same event is imagined and relived without apparent physical connection. He mentions about solidarities formed around international sports. However, this article shows that such fraternity existed much before the proliferation of electronic capitalism as he stresses on. Appadurai, Modernity at Large.
11. Witzig, *The Global Art of Soccer*, 73.
12. Bale and Christensen, *Post-Olympism*; McNamee, 'Olympism, Eurocentricity, and Transcultural Virtues'.
13. Malcolm, *Globalizing Cricket*; Gupta, 'The Globalization of Cricket'; Kaufman and Patterson, 'Cross-National Cultural Diffusion'.
14. Millward, *The Global Football League*; Rowe and Gilmour, 'Global Sport'.
15. Burdsey, *British Asians and Football*; Henry, 'Sport and Multiculturalism'; Booth, 'The Antinomies of Multicultural Sporting Nationalism'.
16. Majumdar, 'Kolkata Colonised', 71.
17. Maynard, *The Aboriginal Soccer Tribe*, 31–2.
18. Bellos, *Futebol*, 13.
19. Majumdar, 'Kolkata Colonised', 72.

20. Levine, 'Sport and Society', 233.
21. Mason, *Passion of the People*, 9–10.
22. Scotland Herald, 'New research reveals the Scottish dye worker who brought football to Brazil, 117 years ago exclusive', March 24, 2011, http://www.heraldscotland.com/sport/more-scottish-football/new-research-reveals-the-scottish-dye-worker-who-brought-football-to-brazil-117-years-ago-exclusive-1.1092220 (accessed March 10, 2013).
23. Majumdar, *Twenty-two Yards to Freedom*, 112–3.
24. Levine, 'Soccer and Society', 234.
25. Lesser, *Immigration, Ethnicity, and National Identity in Brazil*, 100.
26. Sodré, 'Futebol, teatro ou televisao?', 148, cited in Oliven, 'The Production and Consumption of Culture in Brazil', 112.
27. Lopes, 'Class, Ethnicity, and Color in the Making of Brazilian Football', 245–6.
28. Borge, '*Hinchas, Cracks* and *Letrados*', 299.
29. Oliven, 'The Production and Consumption of Culture in Brazil', 112.
30. Lopes, 'Class, Ethnicity, and Color in the Making of Brazilian Football', 256.
31. Levine, 'Soccer and Society', 240.
32. Lopes, 'Class, Ethnicity, and Color in the Making of Brazilian Football', 260.
33. Pelé became a living symbol of Brazilianness. His career reflected the historical development of artistic football as part of the Brazilian discourse in which sport, football in particular, was a means of organising a 'national project of modernity'. Da Silva, 'King Pelé', 3.
34. Nandy, *The Intimate Enemy*; Majumdar and Bandyopadhyay, *Goalless*.
35. Bandyopadhyay, *Scoring Off the Field*.
36. Majumdar, 'Kolkata Colonised', 72.
37. Lowerson, *Sport and the English Middle Classes*, 70.
38. Ibid., 72–3.
39. Mangan, *The Games Ethic and Imperialism*.
40. Nandy, *Tao of Cricket*; Naha, 'Producing the First Indian Cricketing Superhero'.
41. Weber, *The Theory of Social and Economic Organization*, 358.
42. Harris, *Pelé*, 85.
43. Riner, *Pelé*, 60.
44. Brazil's military opened file on Pele', Miami Herald, 23 Aug 2011, http://www.miamiherald.com/2011/08/23/2371376/brazils-military-opened-file-on.html, accessed on.
45. Holt, 'Champions, Heroes and Celebrities', 12.
46. Nandi, *Striker*, 1–4.
47. Ashok Dasgupta, 'Emon Jodi Hoto', *Ananda Bazar Patrika* special supplement, September 24, 1977, 3.
48. Basu, *Footballe Sonar Pori*, 1.
49. The trophy was stolen again in 1983 from the office of the Brazilian Football Federation, and has not been recovered since. It is believed that the trophy was melted down and converted to gold bars.
50. Basu, *Footballe Sonar Pori*, 4.
51. Dutta, *Pelér Diary*, 33.
52. Ibid., 38.
53. Ibid., 66–7.
54. Ibid., 68.
55. Ibid., 75.
56. Ibid., 50–1.
57. Bandopadhyay, *Baller Raja Pelé*.
58. Ibid., 35.
59. Ibid., 55.
60. Ibid., 86.
61. Bandopadhyay, *Football Gharana*, 277.
62. Foster, 'Dreaming of Pelé', 84.
63. Personal interview, July 26, 2013.
64. Personal interview, April 14, 2013.
65. Bhabani Prasad Majumdar, *Dainik Basumati* (*DB*), September 22, 1977, 6. Translated from Bengali by Anirban Bandyopadhyay.

66. *Ananda Bazar Patrika* (hereafter *ABP*), September 13, 1977, 1.
67. *ABP*, September 21, 1977, 7.
68. Binoy Mukherji, 'Pelé-Kapale Der Khusir Line E', *DB*, September 21, 1977, 1.
69. *ABP*, September 19, 1977, 7.
70. *ABP*, September 20, 1977, 1.
71. *ABP*, September 22, 1977, 5.
72. *ABP*, September 22, 1977, 1.
73. *ABP*, September 20, 1977, 8.
74. *DB*, September 21, 1977, 3.
75. *ABP*, September 22, 1977, 8.
76. *DB*, September 23, 1977, 1.
77. *ABP*, September 24, 1977, 4.
78. *DB*, September 24, 1977, 6.
79. *ABP*, September 23, 1977, 8.
80. *ABP* special supplement, September 24, 1977, 2–3.
81. *ABP*, September 13, 1977, 1.
82. *ABP*, September 23, 1977, 4.
83. Santosh Kumar Ghosh, 'Khelateo Tara Baji ?', *ABP*, September 24, 1977, 5.
84. Dipali Kumar Ghosh, 'Pelé Niye Aj Pellai Kando', *DB*, September 24, 1977, 1.
85. *DB*, September 25, 1977, 6.
86. This is not to be confused with Leela Gandhi's 'affective communities'—British colonials who critiqued the imperial and liberal order from hybrid perspectives instead of maintaining their privileged location within it. Gandhi, *Affective Communities*.
87. K. Bhaskaran, 'Pelé magic was missing as Mohun Bagan hold Cosmos', *The Times of India*, September 25, 1977, 14.
88. 'Pelé all Praise for Our Players', *The Times of India*, September 25, 1977, 14.
89. Bandopadhyay, *Cluber Naam Mohun Bagan*, 94.
90. Bandopadhyay, *Football Gharana*, 278.
91. Palit, 'Brazil', 130.
92. Subhro Niyogi, 'City Schools Score with Monday Off', *The Times of India*, July 7, 2006, http://articles.timesofindia.indiatimes.com/2006–07-07/kolkata/27815583_1_city-schools-middle-path-holiday.

References

Appadurai, Arjun. *Modernity at Large: Cultural Dimensions of Globalization*. Minneapolis, MN: University of Minnesota Press, 1996.
Bale, John, and Mette Krogh Christensen, eds. *Post-Olympism? Questioning Sport in the Twenty-first Century*. Oxford: Berg, 2004.
Bandopadhyay, Santipriyo. *Baller Raja Pelé* [Pele, the King of Football]. Calcutta: A. Mukherjee & Co, 1977.
Bandopadhyay, Santipriyo. *Cluber Naam Mohun Bagan* [The Club called Mohun Bagan]. Calcutta: New Bengal Press, 1978.
Bandopadhyay, Prasun. *Football Gharana: Biplab O Bibartan* [The Tradition of Football: Revolution and Transformation]. Calcutta: Pratibhas, 1989.
Bandyopadhyay, Kausik. *Scoring Off the Field: Football Culture in Bengal, 1911–80*. New Delhi: Routledge, 2011.
Basu, Ajoy. *Footballe Sonar Pori* [Football's Golden Angel]. Calcutta: Grantha Prakash, 1971.
Bellos, Alex. *Futebol: The Brazilian Way of Life*. London: Bloomsbury, 2002.
Booth, Douglas. 'The Antinomies of Multicultural Nationalism: A Comparative Analysis of Australia and South Africa'. *International Sports Studies* 21, no. 2 (1999): 4–24.
Borge, Jason. '*Hinchas, Cracks* and *Letrados*: Latin American Intellectuals and the Invention of Soccer Celebrity'. *Revista Canadiense de Estudios Hispánicos* 33, no. 2 (2009): 299–316.
Burdsey, Daniel. *British Asians and Football: Culture, Identity, Exclusion*. London: Routledge, 2007.

Dutta, Jayanta. *Ami Pelé Bolchi* [This is Pele Speaking]. Calcutta: Jnan Tirtha, 1972.

Dutta, Jayanta. *Pelér Diary* [Pele's Diary]. Calcutta: Nath Brothers, 1976.

Foster, Kevin. 'Dreaming of Pelé: Football and Society in England and Brazil in the 1950s and 1960s'. *Football Studies* 6, no. 1 (2003): 70–86.

Gandhi, Leela. *Affective Communities: Anticolonial Thought, Fin-de-Siècle Radicalism, and the Politics of Friendship*. Durham, NC: Duke University Press, 2005.

Gupta, Amit. 'The Globalization of Cricket: The Rise of the Non-West'. *The International Journal of the History of Sport* 21, no. 2 (2004): 257–76.

Harris, Harry. *Pelé: His Life and Times*. London: Robson Books, 2001.

Henry, Ian P. *Sport and Multiculturalism: A European Perspective*.0 Barcelona: Centre d'Estudis Olímpics UAB, 2005, http://olympicstudies.uab.es/pdf/wp102_eng.pdf.

Holt, Richard. 'Champions, Heroes and Celebrities: Sporting Greatness and the British Public'. In *The Book of British Sporting Heroes*, ed. J. Huntington-Whiteley, 10–25, London: National Portrait Gallery, 1999.

Kaufman, Jason, and Orlando Patterson. 'Cross-national Cultural Diffusion: The Global Spread of Cricket'. *American Sociological Review* 70, no. 1 (2005): 82–110.

Lesser, Jeffrey. *Immigration, Ethnicity, and National Identity in Brazil, 1808 to the Present*. New York: Cambridge University Press, 2013.

Levine, Robert M. 'Sport and Society: The Case of Brazilian Futebol'. *Luso-Brazilian Review* 17, no. 2 (1980): 233–52.

Lopes, José Sergio Leite 'Class, Ethnicity, and Color in the Making of Brazilian Football'. *Daedalus* 129, no. 2 (2000): 239–70.

Lowerson, John. *Sport and the English Middle Classes*. Manchester: Manchester University Press, 1993.

Majumdar, Boria. 'Kolkata Colonized: Soccer in a Subcontinental "Brazilian Colony"'. *Soccer & Society* 3, no. 2 (2002): 70–86.

Majumdar, Boria, and Kausik Bandyopadhyay. *Goalless: The Story of a Unique Footballing Nation*. New Delhi: Penguin/Viking, 2006.

Malcolm, Dominic. *Globalizing Cricket: Englishness, Empire and Identity*. London: Bloomsbury, 2012.

Mangan, J.A. *The Games Ethic and Imperialism: Aspects of the Diffusion of an Ideal*. Harmondsworth: Viking, 1986.

Mason, Tony. *Passion of the People? Football in South America*. London: Verso, 1995.

Maynard, John. *The Aboriginal Soccer Tribe: A History of Aboriginal Involvement with the World Game*. Broome: Magabala Books, 2011.

McNamee, Mike. 'Olympism, Eurocentricity, and Transcultural Virtues'. *Journal of the Philosophy of Sport*, no. 33 (2) (2006): 174–87.

Millward, Peter. *The Global Football League*. London: Palgrave Macmillan, 2011.

Naha, Souvik. 'Adams and Eves at the Eden Gardens: Women Cricket Spectators and the Conflict of Feminine Subjectivity in Calcutta, 1920–1970'. *The International Journal of the History of Sport* 29, no. 5 (2012): 711–729.

Naha, Souvik. 'Producing the First Indian Cricketing Superhero: Nationalism, Body Culture, Consumption and the C.K. Nayudu Phenomenon'. *The International Journal of the History of Sport* 29, no. 4 (2012): 562–82.

Nandi, Moti. *Striker*. Calcutta: Ananda, 1973.

Nandy, Ashis. *The Intimate Enemy: Loss and Recovery of Self under Colonialism*. Oxford: Oxford University Press, 1983.

Nandy, Ashis. *The Tao of Cricket: On Games of Destiny and the Destiny of Games*. New Delhi: Viking, 1989.

Oliven, Ruben George. 'The Production and Consumption of Culture in Brazil'. *Latin American Perspectives* 11, no. 1 (1984): 103–15.

Palit, Dibyendu. 'Brazil'. In *Khela Ar Khela* [Sport and Sport], ed. Siddhartha Ghose, 125–32. Calcutta: Ananda, 1994.

Riner, Dax. *Pelé*. Minneapolis, MN: Lerner, 2010.

Rowe, David, and Callum Gilmour. 'Global Sport: Where Wembley Way Meets Bollywood Boulevard'. *Continuum: Journal of Media & Cultural Studies* 23, no. 2 (2009): 171–82.

Da Silva, Ann Paula. 'King Pelé: Race, Professionalism and Football in Brazil'. *The National Black Law Journal* 21, no. 3 (2010): 1–21.

Weber, Max. *The Theory of Social and Economic Organization* Trans. A.M. Henderson and Talcott Parsons, New York: Oxford University Press, 1947.

Witzig, Richard. *The Global Art of Soccer.* New Orleans: CusiBoy, 2006.

Index

For Product Safety Concerns and Information please contact our EU
representative GPSR@taylorandfrancis.com Taylor & Francis Verlag GmbH,
Kaufingerstraße 24, 80331 München, Germany

Batch number: 08153807

Printed by Printforce, the Netherlands